Anna Kavan

For Ben

Anna Kavan

Mid-Century Experimental Fiction

Victoria Walker

Edinburgh University Press is one of the leading university presses in the UK. We publish academic books and journals in our selected subject areas across the humanities and social sciences, combining cutting-edge scholarship with high editorial and production values to produce academic works of lasting importance. For more information visit our website: edinburghuniversitypress.com

© Victoria Walker 2023, 2024

Edinburgh University Press Ltd
13 Infirmary Street,
Edinburgh, EH1 1LT

First published in hardback by Edinburgh University Press 2023

Typeset in 10.5/13 Adobe Sabon
by Manila Typesetting Company

A CIP record for this book is available from the British Library

ISBN 978 1 4744 7894 6 (hardback)
ISBN 978 1 4744 7895 3 (paperback)
ISBN 978 1 4744 7896 0 (webready PDF)
ISBN 978 1 4744 7897 7 (epub)

The right of Victoria Walker to be identified as the author of this work has been asserted in accordance with the Copyright, Designs and Patents Act 1988, and the Copyright and Related Rights Regulations 2003 (SI No. 2498).

Contents

Acknowledgements	vi
Anna Kavan Chronology	vii
Introduction	1
1. Realism and Reality: Helen Ferguson to Anna Kavan	21
2. Psychiatry, Anti-Psychiatry and the Asylum at Mid-Century	45
3. Blackout: Hearts and Minds Under Aerial Bombardment	69
4. The Crowding of Dreams: Postwar Time and Experimentalism	93
5. Experimental Fictions: *Ice* and the Anthropocene	115
Bibliography	139
Index	157

Acknowledgements

This book develops the research I undertook for my PhD at Queen Mary, University of London, which I completed in 2012. My first thanks are to my PhD supervisor, Michèle Barrett, who supported me far beyond the scope and duration of her role. I am grateful to Jackie Jones at Edinburgh University Press for her confidence in this project and to Susannah Butler and Fiona Conn for their editorial assistance. The generosity and friendship of the other scholars I have met working on Kavan have made writing this book a pleasure. I thank all those involved in the Anna Kavan Symposium at the Institute of English Studies in 2014 and those who contributed to the special issue *Anna Kavan: New Readings*. I have benefitted enormously from fruitful conversations with Leigh Wilson, Hannah Van Hove, Carole Sweeney, Andrew Gaedtke, Jennifer Sturm and Nonia Williams. Clara Jones was immensely generous in bringing Helen Ferguson's previously unacknowledged stories to my attention, and Rose Knox-Peebles, Kavan's close friend, has been immensely generous with her time and insights.

Many archivists and librarians have assisted me in my research, and I am indebted to them for helping me to construct an account of Kavan's life and writing which supplements, and sometimes rewrites, the published biographies. I thank especially all those at the McFarlin Library Special Collections at the University of Tulsa; the Harry Ransom Center, University of Texas at Austin; the Alexander Turnbull Library, National Library of New Zealand, Wellington; and the Ludwig Binswanger Archive, Universitätsarchiv, Eberhard Karls Universität Tübingen.

Some material from this book has appeared in different form as 'Hearts and Minds: War Neurosis and the Politics of Madness in Anna Kavan's *I Am Lazarus*' in *Women: A Cultural Review* 28:4 (Winter 2017) and 'Anna Kavan's *Ice*: Postwar Experimentalism and the Fiction of the Anthropocene' in *British Experimental Women's Fiction, 1945–1975: 'Slipping Through the Labels'*, ed. by Andrew Radford and Hannah Van Hove (London: Palgrave, 2021).

Anna Kavan Chronology

1901 Born Helen Emily Woods (10 April) in Cannes to Helen Eliza Woods (née Bright) and Claude Charles Edward Woods.
1905 Family move from England to Rialto, California, to establish an orange farm.
1910 Claude Woods goes missing, leaving his wife with debts.
1911 Claude Woods commits suicide by jumping from a ship in Tuxpan Harbour, Mexico.
Helen educated at boarding schools in England.
1920 Marries Donald Harry Ferguson (10 September) and moves with him to Maymyo, Burma.
1921 Begins writing.
Mother marries Joseph White.
1922 Birth of son Bryan Ferguson.
1923 Leaves Donald Ferguson and returns to England with Bryan.
1925 Attends London Central School of Arts and Crafts.
Meets artist (Leslie) Stuart Edmonds.
1926 Diaries record that she is using heroin.
1927 Divorce from Donald Ferguson (23 July).
1928 Marries Stuart Edmonds (1 October). Couple live at Saunders Close, Bledlow nr Princes Risborough.
1929 *A Charmed Circle* (Jonathan Cape) published.
1930 *The Dark Sisters* (Jonathan Cape) published.
Treated for Tuberculosis at Clinique Miremont, Leysin, Switzerland.
Let Me Alone (Jonathan Cape) published.
1934 Mother marries wealthy American Hugh Tevis and moves with him to South Africa.
1935 *A Stranger Still* (John Lane, The Bodley Head) published.
Solo exhibition of landscape paintings at the Wertheim Gallery, London.

Birth and death of daughter Margaret (21 November) and subsequent adoption of daughter Susanna.
1936   *Goose Cross* (John Lane, The Bodley Head) published.
1937   *Rich Get Rich* (John Lane, The Bodley Head) published.
Two stories published in *Home and Country*.
1938   Stuart Edmonds begins affair with Marjorie Davies; breakdown of marriage. Suicide attempt and treatment at asylum in Switzerland.
1939   Living in London. Treated by Henry Dicks.
Meets pacifist playwright Ian Hamilton and travels with him to Norway.
England enters Second World War.
Travels with Hamilton to New York and Mexico. The couple settle for six months in La Jolla, California.
1940   *Asylum Piece* (Jonathan Cape) published under the name Anna Kavan.
Ian Hamilton sails for New Zealand. Kavan sails towards South Africa via Singapore and meets American publisher Charles Fuller on the ship. Travels in Philippines and Dutch East Indies with Fuller before returning with him to New York City. Several suicide attempts.
1941   Travels to New Zealand to join Ian Hamilton.
Change the Name (Jonathan Cape) published.
1942   Sails for England via New York City. Begins using the name Anna Kavan in her personal life.
1943   Arrives in England, unable to obtain a visa to travel onwards to South Africa to join her mother.
Treated at the Tavistock Clinic.
Finds war work at the Mill Hill Emergency Hospital and later takes secretarial job at *Horizon*.
Attempts and fails to gain custody of Susanna. Divorce from Stuart Edmonds.
Ian Hamilton imprisoned in New Zealand as a 'military defaulter'.
'New Zealand: Answer to an Inquiry' published in *Horizon*.
1944   'The Case of Bill Williams' published in *Horizon*.
Death of son Bryan (22 February).
London flat 'blitzed'.
Begins to be treated by Dr Karl Theodor Bluth.
Serious illness, affecting her heart.
Leaves *Horizon* job.

1945	*I Am Lazarus* (Jonathan Cape) published.
1946	*Asylum Piece* published by Doubleday in US (includes *I Am Lazarus* stories).
	Ian Hamilton released from prison in New Zealand.
1947	Treated for Tuberculosis at Park Sanatorium, Davos, Switzerland. Treated for psychiatric problems and heroin addiction by Ludwig Binswanger at Bellevue Sanatorium, Kreuzlingen, Switzerland.
	The House of Sleep (Doubleday) published in USA.
	Visits mother and stepfather in South Africa.
1948	Second visit to Bellevue Sanatorium.
	Sleep Has His House (Cassell) published in UK.
1949	Visit to mother and stepfather in South Africa.
	The Horse's Tale, co-authored with Karl Theodor Bluth, published by Gaberbocchus Press.
1950	Mother dies, private income reduced.
1956	*A Scarcity of Love* (Angus Downie) – publisher goes into receivership before copies distributed.
1957	*Eagle's Nest* (Peter Owen) published.
1958	Moves to Hillsleigh Rd, W8, her home until her death.
	Car runs over her foot leaving her housebound.
	A Bright Green Field (Peter Owen) published.
1963	*Who Are You?* (Scorpion Press) published.
1964	Karl Bluth dies (5 March), precipitating serious depression.
1967	*Ice* (Peter Owen) published.
1968	Brian Aldiss publishes article naming *Ice* 'best sci-fi novel of 1967'.
	Treated for leukaemia and blood clot in St Charles' Hospital.
	Dies of heart failure (4 December).
	Cremated at Golders Green Crematorium (12 December).
1970	*Julia and the Bazooka* (Peter Owen) published posthumously.
1975	*My Soul in China (Novella & Stories)* (Peter Owen) published posthumously.
1994	*Mercury* (Peter Owen) published posthumously.
1995	*The Parson* (Peter Owen) published posthumously.
2007	*Guilty* (Peter Owen) published posthumously.

Introduction

'My name is Kavan now,' she said, forcing, with difficulty, a slight smile. The words sounded foolish as they came out of her mouth.
Let Me Alone (1930)

I've really succeeded in changing my name to Anna Kavan, but it doesn't seem to have changed my bad luck. . .
Only call me Anna Kavan. I use it always now. . .
Don't forget I'm Anna Kavan.
Anna Kavan to Ian Hamilton (Nov–Dec 1940)

. . . a mistake had certainly been made; I was not the person mentioned in the document he had shown me which probably referred to somebody of the same name. After all, my name was not an uncommon one; I could think of at least two people off-hand – a film actress and a writer of short stories – who were called by it.
Asylum Piece (1940)

'Anna Kavan' first appeared as a character in Helen Ferguson's *Bildungsroman*, *Let Me Alone* (1930); in the first quotation above, she self-consciously claims her new, married name to the publisher whose rejection ended her writing aspirations.[1] Ten years later, after using Anna Kavan as a pen name for less than a year, Helen Ferguson would write to her lover to make this claim herself with more assurance: 'Only call me Anna Kavan.'[2] The parallels between Anna's story and episodes in Helen Ferguson's life have made *Let Me Alone* the source of much apocryphal Kavan biography, yet she did not consider her writing to be autobiographical, claiming towards the end of her career that 'I can only write fiction' and 'I've often started autobiographical things, but never finished them.'[3] Taking the name of her own fictional creation, coupled with her habit of writing un-named and ill-defined protagonists, has worked retroactively on interpretations of both Kavan's life and work, and been taken as an open invitation to read her fiction as autobiography.

Her anonymous characters have been commonly understood as figures that stand in for their author and her rejection of plot and characterisation left a blank space into which others have written their stories of her life and personality.

To the reader who is aware of the origin of her name (and her publishers work hard to ensure they are), the status of both 'Anna Kavan' the character and Anna Kavan the author are subtly altered. In the final quotation above, the anonymous narrator of one of Kavan's *Asylum Piece* (1940) stories (her first publication under her new name) attempts to evade a summons by claiming mistaken identity with 'a writer of short stories'.[4] The 'not uncommon' name of the narrator of *Asylum Piece* is never revealed to the reader, but this allusion is tantalisingly self-referential, actively associating, or rather disassociating, the narrator from Kavan herself. The 'film actress' Helen Ferguson was well known at the time Kavan was writing under that name, but it is Anna Kavan (whose name certainly was uncommon) who is the author of this new collection of stories. This metafictional allusion, indiscernible to her first readers to whom her change of name was not signalled, is ambiguous in artfulness or intent, one of many obscurities in the unreliable narrator's commentary. Yet, Kavan's nameless characters, incognito and fearful of being mistaken for their author as they are, have a habit of calling her to mind.

Kavan's name-change appears to have been largely unplanned and unself-conscious; her personal history was not widely known during her lifetime and her first readers would have been unaware that Anna Kavan and Helen Ferguson were the same writer.[5] Her decision to take the name in her personal life was undoubtedly influenced by the critical acclaim she achieved under her new name; her letters indicate that, in the wake of a second failed marriage, she was glad to leave both Helen Ferguson and Helen Edmonds behind her. That Kavan herself has become the subject of various fictional works further compounds the confusion between her writing and her biography.[6] As the protagonist of other writers, and the namesake of her own character, Anna Kavan became a cult literary icon despite her relative obscurity, and the fascination that her life stimulates in her readers has been central to the reception of her work in the years since her death.[7] Zadie Smith recognised this in her claim that for 'the British avant-garde, autobiographical extremity has become a mark of literary authenticity, the drug use of Alexander Trochi and Anna Kavan being at least as important to their readers as their prose'.[8] Smith's analysis proposes an incentive for the sensational and often inflated narrative of Kavan's life that has circulated since her death in her two biographies and multiple articles and reviews.[9] Her publishers have marketed her work with emphasis on her severe depression, drug use and difficult relationships, laying out the extremes of her life story as bait to tempt new readers to her fiction. Smith's observation, though superficially dismissive of Kavan's readers if not her prose, speaks to a wider shift in the perceived relationship between life and fiction in the latter half of the twentieth century.

Carole Sweeny has described how a 'hodge-podge of truth, half-remembered anecdotes, exaggeration and inference has tended to buttress much of the limited critical work on Kavan' and there is a good argument to be made that she deserves serious consideration as a writer without reference to the (often apocryphal) biographical details of her life.[10] But to ignore the phenomenon of the ambiguous writer/character Anna Kavan is to miss something vital about the way her work has been, and continues to be, read. Scrutinising her status as a 'literary curiosity', as Jane Garrity has described her, offers particular illumination to the notion of 'literary authenticity' identified by Zadie Smith.[11] Throwing the relationship between real-world person and fictional character into stark relief, Kavan's name-change necessarily impacts any study of her work, which either risks falling into the trap of conflating her life and fiction or must acknowledge and address the increasing intimacy between metaphysics and metafiction in twentieth-century writing. Amanda Anderson, Rita Felski and Toril Moi have jointly tackled critically prohibited questions around reader identification and emotional response to character. Tracing the impact of formalism on critical consideration of character in the twentieth century, they take a more open approach to such inquiry and suggest that 'perhaps it is the fictional qualities of characters that make them real: figures in novels and films are alluring, arresting, alive, not in spite of their aesthetic dimensions, but because of them'.[12] Their project sanctions the possibility of critical study that is sensitive to the way in which Kavan's readers continue to empathise not only with her characters (including 'Anna Kavan' and her many nameless first-person narrators) but with her authorial persona as written by others.

Motifs of un-naming and uncertain identity recur throughout Kavan's work, and the transformative potential of renaming is invoked in the title of her novel *Change the Name* (1941). The anonymity of her nameless characters often signifies their alienation and existential insecurity, exemplified by the protagonist of *My Soul in China* 'wandering lost and aimless without even a name to connect me to life' (14). Kavan's play with the category of fictional character was also a feature of her 1944 *Horizon* polemic 'The Case of Bill Williams', in which she presented a psychiatric case study of one of her own minor characters.[13] The effects, if not the intention, of Kavan taking her character's name are illuminated by Patricia Waugh's observation that characters' names (or lack thereof) are employed in metafiction to 'split open the conventional ties between the real and fictive worlds rather than to reinforce them'.[14] Without such 'conventional ties', the reader must interrogate and reforge the relationship between fact and fiction, and in doing so question the nature of knowledge and subjectivity. In this book, I suggest that this renegotiation of the standard contract of suspension of disbelief between author and reader is integral to the way Anna Kavan wrote as much as to the way she has been read, as it was for many mid-century British writers.

Reading Kavan alongside other writers of her era, especially Jean Rhys, Elizabeth Bowen, Muriel Spark and Doris Lessing, I consider how they might be considered together as mid-century experimentalists, challenging perceived divisions between experimental and realist writing, literary and popular genres and (late) modernist and postwar literatures. Many, but not all, of these author comparisons are with women writers who lived for a time in countries other than Britain, and issues of gender, class and colonialism inflect their literary experiment. All share with Kavan a preoccupation with the relationship between reality and fiction, as well as between madness and sanity. Their writing exhibits the common factors that Julia Jordan has identified in relation to the experimentalism of both late modernism and the postwar avant-garde: 'slippage between truth and representation, and a heightened sense of the ethical questions that inhere in the idea of authorial control'.[15] Destabilising the relationship between text and world, this mid-century experimentalism was articulated formally in the critical turn towards reader response theory and 'the death of the author'.

Characters and Authors in Twentieth-Century Fiction

In Virginia Woolf's familiar words, 'on or about December 1910 human character changed', necessitating a revolution in fictional representations of the same.[16] Woolf's account of the intimacy between fiction and the human condition articulates the causal connection between modernism's focus on interiority and historical shifts in relations between classes, genders and generations. But the dramatic change in Kavan's writing of character when she began to publish as Anna Kavan on or about early 1940 has been perceived less as epochal and political as entirely personal and pathological, effectively a symptom of her 'madness' and drug use. Reading Kavan alongside her contemporaries in this book, I maintain that the change in her writing reflects broader trends in the writing of fictional character in mid-century British literature, which in turn were responding to changes in the way persons conceived and constituted their identities, and that of those around them, in their cultural and historical context. Thus, I place emphasis on how Kavan's writing responds to the aftermath of the First World War and the experience of the Second, to Freudian innovations and scientific advances, philosophical existentialism and the alienated, fragmented condition of modernity, as well as her personal experiences of depression, asylum incarceration and both illicit and medically-prescribed drug use.

Addressing many of the same issues that Woolf's *Mr Bennett and Mrs Brown* had done for its times, Nathalie Sarraute's 1950 essay 'The Age of Suspicion' indicates that by the postwar era, something had shifted again in both human relations and the writing of character. For Sarraute, the mid-century reader had 'grown wary of practically everything' and 'not only has the novelist practically ceased to believe in his characters, but the reader, too, is unable to believe in them'.[17] As in Woolf's essay before it, character is the mutual acquaintance of author and reader and, in Hannah Arendt's words, the change Sarraute outlines 'indicates a serious break-down in communication' between them.[18] In Roland Barthes's seminal essay, 'the birth of the reader must be at the cost of the death of the Author',[19] but for Sarraute, the estranged author and reader must find a way to share space and authority: the reader must renounce their 'love of comfort' (70) and be enticed 'into the author's territory' so that they are 'on the inside, exactly where the author is' (71). In Woolf's essay, writer and character are strangers in a railway carriage; in Sarraute's, they must make room for the reader to squeeze in and join them on the common ground of the text. Thus, the fates of author, character and reader were intertwined in twentieth-century literature and its criticism, a factor reflected both in Kavan's writing and the way it has been read.

For Roland Barthes: 'Writing is that neutral, composite, oblique space where our subject slips away, the negative where all identity is lost, starting with the very identity of the body writing' (142). Barthes' statement that to 'give a text an Author is to impose a limit on that text' is pertinent to the extent to which critics' focus on Kavan's life has closed down avenues of interpreting her work.[20] In emptying out her writing of plot and character, Kavan's experimental writing follows Barthes's injunctive to place greater responsibility for interpretation upon the reader. Yet, Zadie Smith's observations over forty years later suggest that her readers have insisted upon resurrecting the author and implicating her in her work. Thus, the more the author attempted to relinquish their authority by subverting the notion of a unified and identifiable writing subject, the more their readers have sought them in the text. Clear evidence for this can be found in the twentieth-century proliferation of literary biography, resulting in what Malcolm Bradbury would describe as the 'double vision of the writer – all too there, and not there at all', a paradox he traces to a rift between the reading public's desires (for author's biography) and those of the academic critic (against it), as well as within the academy itself.[21] But although these impulses appear contrary to one another, the increased focus on both the life and (metaphorical) death of the author, along with developments in literary constructions of character, were determined by the same mid-century shifts in the understanding of knowledge, truth and reality.

John Frow has described literary character as the 'ontologically ambivalent construct which lies at the heart of the life of textual fictions of all kinds'.[22] His study of the relationship between characters and persons, which are 'at once ontologically discontinuous (they have different manners of being) and logically interdependent', describes how a fictional character can be 'a kind of acquaintance' and a 'quasi-human being'.[23] This analysis is useful in considering the anomaly of Anna Kavan, who was once both a fictional character and a real person (significantly, an author), and has now become the protagonist of literary biographies and biographical fictions. If characters are, in Frow's terms, 'ontologically hybrid beings', 'clusters of words' that are 'in some way like persons', to her readers Kavan transgressed the fine boundary between person and character when she took the name of her own fictional creation, amplifying the ontological ambivalence of the character 'Anna Kavan' and implicating her own fictionality.[24] Her simultaneous shift towards writing un-named characters with unfixed, troubled and open-ended identities further disturbs and undermines the distinction between author and character, and consequently between life and fiction. In this, Anna Kavan thus exemplifies, if not redefines, a new kind of acquaintance between author, character and reader in the mid-twentieth century.

Patricia Waugh suggests that experimental writers in the postwar period represent characters who are 'persons?' – that is, written 'in the mode of the *interrogative* rather than that of the *affirmative*' – a model that not only illuminates the uncertain identity that defines many of Kavan's characters but identifies the writing of fictional character as ontological enquiry.[25] In *Mimesis*, Erich Auerbach takes Virginia Woolf's narrative technique as exemplary of such characterisation in the modern novel, describing how 'the author' represents 'herself to be someone who doubts, wonders, hesitates, as though the truth about her characters were not better known to her than it is to them or to the reader'.[26] This doubt and hesitation, signalling the decline of the omniscient authorial voice, reveals the writer as someone who asks questions rather than gives answers, a process which Kavan takes to a further extreme; like the brain-fever bird's endless repetition 'who-are-you?' in her novel of the same name, Kavan's texts constantly press the question of identity. It was against this mid-century backdrop of authorial, epistemological and ontological uncertainty that Helen Ferguson took the name of her own fictional character and began to write representations of un-named and empty protagonists.

Mid-Century Experimental Fiction

Finding a pre-existing category into which to fit Kavan's work has been an ongoing challenge for literary scholars. The longevity of her publishing career (1929–1967) and the diversity of her writing qualify her for inclusion in a broad range of literary taxonomies, but conversely it has led to her work being critically sequestered for failing to show allegiance to any one style or movement. Frequently, her writing has been described as unique or unusual for its times, accolades that repudiate any literary lineage or alliance. Recent engagement with her literary and cultural influences has begun to challenge this narrative of solipsism, and comparative studies have traced connections between her experiment and that of her contemporaries including Muriel Spark, Jean Rhys, Graham Greene, Malcolm Lowry, Patrick Hamilton and Alan Burns.[27] This growing reconsideration of Kavan's writing brings together diverse writers and offers fresh perspective on experimental writing in the mid-century. For many years, Kavan's fiction received greater attention from other writers than from the literary academy and several of those against whose work I read her in this book were her admirers, or were at least familiar with her work. My 'Introduction' to the special issue of *Women: A Cultural Review*, *Anna Kavan: New Readings* (2017) provides an overview of the limited critical engagement with her writing up to that time; since then, references to her work have appeared with increasing frequency in studies of twentieth-century literature, demonstrating its relevancy beyond the discrete category of 'Kavan studies' into diffuse areas of literary scholarship.[28]

In 1943, Kavan lamented:

> There's absolutely no chance of getting any of my stuff published now [. . .] My sort of experimental writing is completely out under present conditions, so I may as well resign myself to the fact that as a writer I'm just liquidated until after the war – if not forever.[29]

Kavan's self-application of the term 'experimental', here and elsewhere, indicates that it held none of the pejorative connotations for her that it would accrue for writers later in the twentieth century.[30] She was unconcerned by the word's associations with the potential for failure, applying it both to her own work and that which she most admired. Her prediction about the wartime appetite for 'her sort' of experimentalism proved inaccurate; she achieved critical success with *I Am Lazarus*, her second collection of stories published in March 1945, but her postwar writing in both realist and more experimental styles brought her two decades of near obscurity and critical failure until her final novel *Ice* (1967) drew a new generation of admirers to her writing.

The most striking change in her writing when she first began to publish under the name Anna Kavan in 1940 was its sparsity. Distilling and dispensing with descriptive language, paring down dialogue and plot, her narratives became fragmented, settings became unidentifiable, and protagonists lost both names and characterisation. She began to write in the first person and her narrator's voice was unsettling and unreliable, making the reality of her fictional worlds difficult to locate. Although many of these features would recur throughout her later career, despite her success with *Asylum Piece* her writing did not consistently develop in the same manner; as Anna Kavan she had discovered not so much a new style as a taste for experimentation, and she continued to change her approach to representing selfhood, in both conscious and unconscious states, across the next three decades. Following Roland Barthes's model of the text as 'a tissue of quotations drawn from the innumerable centres of culture', Kavan wove together elements of disparate narrative styles and genres and incorporated influences from theatre, film and, later, television.[31] Far from being unique, this hybridity conforms to a trend in mid-century fiction described by Andrzej Gasiorek as the 'interanimation of forms, styles and techniques' from writers who 'cross-breed narrative modes, taking what suits them from a variety of genres, and creating new forms that cannot easily be classified'.[32]

The impact of Kavan's retroactive name-change highlights the extent to which hindsight affects literary interpretation, a factor which informs my reading of her final novel against the contemporary concept of the Anthropocene, whose mid-century foundations have only recently been established. If an author naming their character after themselves makes for a metafictional text, naming themselves after their character makes for a metafictional author, extending its effect from the two 'Anna Kavan' novels she published as Helen Ferguson to the entire body of her writing. Kavan's use of narrative repetition and her reworking of her own, and other, fiction indicates the significance of retrospection and return in her writing, a feature that became increasingly important in her 1960s output.

Jane Garrity has contemplated Kavan's 'invisibility within the modernist canon', identifying persistent focus on her biography, the disparate nature of her writing, the post-1940 beginnings of her experimentalism and a wider critical neglect of British experimentalists as contributing factors.[33] As Garrity suggests, Helen Ferguson's earlier publication dates (1929–1938) fit more comfortably into a chronology of late or intermodernism, but her more fragmented narratives as Anna Kavan (1940–1967) were arguably more formally modernist in their aesthetic experimentation. However, interpreting her name-change as conveniently marking a break between non-modernist and modernist styles oversimplifies the diversity of Kavan's oeuvre. Tyrus Miller's account of late modernist writing in the interwar years, which confronted 'the survival of individual selves in a world of technological culture, mass politics, and shock experience', fits the defining preoccupations of both her Helen Ferguson writing in this period and beyond it in her work as Anna Kavan.[34] Marina MacKay and Lyndsey Stonebridge remind us that mid-century writers were 'modernism's first readers', 'whose respect for the modernist enterprise is apparent throughout their complex and sometimes introspective fiction'.[35] Kavan was both influenced by and writing alongside late Anglo-American and European modernism; her reviews, correspondence and intertextual allusions reveal her particular affinities with Kafka and T. S. Eliot. Yet, it is easier to make an argument for the modernist attributes of a single Kavan text, as critics such as Jane Garrity and Hannah Van Hove have done with the surrealist, oneiric *Sleep Has His House*, than to present her as an unambiguously (late) modernist writer throughout her career.[36] Garrity lucidly identifies this novel's 'conjunction of feminist literary discourse and modernist practice' (255), but such analysis would be inappropriate for her more stylistically conventional interwar texts such as *A Charmed Circle* at one end of her publishing career, as it would be for her postwar experiment in *Ice* at the other. Despite the evolution and expansion of standard definitions of modernism, the category cannot accommodate Kavan's writing in its entirety.

Scholarly attention to British postwar experimental writing in recent years has embraced Kavan's work, but the parameters of this category exclude her writing during the interwar and wartime periods (more than half the work she published in her lifetime).[37] As Hannah Van Hove has argued, reading Kavan's oeuvre as a whole 'allows us to trace a continuity between pre- and postwar experimentalism' and I identify her predominantly as a mid-century writer, a category that unifies writing across the interwar, wartime and postwar decades.[38] MacKay and Stonebridge have described the mid-century in 2007 as 'a critically awkward phase of twentieth-century writing', and few writers of the period have escaped a scholarly bias that situates them qualitatively, as well as chronologically, 'after modernism'.[39] But Claire Seiler's recent work asks: 'What might we gain from reading the century not forward from the modernist heave, but outward from its historical middle? Or from broaching midcentury as a substantive alternative to periodisation by ostensibly discrete wartimes?'[40] Following Seiler's incitement to view the mid-century not as a transitional phase between modernist and contemporary writing but as an autonomous category which can accommodate the experiments of late or inter-modernism as well as those of the postwar avant-garde, this broad grouping encourages a freer examination of developments in fiction that spanned the twentieth century. Although many of the features of Kavan's writing appear to predict concepts and movements whose initiation has been dated later in the century or into the next (for example the ontological insecurity of R. D. Laing's divided self in the 1960s, and the recent concept of the Anthropocene), I do not deduce from this that Kavan's work was 'before its time'. Rather, I suggest that the retrospectively imposed break between pre- and post-Second World War in critical considerations of intellectual and aesthetic ideas and methodologies has obscured the long, slow development of these ways of thinking about self and world.

In a late, self-defensive and self-reflective letter to her publisher Peter Owen, Kavan justified the diversity of her style:

> I can't keep on all my life writing in the same way. [. . .] The world now is quite different and so is my life in it. One reacts to the environment and atmosphere one lives in, one absorbs outside influences, and my writing changes with the conditions outside.[41]

These 'outside influences' and 'conditions' indicate Kavan's sensitivity to the political, intellectual and literary climate of her times. Her journalism and personal correspondence reinforce the extent to which her writing responded to cultural shifts and world events and, as Rhys Davies testified, 'she was a ceaseless reader of fiction'.[42] Kavan's protestation that 'I can't keep on all my life writing in the same way' is a mantra for her break from Helen Ferguson's narrative style and her ongoing experiment beyond it. Although lacking a single methodology, her innovation was consistent in attempting to undermine and renegotiate the concepts of definite identity and objective reality. Writing as Helen Ferguson, her early third-person novels represent characters plagued by feelings of de-realisation, self-division and alienation; as Anna Kavan, her elliptical style, combination of third- and first-person voices and disruption of linear narrative work to draw the reader into interrogating the 'real' in both her fictional worlds and beyond. Combining elements of psychological realism, gothic fantastic, surrealism, science fiction and metafiction, Kavan's fiction, in its various forms, reflects and explores what Christine Brooke-Rose would describe as the twentieth century's 'reality crisis'.[43]

Women's Writing, Madness and Experiment

Kavan's profound and long-term clinical depression, her associated suicide attempts and periods of psychiatric incarceration undoubtedly shaped both the writing and reception of her fiction and interpretations of her life and character. Her experience of mental illness has been closely associated with her asylum incarceration in the late 1930s and the occasion of her name-change, but Carole Sweeney makes a convincing case for the origins of her heroin addiction, beginning in the 1920s, in a prescription of morphia for major depression.[44] The likelihood that she experienced mental illness prior to her asylum treatment in the late 1930s is supported by her descriptions of the 'inexplicable glooms' of 'my unhappy school days' and by the despair and dissociation experienced by the characters in her Helen Ferguson novels.[45] Muriel Spark, who authored reader's reports on several of Kavan's submissions to her publisher Peter Owen in the 1950s, perhaps invokes her writing directly when the narrator of *Loitering with Intent* (1981), aspiring writer Fleur Talbot, describes feeling 'like a grey figment, the "I" of a novel whose physical description the author had decided not to set forth'.[46] What is a momentary faint for Fleur Talbot is a permanent state of existential being for many of Kavan's characters; these 'grey figments', without names, histories or physical characteristics, represent a mode of life that appears inimical to any faithful representation of human character. In Chapter 2 of this book, I suggest that these emptied-out, disembodied and often affect-less characters are shaped in part by Kavan's experience and representation of major depression.

Despite the central place of psychiatric illness and treatment in her writing and journalism, Kavan's work has been neglected in studies of madness and literature. Nonetheless, her mental illness has made her subject to many of the same critical moves and pejorative presumptions that have plagued more prominent women writers known for their 'madness', principally Virginia Woolf and Sylvia Plath, and she has been presented as being self-obsessed, over-privileged and a bad mother. The heavy reliance on Kavan's biography in some earlier readings of her fiction was, at least in part, fuelled by the political urgency of feminist critics and readers seeking to rediscover women's voices, but feminist readings of Kavan's work in the 1980s paradoxically failed to recognise many of the political aspects of her fiction in their preoccupation with her biography, maintaining that her writing was dominated by personal psychological trauma.[47] Jacqueline Rose has argued that Plath's work has often been judged in relation to a 'false antagonism' between history and subjectivity:

> There is no history outside its subjective realisation, its being-for-the-subject, just as there is no subjectivity uncoloured by the history to which it belongs. The division between history and subjectivity, between external and internal reality, between the trials of the world and the trials of the mind, is a false one.[48]

This observation is demonstrably true for Kavan, whose journalism and correspondence press the historical contingency of her fiction (although this has often been ignored), and whose writing consistently undermines the partition of mind/world and external/internal reality.

Christine Brooke-Rose's oft-quoted 'speculation on ancient prejudices' against 'experimental women writers' continues to bear relevance, and the sometimes competing strategies of feminist literary criticism to redress such discrimination has, at times, only compounded these issues.[49] What remains clear is that when it comes to experimental writing, the work of redressing the invisibility and dismissal of women writers who, as Kaye Mitchell has recently observed, 'suffer a kind of double exclusion, from both masculinist and feminist canons', is still ongoing.[50] Responding to this neglect, recent focus on women's experimental writing has brought attention to Kavan's work, but she herself was silent on her status as a woman writer and on feminist politics.[51] Claims that she indiscriminately despised other women, established after her death by her male publisher and executors, are contradicted by her close female friends and her public and private admiration of other women writers. Yet, although gender inequality and violence against women were recurring themes in her fiction, Kavan's writing consistently resists any notion of collective identity in its representation of marginalised and isolated individuals, making defining it as women's writing problematic. Frequently, her writing performs what Mitchell has described as a 'voiding of identity in experimental texts [that] works in tension with earlier feminist imperatives to self-discovery and self-expression'.[52]

Comparisons between Kavan and Anaïs Nin have largely followed from Nin's own feelings of a 'great affinity' with Kavan's writing and her praise of the 'clarity and compassion' of her representations of 'the world of madness'.[53] Taking her lead, Nin scholars have identified parallels between her explorations of her writing identity and Kavan's status as a writer who (unbeknownst to Nin) took the name of her own fictional creation.[54] Kavan's name-change, coupled with her frequent use of first-person narrative in her experimental texts, have again skewed such readings, for her writing of vacant and unidentifiable characters, as much as her repeated emphasis on the fictional nature of her own writing, sits at odds with Nin's life-writing project.[55] Jeanette Winterson addresses the tendency to read women's fiction biographically in her retrospective 'Introduction' to *Oranges are Not the Only Fruit*, in which she explains that: 'Learning to read yourself as a fiction as well as a fact is liberating':[56]

> If I call myself Jeanette why must I be writing an autobiography? Henry Miller calls his hero Henry. Paul Auster and Milan Kundra call themselves by name in some of their work. So does Philip Roth. This is understood by critics as playful meta-fiction. For a woman it is assumed to be confessional. Is this assumption about gender? Something to do with creative authority? Why shouldn't a woman be her own experiment?[57]

Winterson identifies the gender politics underlying interpretations of metafictional experiment with the figures of character and author, founded upon the premise that men perform innovative feats of artistic creativity and women confess their lives. Reading Kavan's fiction as confessional or self-actualising is not only incommensurate with her own views of her writing practice, but also with the majority of her work which features protagonists who do not resemble her or her life experience. I interpret Kavan's name-change and her first-person narratives in the spirit suggested by Winterson, not as a means of writing her own identity, but rather as a means of emphasising and exploring the relationship between fiction and the real world. Kate Aughterson and Deborah Philips have mapped a longer trajectory of women's experimental writing beyond the twentieth century, observing that 'this experimentalism is one which has a history that is anchored not to modernism and postmodernism but rather the experiences women writers had as outsiders to the literary or cultural establishment'.[58] Such an approach is fitting for Kavan's writing since it acknowledges the importance of gender to both her experiences and those she represents yet avoids attributing a consciously feminist agenda to her work or essentialising her experimentalism beyond the assertion that 'by being outsiders, women became innovators'.[59]

The absence of detailed plot and characterisation in Kavan's more oblique texts has led critics to reason that without depth or personal history, her characters lack political identity; that without temporal movement, their experiences signify isolated moments of extreme pain;

and that without defining features to indicate otherwise, they automatically represent only their author. Thus, her writing has been largely interpreted as apolitical. To date, little attention has been given to her 1940s journalism, in which her anarchistic approach to the politics of madness is made clear. Only in recent years has the political potential of Kavan's fiction, as fiction, been recognised, notably for feminist politics by Leigh Wilson, and for the politics of mental health by Andrew Gaedtke.[60] Other studies have shifted attention away from her personal experience and trauma to consider the ways in which her writing is more broadly concerned with the fate of marginalised outsiders.[61]

Defining Kavan's writing as 'mid-century experimental fiction' ultimately excludes less than other available categories – it does not take the war as a breaking point; does not imply a response to, or against, particular forebears, especially modernism; makes no distinctions based on the whims of critics or publishers of its own time or ours, allowing for the influence and inclusion of popular genre; does not take her status as a woman writer as a defining feature; does not impose any set of essential characteristics. Indeed, it is the only category into which the whole of Kavan's diverse oeuvre will comfortably fit, allowing only that her writing was of its times, which she herself felt keenly, and that she was experimenting with her writing, which again consistently matches her own description.

It has not been my purpose to provide a detailed account of Kavan's life in this book. Any relevant biographical details I have drawn on are supported by archival research; where these differ from her published biographies I have provided references in end-of-chapter notes. I have not covered in detail every publication from Kavan's long writing career, nor drawn extensively from her unpublished manuscripts in the McFarlin Library Special Collections at the University of Tulsa. Her late flush of success with *Ice* in the year before her death encouraged her executors and publishers to issue posthumous publications as well as revelations about her life, most of which I do not substantially engage with. *My Soul in China* (1975), originally a novel, was heavily edited to less than half its length by Rhys Davies and published with a selection of stories that Peter Owen had previously rejected for being 'without real spark or outstanding original creativity'.[62] *Mercury* (1994) is a draft of *Ice* which is perhaps most useful to scholars in its potential for tracking her writing technique than as a text in its own right. *Guilty* (2007), another novel Peter Owen originally rejected in 1956, citing the probability that 'critics would slash' it, has affinities with the novel he did publish, *Eagle's Nest* (1957).[63]

Although this book takes a roughly chronological approach to Kavan's oeuvre, it aims to demonstrate how tropes and motifs recur across her career and I draw comparisons between her earlier and later work. Chapter 1 looks at her interwar writing as Helen Ferguson, taking its frequent designation as 'conventional Home Counties novels' as ground from which to consider her representations of rural tradition and urban modernity; war; British colonialism and social conventionality. Closely examining her direct reworking of her 1930s writing in the 1960s to assess the continuities and discontinuities between these phases of her writing, the chapter tracks the development of her distinctive narrative voice and considers how her work intersects with changing understanding of realism and reality in the mid-century. Chapter 2 addresses how Kavan's narrative experiment began with writing the encounter with psychiatric treatment and the asylum, and focuses on her 1940s texts *Asylum Piece*, *I Am Lazarus* and *The Horse's Tale*. Mindful of how developments in mid-century psychiatry both reflected and effected wider changes in subject formation and social relations, the chapter draws evidence from her article 'The Case of Bill Williams' to demonstrate that her writing of psychiatric treatment was political rather than purely subjective in focus, strongly anticipating the work of the anti-psychiatry movement. Examining her experimental narrative strategies to formally represent the existential experiences of depression, psychiatric treatment and incarceration, I explore how these factors subtly alter the reader's relationship to the text, its narrators and protagonists.

In Chapter 3 I consider the impact of the Second World War on Kavan's writing, with reference to her work with soldiers suffering from effort syndrome. Considering how the psychosomatic symptoms of the syndrome inflect the increasingly hallucinatory and surrealist prose of her *I Am Lazarus* stories, blurring divisions between mind/body and person/object, I observe how these factors manifest too in the work of other Blitz writers, especially Elizabeth Bowen. Chapter 4 considers the importance of dream to Kavan's postwar writing, and the psychoanalytical and existential inflections in two of her postwar novels, *Sleep Has His House* and *Who Are You?*. Taking Kavan's thoughts on a postwar cultural impulse to look backwards as a starting point, the chapter considers how the concept of the postwar inflects Kavan's experiments with time, and those of her contemporaries. Examining the influence of heroin and surrealism on her representations of the unconscious, I also suggest that her earlier representations of ontological uncertainty become a conscious engagement with existential angst. Chapter 5 examines how Kavan's mid-century experimental writing, at its peak in her final novel *Ice*, anticipates the later concept of the Anthropocene. Maintaining that the novel continues the experimental strategies and concerns of her early writing while absorbing new influences, it considers how she experiments with, and subverts, genre. Closely examining the novel's troubling depictions of sexual violence, its narrative temporality and its use of the trial as a formal device to explore postwar culpability, it draws on Kavan's own thoughts on the ethical significance of experimental fiction.

From the turning of the 'first bright infantile page' of the fictional 'Anna Kavan's' life, via the 'honourable and precious' books of the narrator of 'Our City' which are 'like members of a suicide squad' engaging the enemy of life (140), to the figure of B in *Sleep Has His House* reading and writing to retreat into a private world, Kavan's oeuvre is littered with clues hinting at the significance of fiction both as a consolation for her characters and as a medium for understanding and exploring self and world. Her character's claim of mistaken identity with her author is one that I keep present in my readings of her work, taking her at her word in her statements about the fictional rather than autobiographical nature of her writing. Her sustained interrogation of 'reality' across her career presses home the conviction that the relationship between life and fiction is profoundly more complex than mimetic representation. As the legitimate arena in which subjectivity and reality can be fashioned, in Kavan's writing fiction becomes a lodestar by which to navigate existential issues of subject formation and reality in the 'real' world.

Notes

1. Anna Kavan, *Let Me Alone* [1930] (London: Peter Owen, 2002), p. 204.
2. Anna Kavan to Ian Hamilton, 11 November; 14 November; 7 December 1940, *NLNZ*.
3. Anna Kavan to Francis King, 30 December 1965, Francis Henry King Collection, *HRC*; Anna Kavan to Peter Owen, 19 September 1958, Peter Owen Ltd Records, *HRC*.
4. Anna Kavan, *Asylum Piece* (London: Jonathan Cape, 1940), pp. 93–4.
5. Since her death, several of her Helen Ferguson novels have been reissued under the name Anna Kavan.
6. Fictions about Anna Kavan include Rhys Davies's novel based on her marriage to Stuart Edmonds, *Honeysuckle Girl* (London: Heinemann, 1975); D. J. Britton's play *Silverglass* based on Kavan's friendship with Rhys Davies (Swansea University, 13 September 2013, Performance); Catherine LeNoble's novel in French, *Anna K* (Orléans: HYX, 2016), and Jeremy Reed's collection of poems about her life, *Red China Smoke* (Pociao, 2017), which follows his earlier biography.

7. See, for example, Emily Hill, 'Cult VIP/Anna Kavan: Kafka's Sister', *Dazed and Confused*, August 2010.
8. Zadie Smith, 'Two Paths for the Novel', *The New York Review of Books*, 20 November 2008.
9. See David Callard, *The Case of Anna Kavan: A Biography* (London: Peter Owen, 1992); Jeremy Reed, *A Stranger on Earth: The Life and Work of Anna Kavan* (London: Peter Owen, 2006).
10. Carole Sweeney, *Vagabond Fictions: Gender and Experiment in British Women's Writing, 1945–1970* (Edinburgh: Edinburgh University Press, 2020); Andrew Radford and Hannah Van Hove (eds), *British Experimental Women's Fiction, 1945–1975: Slipping Through the Labels* (Basingstoke: Palgrave Macmillan, 2021), p. 38.
11. Jane Garrity, 'Nocturnal Transgressions in *The House of Sleep*: Anna Kavan's Maternal Registers', *Modern Fiction Studies*, 40:2 (Summer 1994), 253–77, p. 253.
12. Amanda Anderson, Rita Felski and Toril Moi, *Character: Three Inquiries in Literary Studies* (Chicago and London: University of Chicago Press, 2019), p. 19.
13. Bill Williams appeared as a character in Anna Kavan, 'The Case of Bill Williams', *Horizon*, 50 (February 1944) and soon after in 'Face of My People', *Horizon*, 53 (May 1944), later collected in *I Am Lazarus*.
14. Patricia Waugh, *Metafiction: The Theory and Practice of Self-Conscious Fiction* (London and New York: Routledge, 1984), p. 94.
15. Julia Jordan, 'Late Modernism and the Avant-Garde Renaissance', in *The Cambridge Companion to British Fiction Since 1945*, ed. David James (Cambridge: Cambridge University Press, 2015), 145–59, p. 146.
16. Virginia Woolf, *Mr Bennett and Mrs Brown* (London: Hogarth Press, 1924), p. 4.
17. Nathalie Sarraute, 'The Age of Suspicion' [1950], in *The Age of Suspicion: Essays on the Novel*, trans. by Maria Jolas (New York: George Braziller, 1963), pp. 61, 54.
18. Hannah Arendt, 'Nathalie Sarraute', *The New York Review of Books* (5 March 1964), 5–6, p. 5.
19. Roland Barthes, 'The Death of the Author' in *Image, Music, Text*, trans. by S. Heath (London: Fontana, 1977), 142–8, p. 148.
20. Barthes, 'Death of the Author', p. 147.
21. Malcolm Bradbury, 'The Telling Life', in *No, Not Bloomsbury* (London: Andre Deutsche, 1987), 309–15, p. 312.
22. John Frow, *Character and Person* (Oxford: Oxford University Press, 2014), p. vi.
23. Frow, *Character and Person*, pp. vii, vi, vii.
24. Frow, p. 1.
25. Patricia Waugh, *Feminine Fictions: Revisiting the Postmodern* (London and New York: Routledge, 1989), p. 217.
26. Erich Auerbach, *Mimesis: The Representation of Reality in Western Literature* [1946], trans. by Willard R. Trask (Princeton NJ: Princeton University Press, 1968), p. 535.
27. See Andrew Gaedtke, *Modernism and the Machinery of Madness: Psychosis, Technology and Narrative Worlds* (Cambridge: Cambridge University

Press, 2017); Victoria Walker, 'Ornithology and Ontology: The Existential Birdcall in Jean Rhys's *Wide Sargasso Sea* and Anna Kavan's *Who Are You?*', *Women: A Cultural Review*, 23:4 (December 2012), 490–509; Geoff Ward, 'The Wibberlee Wobberlee Walk: Lowry, Hamilton, Kavan and the Addictions of 1940s Fiction', in *The Fiction of the 1940s: Stories of Survival*, ed. by Rod Mengham and N. H. Reeve (Basingstoke: Palgrave Macmillan, 2001), 26–45; Sara Wasson, *Urban Gothic of the Second World War: Dark London* (Basingstoke: Palgrave Macmillan, 2010); Leigh Wilson, 'Anna Kavan's *Ice* and Alan Burns' *Europe After the Rain*: Repetition with a Difference', *Women: A Cultural Review*, 28:4 (Winter 2017), 327–42.

28. Victoria Walker, 'An Introduction to Anna Kavan: New Readings', *Women: A Cultural Review*, 28:4 (Winter 2017), 285–94.
29. Anna Kavan to Ian Hamilton, 6 February 1943, *NLNZ*.
30. See Kaye Mitchell, 'The avant-garde must not be romanticized. The avant-garde must not be dismissed', in Kaye Mitchell and Nonia Williams (eds), *British Avant-Garde Fiction of the 1960s* (Edinburgh: Edinburgh University Press, 2019), 107–24, p. 5; Julia Jordan, *Late Modernism and the Avant-Garde British Novel: Oblique Strategies* (Oxford: Oxford University Press, 2020), pp. 12–13.
31. Barthes, 'Death of the Author', p. 146.
32. Andrzej Gasiorek, *Post-War British Fiction: Realism and After* (London: Edward Arnold, 1995), p. 19.
33. Garrity, 'Nocturnal Transgressions', p. 254.
34. Tyrus Miller, *Late Modernism: Politics, Fiction, and the Arts Between the Wars* (Berkeley: University of California Press, 1999), p. 24.
35. Marina MacKay and Lyndsey Stonebridge (eds), *British Fiction after Modernism: The Novel at Mid-Century* (Basingstoke: Palgrave, 2007), p. 5.
36. See Garrity, 'Nocturnal Transgressions' and Hannah Van Hove, 'Exploring the Realm of the Unconscious in Anna Kavan's *Sleep Has His House*', *Women: A Cultural Review*, 28:4 (Winter 2017), 358–74.
37. See, for example, Kaye Mitchell and Nonia Williams (eds), *British Avant-Garde Fiction of the 1960s* (Edinburgh: Edinburgh University Press, 2019); Carole Sweeney, *Vagabond Fictions: Gender and Experiment in British Women's Writing, 1945–1970* (Edinburgh: Edinburgh University Press, 2020); Andrew Radford and Hannah Van Hove (eds), *British Experimental Women's Fiction, 1945–1975: Slipping Through the Labels* (Basingstoke: Palgrave Macmillan, 2021).
38. Hannah Van Hove, 'Anna Kavan: Pursuing the "in-between reality" hidden by the "ordinary surface of things"', in *British Avant-Garde Fiction of the 1960s*, ed. by Kaye Mitchell and Nonia Williams (Edinburgh: Edinburgh University Press, 2019) 107–24, p. 121.
39. MacKay and Stonebridge, *British Fiction after Modernism*, p. 1.
40. Claire Seiler, *Midcentury Suspension: Literature and Feeling in the Wake of World War II* (New York: Columbia University Press, 2020), p. 5.
41. Anna Kavan to Peter Owen, 29 March [1966], *HRC*.
42. Rhys Davies, 'The Bazooka Girl: A Note on Anna Kavan', *London Magazine*, 1970, p. 14 and also in Davies, 'Anna Kavan', *Books and Bookmen*, February 1971, p. 9.

43. Christine Brooke-Rose, *A Rhetoric of the Unreal: Studies in Narrative and Structure, Especially of the Fantastic* (Cambridge: Cambridge University Press, 1981), p. 3.
44. See Carole Sweeney, '"Keeping the Ruins 'Private'Private": Anna Kavan and Heroin Addiction', *Women: A Cultural Review*, 28:4 (Winter 2017), 312–26.
45. Anna Kavan to George Bullock, Letters from Bellevue, Kreuzlingen, 'Monday night' [Easter Monday 1947], Tulsa, Series II, Box 1, Folder 5. p. 62.
46. Muriel Spark, *Loitering with Intent* [1981] (London: Virago, 2014), p. 69. For Spark's notes on Kavan's submissions to Peter Owen, see Peter Owen Archives, Harry Ransom Center, Austin.
47. Margaret Crosland, *Beyond the Lighthouse: English Women Novelists in the Twentieth Century* (London: Constable, 1981); Vivian Gornick, 'The Great Depression of Anna Kavan', *The Village Voice* (December 2–8 1981), 49–113 and *The End of the Novel of Love* (London: Virago, 1999).
48. Jacqueline Rose, *The Haunting of Sylvia Plath* (London: Virago, 2013), p. 8.
49. Christine Brooke-Rose, 'Illiterations', in *Stories, Theories and Things* (Cambridge: Cambridge University Press, 1991), 250–64, p. 250.
50. Kaye Mitchell, 'Introduction: The Gender Politics of Experiment', *Contemporary Women's Writing*, 9:1 (1 March 2015), 1–15, p. 2.
51. See Sweeney, *Vagabond Fictions*.
52. Mitchell, 'The Gender Politics of Experiment', p. 9.
53. Anaïs Nin to Anna Kavan, 9 March 1959, reproduced in *Anaïs*, Vol 3, 1985, p. 63. See also Nin to Kavan, 4 September 1963 reproduced in *Anaïs*, Vol 3, 1985, p. 64; Nin on Kavan in *The Journals of Anaïs Nin*, 7 vols (London: Peter Owen, 1980), see vols 1944–7 and 47–55 and in 'The Novel of the Future' in *The Novel of the Future* (London: Peter Owen, 1968).
54. See Richard R. Centing, 'Anna Kavan's Shout of Red', *Under the Sign of Pisces: Anaïs Nin and her Circle*, 1:3 (Summer 1970), 1–9; Helen Tookey, *Anaïs Nin, Fictionality and Femininity: Playing a Thousand Roles* (Oxford: Clarendon Press, 2003), p. 39.
55. Kavan never responded to Nin's overtures of friendship, only having a copy of *Who Are You?* forwarded to her on publication and admitting: 'I always feel guilty about not answering her letter, which followed me around the world and reached me nearly a year after it was written. It then seemed too late to answer.' Anna Kavan to John Rolph, 16 July 1963, Scorpion Press Archive, UT.
56. Jeanette Winterson, 'Introduction', *Oranges Are Not the Only Fruit* (London: Vintage, 2014), p. xii.
57. Winterson, 'Introduction', p. xiv.
58. Kate Aughterson and Deborah Philips (eds), *Women Writers and Experimental Narratives: Early Modern to Contemporary* (Basingstoke: Palgrave, 2021), p. 4.
59. Aughterson and Philips, p. 4.
60. See Wilson, 'Anna Kavan's *Ice*', and Gaedtke, *Modernism and the Machinery of Madness*.

61. See Ward, 'The Wibberlee Wobberlee Walk'; Sara Wasson, 'Carceral City, Cryptic Signs: Wartime Fiction by Anna Kavan and Graham Greene', in *Urban Gothic of the Second World War*.
62. Reader's Report, December 1967, Peter Owen Archive, *HRC*.
63. Peter Owen to Anna Kavan, 1 October 1956, *HRC*. For more detail on Peter Owen's publishing of Kavan's writing, including posthumous works, see Leigh Wilson, 'Whose Sister? "Convenient Pigeonholes", Peter Owen and the Publishing of Anna Kavan', in Andrew Radford and Hannah Van Hove (eds), *British Experimental Women's Fiction, 1945–1975: Slipping Through the Labels* (Basingstoke: Palgrave Macmillan, 2021), 83–101.

Chapter 1

Realism and Reality: Helen Ferguson to Anna Kavan

> She did the things that were required of her, the things everyone else did. But whatever she was doing remained unreal to her, nothing had any significance. She went to the club; the talk which she heard and in which she joined was like a dialogue heard in a theatre, she seemed to listen to it from outside. With a vague surprise she heard her own voice speaking. But it was not she herself who spoke. She was simply not there. She had no contact with anything. There was no meaning in the world in which she now moved, it was made up of shapes and noises, without reality or consequence.
>
> During the greater part of the time she was alone in the house. Then everything became blank. The loneliness completely extinguished her, it washed over even her fictitious self. She was nothing.
>
> Let Me Alone

This account of the fictional 'Anna Kavan' in Helen Ferguson's *Let Me Alone* (1930) shows her becoming increasingly estranged from others, herself and her environment. Trapped in a loveless and abusive marriage, alienated from British colonial society as well as the native land and its people, de-realisation and meaninglessness eventually overwhelm her and she succumbs to existential annihilation, becoming 'nothing', 'simply not there'. Anna's symptoms of 'a sort of empty madness, a madness of vacancy' (286) are those of the existential crisis that plagues Kavan's characters throughout her writing career. She observes her 'fictitious self' in a psychic division that suggests both the dissociation of major depression and the gendered experience of the male gaze, captured in John Berger's seminal statement that '[w]omen watch themselves being looked at'.[1] The colonial social world Anna inhabits exemplifies the traditional patriarchal frameworks under which Berger maintains women's sense of self is shaped by their position as an object of spectacle for men, resulting in 'a woman's self being split into two' (40). Under the gaze of her husband, Anna becomes her own spectator, watching herself performing her social role as a woman; at times she feels 'as if he would stare her out of existence altogether' (131). In this early novel, Anna's sensations of unreality are symptoms of her difficult material circumstances and psychological breakdown, but they also reflect a philosophical and cultural shift towards existential and epistemological uncertainty that emerges across, and reflects back upon, mid-century fiction.

Of the six Helen Ferguson novels, *Let Me Alone* has attracted the most critical attention because the story of 'Anna Kavan' was clearly shaped by her own early life. But this novel is also significant both in its specific ties to her later writing (she would rewrite a section of the story for her 1963 novel *Who Are You?*) and in exemplifying the major themes of the Ferguson novels that carried across her entire career. Its colonial setting and representation of sexual violence are features she would return to, and the fictional Anna's depression, psychic division and de-realisation all anticipate the experiences of her later characters. She prefigures the nameless 'girls' of Kavan's postwar novels; a blonde, fragile and childishly slender woman, frequently the object of male domination and sexual violence, which critics have interpreted as multiple iterations of the same heroine and often as representations of their author.[2]

Rhys Davies, Kavan's close friend and literary executor, was the first to describe her Helen Ferguson books as 'conventional Home Counties novels' and this phrase has stuck in later critical reference to these works.[3] Davies employed the term 'conventional' as a measure relative to the fantastic elements and narrative experimentation of Kavan's later work. The coyly pejorative 'Home Counties' conflates her fiction (which has varied settings) with his description of her 'gracing the Chilterns' and breeding bulldogs.[4] In the manuscript of her unpublished *The Cactus Sign*, later struck through as she made revisions, Kavan passed judgement on the two phases of her writing career:

> Poor Jonathan Cape. Over a period of years he published my unsuccessful work. He did it because he believed in me as a writer. At last I did produce something really good, something quite out of the ordinary, if I say it myself.[5]

Kavan herself thus described her Helen Ferguson writing as 'unsuccessful' and her early Anna Kavan work as 'out of the ordinary'. But although their style is less experimental than much of her later work, the unremarkable nature of these novels was exaggerated by Davies to support his account of Kavan's dramatic transformation from unexceptional minor novelist to glamorous writer of noteworthy fiction. In fact, there is much in these early texts that is thematically unconventional and fantastic, and which continues into her writing as Anna Kavan; Helen Ferguson's characters are misfits and outsiders, failing to fully integrate into conventional British society and beset by the misanthropy and sensations of unreality that would become the distinguishing tone of her later narrators and protagonists.

Kavan began to write in the early 1920s while living in Burma and married to Donald Ferguson.[6] The lengthy process of getting into print is a likely reason for her publishing her first novels as Helen Ferguson, rather than under her new married name, Edmonds. *A Charmed Circle* (1929) and *The Dark Sisters* (1930) appeared within six months of each other, closely followed by *Let Me Alone* (1930), all with Jonathan Cape. Cape rejected her next novel and five years passed before she published another three with John Lane; *A Stranger Still* (1935), *Goose Cross* (1936) and *Rich Get Rich* (1937). As Helen Ferguson, she also published three short stories in *Home and Country: The Magazine of the National Federation of the Women's Institutes* during 1937–1938.[7] Details of her time living as Helen Edmonds and writing as Helen Ferguson are sparse. Her later biographers followed Rhys Davies's lead in presenting her life at this time as sedate and conservative. Archival sources suggest a more complex and erratic mode of living during these years. Helen Edmonds spent long stretches in Paris in the late 1920s and early 1930s.[8] Her letters to Jonathan Cape in 1930 indicate that she had temporarily split from her husband and was drifting around France staying with friends and acquaintances in St Tropez and the Pyrenees and describing herself as 'broke'.[9] The couple reconciled, but in 1933–1934 she was in France again, visiting American writer Marjorie Worthington and seeking a new publisher.[10] A transcript of a late interview with Ian Hamilton also offers insight into her life as Helen Edmonds; he describes her close friendship with Rex Warner whom he cites as being influential to her writing and in combating her drug addiction, a serious affair with playwright Ernst Toller, and participation at a political meeting organised by Cecil Day-Lewis.[11] These scattered references offer a glimpse into Helen Edmonds's unsettled domestic and personal life during the 1930s and suggest peripheral involvement in both wider literary circles and radical left-wing politics.

Kavan did not abandon her earlier realist style under her new name, returning to this mode in *Change the Name* (1941), *A Scarcity of Love* (1956) and the posthumously published *The Parson* (1995), as well as in some of her short stories, and much of her more experimental writing as Anna Kavan is characterised by a hybridity of realism and fantasy. Likewise, her move to the first person was not a clear break from her former third-person narratives; in the *Asylum Piece* stories and beyond she used third- and first-person voices interchangeably, and the subtle relationship between these modes is essential to her distinctive style.

Madness and depression, the defining motifs of Anna Kavan's 1940s fiction, are already prevalent in Helen Ferguson's psychological novels, which are deeply concerned with the workings of the mind and its pathology. Uncanny mannequins and hints at bewitchment haunt these ostensibly realist narratives, drawing on the gothic trope that spans her writing career. Climatic and emotional tensions coincide as they continue to do throughout her writing as Anna Kavan; the oppressive heat and gathering storm of *A Charmed Circle* and *Let Me Alone* foreshadow the tropical atmosphere of *Who Are You?*, and fantastic wintry landscapes in *The Dark Sisters*, *Goose Cross* and *Rich Get Rich* prefigure the frozen apocalypse of *Ice*. Human nature and the natural world are sublime forces throughout her writing career, the converse of the dead mechanisation that characterises modern society and the landscapes and environments of her texts are, beyond pathetic fallacy, extensions of her characters' internal worlds.

Critical focus on Kavan's writing of subjectivity has largely excluded any attention to her engagement with the political upheaval and crises of her times and little attempt has been made to read the Ferguson novels alongside other interwar fiction. Their 'conventional' label has invited assumptions of both literary realism and political quietism. However, her formally 'realist' writing in this period allows for more explicit references than in her later work to the legacy of the First and the anticipation of the Second World Wars, the decline of the British Empire and the shifting politics of class and gender. This chapter takes the orthodox description of Helen Ferguson's writing as 'conventional' as ground from which to explore these early texts, reassessing the perceived disjoin between her writing under that name and as Anna Kavan, and the extent of her move from conventional to experimental narrative, from realism to fantasy and from romance to a late modernist aesthetic. Reading *Let Me Alone* as exemplary of the continuities and discontinuities in her writing under her two names, I suggest that the move from Ferguson to Kavan was less dramatic than has been presented yet marked a significant shift in the relationship between reader and narrator that was both integral to her evolving representation of a depressed subject and metonymic of a broader trend in mid-century writing.

The Fictional 'Anna Kavan'

A 1930 *Times Literary Supplement* review of *Let Me Alone* exemplifies contemporary responses to Ferguson's novels in its admiration of her writing and psychological insight, but ultimate dissatisfaction with her subject matter:

> ... the reader can hardly fail to be depressed by the book's persistently gloomy note. The study of a young girl who never experiences a single moment of true happiness is not calculated to raise the spirits: and Anna-Marie, though an interesting, is not a very attractive personality. But at least she has our sympathy, which is more than can be said for most of the other characters. For either they are verging on madness, or else they are jealous, or cruel, or designing, or brutal and insensitive, or merely weak.[12]

As this reviewer notes, there is not much to like about Helen Ferguson's protagonists; their ventures are unsuccessful, their personalities unattractive and their depression relentless. This judgement might well apply to any of her first three novels, which all feature young, middle-class women of limited income and education and their attempts to gain independence from oppressive domestic circumstances. None are attractive or uncomplicated heroines who escape into loving marriages; for some there is no option but to remain in thrall to their tyrannical relatives and those that attempt to break away find themselves no better off.

Anna begins life as Anna-Marie Forrester (the resonance with Helen Ferguson's own maiden name, Woods, supports the implication that this character is modelled on her early life). In Ferguson's typically gothic style, Anna is raised by her shadowy and misanthropic father; his ill-defined but ominous intentions towards her take on a sexual aspect when she reaches her teens, and their disturbing relationship ends when he shoots and kills himself. From this point, Anna's time at school and at home with her Aunt Lauretta is a catalogue of ill-fated friendships and social failures. Her adult life is coloured by deep depression and despair but, distinct from the sparsity of Kavan's later writing of these experiences, the text is hyperbolic in its reiteration of her fear, horror and longing for death. Her ambitions to become a writer are crushed when she fails to secure a publisher for her poems and her aunt refuses to support her in taking up a place at Oxford. Instead, she is pressed into marrying Matthew Kavan, a man she barely knows, and returns with him to his post in colonial Burma; when she resists his sexual advances, he rapes her. Estranged and isolated in colonial society, Anna finds herself pregnant; after a confrontation with her husband, she flees into the monsoon rains, miscarries and resolves to leave him.

Anna's dread of physical and sexual intimacy can be traced to a scene early in the novel in which her father approaches her while she is bathing:

> Anna would have liked to jump away from the stealthy touch; but she was ashamed to do that. So she sat still, very tense and uncomfortable, while

> James Forrester's hand moved down her arm with the strangest, softest, most disturbing touch imaginable. Then raised itself and touched, just lightly touched with bent fingers, the cool curve of her neck where tiny runnels of water were still creeping from her wet hair. (39)

James Forrester does not act further on his desire for his thirteen-year-old daughter, but Anna feels an 'obscure terror', a 'nightmare fear' and 'a vague, increasing dread of him' while he watches her 'secretly it seemed, as one might spy upon an enemy; or a victim' (38). When she later marries Matthew Kavan to escape her stifling home life, the thought of sexual contact with him horrifies Anna as 'something shocking and unnatural' (125) and the idea of conceiving a child by him is again 'unnatural, almost shocking' (290), feelings more appropriate to the childhood encounter with her father. As their relationship deteriorates, Anna's indifference to Matthew makes him 'feel he could kill her' (289); like her father before him, he experiences a combination of sexual desire and murderous intent towards her, and martial rape becomes commonplace in their relationship. It is under these circumstances that Anna begins to experience doubts about her own reality and existence. The sexual violence of *Let Me Alone* is a motif that recurs in Ferguson's later novel *Goose Cross* (1938) and carries across the Ferguson–Kavan divide to *Who Are You?* and *Ice*. Referenced obliquely in these early works, such taboo subjects nonetheless undermine their 'conventional' label.

Anna Kavan reappears in Ferguson's next novel, *A Stranger Still*, published five years after *Let Me Alone*. Separated from Matthew and living in London, Anna attempts to navigate her financial precarity as a single woman, still pursued by 'a sensation of unreality' (47). Anticipating the pervasive feelings of homelessness and exile that plague Kavan's later characters, she comes to realise that she is 'a foreigner everywhere' (180) and will be 'condemned to remain a stranger until she died' (231). This segment of Anna's story centres on her ultimately failed love affair with artist Martin Lewison, who decides to paint the portrait of 'the girl Anna Kavan' (297). Animated with life-like characteristics, the painting embodies in a literal sense the reciprocal gaze of the artwork captured in Walter Benjamin's description of its 'aura' which, to be perceived, invests it 'with the ability to look at us in return': 'from the canvas the woman gazed back at him with her blue-grey eyes, innocent, serious, remote, glamorous, strangely moving, as if watching him from a dream' (301).[13] In a 'transposition of a response common in human relationships to the relationship between the inanimate or natural object and man', Martin's feelings towards the portrait echo those he had for Anna when they were in love.[14] But Martin is more beguiled by the aura of the painting than by Anna herself, for he has already ended their affair; it is an undemanding substitute for the woman he has abandoned, without her emotional or economic needs. This work of art, a painting of a dream figure, is the final representation of the fictional 'Anna Kavan' in Helen Ferguson's writing before she claimed the name as her own.[15]

Many of Helen Ferguson's characters have literary aspirations; 'Anna Kavan' had hoped to be a poet and Adam Green in *Goose Cross* is one, both Swithin Chance in *Rich Get Rich* and Gwenda Lewison in *A Stranger Still* are writing novels and Celia Henzell in *Change the Name* (1941), which returns to Ferguson's realist style, is also a writer. These writer-protagonists reflect the literary focus of the Ferguson novels. Early in *Let Me Alone*, the narrator describes how 'the first bright infantile page of Anna's life was turned' (23), serving less to make her status as a fictional character explicit than to make any human life the model for a book. Anna too understands her world through its relation to literary trope and genre; Burmese colonial society is identified with 'the sort of atmosphere which one expects to meet in mid-Victorian fiction' (244) and her first impressions of the landscape are of 'a fairy-tale country come alive' (245). Using existing modes of writing to define her setting, Ferguson marks the distinction of her own novel's style, for Anna's story does not fit into either of these genres; one is an outdated and restrictive mode into which she fails to reconcile her modern existence, the other a magical fantasy that, despite its appeal, must necessarily remain unreal to her. Anna's relationship to fictionality is further intensified when she comes to repeatedly question her own reality and that of those around her, and in modern editions published under the name Anna Kavan, the fictional Anna becomes ontologically unsettled to a further degree.

'Conventional Home Counties Novels'

The repeated association of Helen Ferguson's writing with the 'conventional Home Counties' evokes a timeless and bucolic England which fails to acknowledge how these texts foreground their wider context, especially the past and future World Wars, increasing industrialisation and the ongoing colonial enterprise of the British Empire. Social conventionality is a central theme, but it is critiqued as a normative and alienating force. Janet Wilson has described how Kavan's 'defiant flouting of social convention [...] underpinned her deliberate engagement with otherness', and in the Ferguson novels, her characters approach such contraventions, and pay the price for it.[16] Her first two novels, *A Charmed Circle* and *The Dark Sisters*, explicitly highlight and problematise a perceived divide between traditional middle-class rural respectability and bohemian urban modernity. Beryl Deane in *A Charmed Circle*, frustrated with life at home in Hannington where her family seclude themselves in the Old Vicarage in a desperate attempt to shut out encroaching modernisation, is torn between her love for the countryside and her desire for new possibilities in metropolitan London. Ferguson's representation of tradition versus modernity reflects modernist artistic development; Molly Aguilar, the epitome of urban sophistication, appears to Beryl 'like a lily; not an ordinary, wholesome, common or garden lily, but some eccentric futurist creation' (181). If Molly personifies modernity, its new forms of aesthetic representation manifest an artificial beauty – rare, exotic, but unnatural and unwholesome. In *The Dark Sisters*, the eponymous Emerald and Karen Lamond respectively embody bohemian modernity and rural tradition, but neither succeeds in achieving fulfilment or in breaking away from the other; they remain tied together by bonds of love and hate. The conflict of tradition and modernity remains unresolved in these novels, and if the Home Counties represent the conservatism of affluent country life in Southern England, Helen Ferguson both subverts this and sets it in contrast to metropolitan and colonial spaces. Her representations of conventional British life are given from the perspective of protagonists who consistently fail to succeed within it and who inhabit its margins.

No tender relationship in these early novels is unmarred by the confrontation of opposing personalities and what is described in *The Dark Sisters* as 'the tyranny of love' (202); deeply felt antagonism seethes beneath casual exchanges between family members, friends and lovers. Frequent possibilities of romantic love, self-fulfilment and new ways of living culminate in disappointment. Olive and Beryl Deane in *A Charmed Circle* and Emerald and Karen Lamond in *The Dark Sisters* establish that in Ferguson's writing there is no sisterhood, even between sisters. Kavan's first biographer, David Callard, makes claims for 'the influence of D. H. Lawrence' on her Helen Ferguson period, and her characters struggle with the conflict between personal independence and love, described in a Lawrentian idiom of domination, submission, victory and defeat.[17] In her later writing as Anna Kavan, this detailed elaboration of characters' temperament and motivations disappears, and her isolated protagonists are alienated from the entire world rather than from other individuals; no connection of either love or hate is possible.

When she began publishing as Anna Kavan, the sparsity of her new style necessitated a move from Helen Ferguson's lengthy novels to stories and novellas; but again this break between Ferguson and Kavan is deceptive, for she was already writing in shorter forms before her name-change. In a letter to the Paris-based agent William Bradley, Helen Ferguson described her hopes of placing 'a number of short stories which are not quite of the conventional type or length'.[18] Offering a rare glimpse into her perception of her own writing during these years, 'not quite conventional' suggests a more nuanced category for her Ferguson writing. Bradley ultimately could not sell the stories, but her description predicts her coming departure in both form and genre. The three stories she published in *Home and Country* in 1937–1938, 'Martin's Wife', 'Christmas Afternoon in Burma' and 'Wives' Encounter', are written in the same style as her Ferguson books and share similar settings, scenarios and characters. Clara Jones has outlined the magazine's anxieties around publishing fiction and their preference for 'recognised and respectable middlebrow writers', testimony to Helen Ferguson's established status as a writer in this period.[19] The darker themes and gothic inflections of her novels are missing from these stories and their protagonists are socially unsuccessful but not alienated to the same extent. It is likely that the Women's Institute was familiar to the writer who 'graced the Chilterns' and that she shaped these short fictions for the *Home and Country* audience of middle-class Women's Institute members, invoking the 'conventional Home Counties' more explicitly than in her novels. As their titles suggest, each story centres on the life of a woman whose identity is defined by her husband, to whom they are, to varying degrees, inscrutable. These protagonists again fail to fully inhabit their social roles and long for something more 'real' than the performance of respectable British life; the grist to the plot in each story is a transgression from social convention.

In 'Martin's Wife', a husband's failure to introduce his bride to his tight-knit family before their marriage ultimately dooms its success. The Martin of this story bears close resemblance to Martin Lewison in *A Stranger Still*, and his enigmatic wife Fleur could be the character Anna Kavan, described in precisely the same terms as 'a stranger still, remote and incomprehensible'.[20] Fleur is an outsider who is never admitted into the circle of established family life; she remains a mystery to Martin until she eventually leaves him. In 'Wives' Encounter', Margaret's husband Arthur has invited his former wife for lunch and although Margaret is 'not old-fashioned or straight-laced or anything of that kind' (407), she finds the invitation peculiar.[21] Ann arrives looking young and stylish with her shingled hair; she is free from the domestic and maternal responsibilities that harry Margaret and, most of all, she is free from Arthur. Like Fleur and Martin, Margaret's inner life is a mystery to Arthur but she perceives with acuity that her husband's unusually attentive behaviour towards his new family is a performance of domestic happiness for the benefit of his former wife, and she refuses to support his charade.

The interwar setting of Helen Ferguson's writing makes the damage of the First World War and the anticipation of the Second integral to its backdrop. Her fifth novel, *Goose Cross*, is set in an English village, but in this instance the Home Counties are not so conventional. The superficial plot intrigue of a disputed cricket match is secondary to supernatural happenings, an ancient mystery, uncanny signs, demonic possession, madness, infidelity, incestuous desire, malevolent genius loci and death incarnated. This novel's fantastical elements, rustic setting and abundance of syncretically combined Christian and pagan imagery recall the rural fantastic of John Cowper Powys's *A Glastonbury Romance* (1932) and Sylvia Townsend Warner's *Lolly Willowes* (1926). Again, many themes of this text presage Kavan's later writing, especially madness and the clandestine life of inanimate objects. Thomas Spender is a veteran of the First World War (fittingly evoking the British 'Tommy') who finds himself subject to the psychic rift that affects many of Kavan's characters, 'torn, like the divided personality he was, between the two conflicting parts of his nature' (32). He is afflicted by a 'peculiar mental persecution' (30), believing himself to be possessed by a small china figure of Admiral Horatio Nelson. This seemingly inconsequential ornament embodies the weight of English patriotism, for Nelson's signal before the Battle of Trafalgar, 'England expects every man to do his duty', was taken up as a recruiting slogan for the First World War. Thus, the china Horatio evokes Thomas's wartime experiences; during the war 'his wakeful imagination had taken some strange twists' (65) and now he dreams of 'a vast sequence of disastrous events, huge, nameless catastrophes, ruinous wars and blood' (60).

Thomas both experiences and represents 'the blocked-up dam of bad memories, nightmares, trauma' which Valentine Cunningham has described as pouring forth into 'a whole battalion of War-minded books' in the late 1920s and 1930s.[22] His wife Judith's miscarriage has ended her physical desire for him; when he rapes her, the incident is only one of several sexual transgressions in the novel's complex web of plotlines. The psychological damage Thomas has endured is implicated in his estrangement from his wife and the injury he inflicts upon her, lending emphasis to the fact that Matthew Kavan in *Let Me Alone*, who also rapes his wife, is likewise a veteran of the war. There are soldiers everywhere in the village of Goose Cross, from the excavated bones of a Roman warrior to the toy armies assembled by Mr Vyse. Thomas manifests in the extreme the symptoms of automation that afflict Helen Ferguson's interwar characters, conforming to Tyrus Miller's identification of a late modernist perception of 'all-pervasive, collective, and incurable shell-shock, from which all suffer and which need not have trench experience as its precondition (though for many, of course, it did)'.[23] Late modernist writers suggest, in Miller's account, that everyone 'has a bit of the automaton about him or her, it follows from the conditions of history within which we must make our selves, our lives, our cities'.[24]

The final novel Kavan published as Helen Ferguson, *Rich Get Rich* (1937), shifts focus onto a male protagonist, Swithin Chance, but in doing so subverts the traditional economics of gender inequality. Driven by a longing for comfort and beauty, Swithin marries a wealthy woman in order to raise himself from his middle-class but impoverished beginnings; finding himself restrained and objectified by his dependence, he leaves her to become 'a sort of male governess' (211). Swithin is an aesthete, quoting from Auden and Lawrence and working on a never-to-be-completed novel; his deep horror of mechanisation and his pacifism are motifs that continue into Kavan's later writing. Perceiving the folly of his youthful ambition for wealth, Swithin finds himself involved on the fringes of a group of left-wing radicals. Ferguson again subverts the traditional *Bildungsroman* by marking Swithin for death from the novel's outset and despite the 'chance' of his name, he is fated to die. The past war claims another victim in *Rich Get Rich* when Swithin's friend Captain Evans dies from the tuberculosis which had 'slowly developed as a result of being gassed in the war' (77). Evans, whose name echoes that of Septimus Smith's dead comrade in Woolf's *Mrs Dalloway* (1925), serves as a reminder to both Swithin and the reader of the extent to which the First World War haunts interwar fiction. Swithin's resolve to make Evans the protagonist of his own pacifist novel, in the hope that his story will help to prevent future wars, also acknowledges anxieties of approaching war. Violence lingers and accumulates in Ferguson's novels, reflecting their literary times for, as Marina MacKay has observed, there are 'few corners in the 1930s novel into which the threat of violent upheaval does not intrude'.[25] In Helen Ferguson's writing, physically damaged veterans continue to die slowly, and psychically damaged veterans have brought the brutality of the battlefield home to their domestic lives. The manifestation of war-induced trauma in these novels, and its indiscriminate effect on both soldiers and civilians, presages Kavan's Second World War stories. In her postwar writing, especially *Ice*, she would amplify her representations of sexual violence, and in line with other British experimentalists such as J. G. Ballard, Ann Quin, Angela Carter and Alan Burns, it would continue to be metonymic of the effects of global conflict on subjectivity formation and social interaction.

Empire and Unreality

Although she spent the greater part of her life in England and is ostensibly a British writer, Kavan had a restless existence; she was born in

France, lived in California in her early childhood and in Burma with her first husband, spent regular stretches in France during the 1920s and 1930s, travelled extensively during the Second World War (in Northern Europe, the Dutch East Indies, the United States and Mexico), settling for periods in Southern California, New York and New Zealand, and later spent stretches of time at her mother's home in South Africa. This itinerant lifestyle left her with little sense of national belonging and appears to have inflected the enduring sense of psychological exile in her writing, which she described as 'the refugee mind'.[26] Recent critical reappraisals of her work have begun to examine how the time she spent out of Britain, especially in Burma and New Zealand, profoundly shaped her fiction.[27]

In Ferguson's second story for *Home and Country*, 'Christmas Afternoon in Burma', Dennis and Clare are a British couple celebrating with friends in a remote hillside outpost. Clare, recently arrived in the country, finds colonial attitudes repressive: 'You mustn't go for a walk alone. You mustn't speak to the natives. You mustn't pick flowers. Or eat fruit. You mustn't this, you mustn't that. Everything was hidden away behind a mysterious taboo' (630). Like Anna in *Let Me Alone*, Clare perceives her British compatriots as 'unreal', 'just ghosts playing at Christmas' (631). Depressed by their charade of festive cheer, she strays outside the compound into the native landscape and finds release: 'Ah, but this was perfect, this was real.' She feels how 'good it was to slip away and find reality at last; to creep under the edges of the taboo' (631) and thus, the 'unreality' of the story, as in Ferguson's other writing, is the performance of British social convention, made explicit in this colonial setting. Just as George Orwell's *Burmese Days* (1934) identifies the 'stifling, stultifying world' of colonial life in which '[f]ree speech is unthinkable', Ferguson's writing demonstrates how rigid adherence to what Orwell describes as the 'pukka sahibs' code' suppresses and ultimately destroys internal life.[28] For Ferguson, whose time in the country was coincident with Orwell's, Burma shaped not only her depictions of the British Empire, but her representations of psychic life; Clare's nascent experience as a colonial wife in 'Christmas Afternoon' is a shadow of the existential annihilation that overwhelms Anna Kavan in *Let Me Alone*.

Helen Ferguson's anti-imperialism is explicit in her writing, but although the marginal position of her characters within British colonial society allows her to critique the dominance and prestige of Empire, her representations of colonial life are always from the perspective of coloniser and blind to the situations and selfhood of those colonised. In her fiction set in colonial Burma, the indigenous people appear gay and charming, but they are mere ciphers in contrast to the complex subjectivity of her protagonists and there is no possibility of any connection between her estranged characters and native others. The natural landscape in her Burmese writings remains remote or hostile, and as Lara Vetter has observed, Anna's descriptions of the blank evil of the Burmese landscape in *Let Me Alone* only reflect her marriage.[29]

Later in her career, Kavan would approach race and colonialism more directly in several of her lesser-known short stories. 'Annunciation' (1958) is a gothic tale of a young girl incarcerated in the house of her white, racist grandmother.[30] Although the story makes no explicit references to its location, it is clearly influenced by Kavan's visits to her mother and stepfather in South Africa in the late 1940s around the time that apartheid was instituted; their already strained relationship was further complicated by disagreements over 'the colour question'.[31] In 'Annunciation' Mary is kept out of sight for obscure reasons connected to her dead mother's disgrace and the insinuation that she is 'not quite like other children of her age' (21). Her grandmother takes Mary's first period as evidence of her potential sexual promiscuity, making her 'disgusting' (27) and associating her with blackness. Mary's name and the title's allusion to the immaculate conception throw her grandmother's disturbing insistence on sexual and racial purity into stark relief. Another (posthumously published) story written during Kavan's time in New Zealand relates a conversation with an indigenous man who feels himself a traitor to his own race. He is a 'man with two faces' – 'one was white and the other one brown' – but neither fits him comfortably and 'the strain of the indecision was driving him mad'.[32] In these stories, writing as Anna Kavan, she more explicitly indicts the racial prejudice of white colonists, incorporating race into her exploration of liminal identities and probing the complex psychological impact of racism and colonisation.

Kavan's interludes in colonial and postcolonial locations had clear effects on her representations of subjectivity, aligning her work with that of other mid-century writers whose protagonists simultaneously benefit from Empire and fail to succeed within it, with disintegrating psychological consequences. Parallels between her writing and that of Jean Rhys have been noted by various scholars and reading their work comparatively illuminates some of the 'not quite conventional' aspects of their early novels. As Erica L. Johnson and Patricia Moran have observed, the two were mutual admirers, and Rhys's readers, like Kavan's, 'have found her work dark and dispiriting'.[33] Kavan's Helen Ferguson period was coincident with Jean Rhys's early novels, and both detail the daily humiliations of women navigating financially precarious and sometimes morally dubious existences on the fringes of respectable British society, at times in colonial and continental European locations. While Rhys's heroines often inhabit the seamy world of boarding houses, Ferguson's characters have greater access to 'respectable' society but still consistently fail to make a success of their opportunities. As Mary L. Emery has described it, in Rhys's novels 'the heroine attempts to follow conventional romance sequencing' but consistently fails to achieve a happy ending, and this same structure of established plotting with thwarted expectations frames the Ferguson novels.[34] Unmoored and friendless, reliant upon men who make use of them and family members who disapprove of them, these protagonists make poor choices and fail to extricate themselves from their unhappy circumstances with an apparent complicity that has posed difficulties for some feminist scholars.

Both Rhys and Kavan frankly represent extramarital sex and sexual assault as well as traumatic experiences of pregnancy, miscarriage, abortion and early infant death. For Rhys's early heroines, sex is tied up with economic dependence, for Kavan's it is often complicated by the expectation of sexual availability within marriage. In Rhys's fiction, the Caribbean is frequently a lost paradise, the counterpoint to restrictive European society; in Helen Ferguson's writing, British social conventionality, which inflects the unsettled experiences of reality that recur throughout her fiction, is never more stifling and damaging than as it manifests in its colonies. Johnson and Moran have described Rhys's representations of 'the mind of the isolated and socially marginalised woman whose very existence appears unreal and insubstantial, a woman whose mind is, to more socially integrated subjects, at best illegible and invisible, at worst "potty", neurotic and pathological'.[35] For Rhys's characters, as with Ferguson's, their 'unreal and insubstantial' existence is something they themselves become acutely aware of and which frequently develops from their abusive and exploitative relationships with men. Just as the character Anna Kavan feels herself to be 'fictious' (286) in her violent marriage, Julia Martin in *After Leaving Mr Mackenzie* finds that following her affair she 'didn't believe in [her] self any more'.[36] The fragmented existence of Ferguson's Anna Kavan can be seen too in Rhys's early heroines who frequently must 'pull themselves together'.[37] Kavan's early reflections on her own name-change – 'I've really succeeded in changing my name to Anna Kavan, but it doesn't seem to have changed my bad luck' – echo Sasha Jansen's in *Good Morning, Midnight*: 'I thought it might change my luck if I changed my name'.[38] Luck, or fate, is the determining force in the lives of Rhys's and Ferguson's protagonists; their limited choices make free will a luxury afforded to those with more money, more friends, more respectability and more confidence, highlighting the iron grip and potentially destructive force of British social convention by telling it from its margins.

In the face of formidable social expectations and disapproval, these profoundly unhappy heroines are plagued by feelings of unreality, fictionality, loss of selfhood, and psychic division, experiences which would remain central to Rhys's and Kavan's later writing and become increasingly significant across mid-century fiction.

Realism and Reality at Mid-Century

From the feelings of unreality and fictitiousness that plague 'Anna Kavan' in *Let Me Alone*, to the narrator of *Ice* who casually notes: 'Reality had always been something of an unknown quantity to me' (6), Kavan's characters display consistently tenuous relations to the reality of their fictional worlds, a preoccupation of her Helen Ferguson period that deepened and became more self-reflexive in her writing as Anna Kavan. Whether their difficulty maintaining contact with a shared 'reality' is a symptom of, or incitement to, madness (like 'Anna Kavan' or the narrators of her asylum stories), or whether they thrive on undermining the concept of the real (like the narrator of *Ice*), her protagonists are driven and shaped by reality's contingency. As Eleonora Rao has described it: 'Kavan's fiction emphasises the impossibility of an unmediated real world of which the attainment of concrete knowledge could be possible'.[39] Ironically, what has been perceived as the conventional 'realism' of Helen Ferguson's novels often describes her protagonists' perception of themselves and their world as 'unreal'. Her more mimetically realist texts (as Helen Ferguson and after) represent characters experiencing alienation, psychiatric breakdown and feelings of unreality that the reader understands to be subjective experiences within the 'real' world of the text; her more experimental narratives, which almost always make some use of the first person, represent worlds that reflect those inner experiences, encouraging the reader to share these sensations with her characters. Writing as Anna Kavan, she began to experiment formally with the themes she had introduced as Helen Ferguson, levelling the disparity between the Ferguson novels' broadly conventional narrative style and their often intense and unnerving subject matter, as her characters desperately attempt, and frequently fail, to negotiate 'conventional' British social life. Thus, the emotional and psychological torment of Kavan's later protagonists becomes embodied in the world of the text, manifest as unfathomable machines, insistent birdcall or the onslaught of a new ice age.

In one of Kavan's most polemical *Horizon* reviews from 1946, in which she censures postwar literature's nostalgic escapism back to the 'smug, self-confident era' of the Victorian age, she evokes Kafka as an exemplary writer:[40]

> The mature artist's work is the outcome of his own experience; his own thought, imagination, emotion. It is his own death which Kafka describes in the terrible last paragraph of *The Trial* when the knife is turned twice in K's heart. The whole of Kafka's life is in the book as well as his last moments. And the poor, crazy man in *The Overcoat* is mad Gogol himself.
> Writers of the quality of Kafka and Gogol do not run away from reality. They have too much integrity, both as artists and human beings, to indulge in escapist flights. Especially sensitive, they are especially vulnerable, and they escape nothing. When life frightens and hurts them, they do not look back at the nursery windows with longing eyes, but incorporate in themselves a part of life's fear and pain. The artistic value of their work endures because it is also a part of reality. It is conscious, uncompromising, personal, true. It is life.[41]

Here, Kavan invokes the death of the author over twenty years before Roland Barthes's seminal essay. For Barthes, this death is a figurative relinquishing of authority, not the demise of the individual writer, but of their power to determine meaning; for Kavan, the association between reality and fiction is so intimate that the author 'describes his own death' in the killing of his protagonist. This interpretation of the writers she most esteemed offers insight into Kavan's relationship with her own characters, suggesting that she invested them not with the circumstances of her life but, in the spirit of Gustave Flaubert's 'Madame Bovary, c'est moi', with the psychological and emotional experiences she had accumulated. Without this, she believed, fiction (realist or not) is flight from reality. Kavan thus aimed to incorporate the whole of her life in her work not by detailing its events and relationships but by writing a 'true' reality which drew from her experience, imagination and emotion, and encompassed something other than mimetic representation.

As the mid-century progressed, Kavan remained attentive to matters concerning reality and representation; in a 1964 letter to Raymond Marriott about reluctant media coverage of the first London 'happening', she asked:

> Haven't we had enough of realistic descriptions by now? I thought they'd been done so well as they can be done over and over again, and as long ago as Zola etc. I find it hard to make out a convincing case for the continuance of factual writing, when the microphone catches reality and transmits it to millions, who thus acquire their facts far more easily and quickly than by reading the shortest book or seeing a one act play. It certainly seems time for a movement away from realism. [. . .]
> You know I'm very interested in this reality thing – in the changes that continually shatter the seemingly objective world, which only our mental and

physical health hold together in some sort of equilibrium, and which the least indisposition causes to slip and dissolve in confusion.[42]

Kavan's sentiments echo earlier anxieties about the effects on the literary and visual arts of twentieth-century sound recording, universal transmission and mechanical reproduction, notably articulated by Walter Benjamin.[43] Benjamin's attention to the 'authenticity' of the artwork in the modern age lies at a tangent to the 'literary authenticity' that Zadie Smith interrogates in her observations on Kavan's reputation for autobiographical extremity, but both emphasise the need for a sense of veracity in the aesthetic experience of the artwork. What Kavan describes as her interest in 'this reality thing' in the 1960s can be charted throughout her fiction from the 1930s onward. But her call for 'a movement away from realism', which she associates with the nineteenth-century novel, shows her engaging with postwar debates around this term which demonstrated, as Raymond Williams would put it, 'what a powerful, and yet vague, word "realism" can be'.[44] That Kavan evokes Émile Zola as an exemplary writer of 'realistic descriptions', while he referred to his own 'experimental method' of writing seventy years earlier, intimates what a vague and contingent word 'experimental' can also be.[45]

The relationship between reality and realism, and the definition of these terms, was thus shifting in the mid-century. Alain Robbe-Grillet would claim:

> Every writer thinks he is a realist. No writer ever calls himself abstract, an illusionist, a visionary, a fantasist, a falsifier [. . .] Realism is not a clearly defined theory by reference to which we can classify some writers as being opposed to others.[46]

For Robbe-Grillet, what interests any writer 'is the real world' and each has their own 'idea of reality' (153). Corresponding intimately to Kavan's earlier reflections on the integrity of the artist, Robbe-Grillet maintains that the author creates reality in the writing of fiction. The clear affinities between Kavan's experimental style and that of the *nouveau roman*, especially in undermining character and plot, are reinforced by resonances between her thinking and the theoretical formulations of writers such as Robbe-Grillet and Nathalie Sarraute. Yet her narrative experiment, which began with *Asylum Piece* in 1940, predates (or was at best simultaneous with) the earliest examples of what would later be termed the *nouveau roman*, and certainly before translations appeared in Britain. These resemblances, rather than demonstrating any direct influence, indicate the emergence of common features across mid-century experimental writing, encouraging readings of Kavan's fiction in a

European tradition and countering notions of British literature in this period as insular and parochial.[47]

Later assessments have largely concluded that, in Dominic Head's words, 'the realism/ experimentalism furore [...] is rarely reflected in the actual practice of writing'.[48] In her study of British women experimentalists, Carole Sweeney maintains that the writers she considers, including Kavan, 'experimented with language and narrative in ways that did not necessitate a polarisation between realism and, its putative opposite, experimentalism', rather they were engaged in '[a]dapting and extending realism's boundaries and codes'.[49] Kavan's diverse and hybrid style shows her shifting between and merging styles and genres; what remains constant throughout her work is a more or less prominent probing of 'reality'. The supernatural features of the Helen Ferguson texts, most explicit in *Goose Cross*, already presage the more definite use of the fantastic in her later writing. As Christine Brooke-Rose maintained in her postwar study, endeavouring to 'account for the return of the fantastic in all its forms' (7), its various literary manifestations, as well as the range of critical approaches to interpreting these, were all responding to, and attempting to reconcile, the twentieth century's 'reality crisis' (3) fuelled by global conflict, scientific advances, the decline of Empire, and gender and class politics.[50]

Julia Jordan has demonstrated how the disputes between realism and experimentalism that accompanied mid-century writing 'marked the paradigm shift that took place in the postwar period in the cultural, aesthetic, and philosophical apprehension of uncertainty', identifying how experimentalists in this age 'attempted to disrupt the epistemological foundations on which realism is made possible – even when remaining faithful to realist techniques'.[51] Kavan's oeuvre spans the line that Jordan traces from late modernism to the postwar avant-garde, and the interrogation of reality in her early writing is indicative of the already-present uncertainty underlying the anxieties which would later accrue around 'realism' when the term, especially for those who stood against it, came to signify absolute knowledge. Helen Ferguson's novels, which largely remained faithful to realist strategies, predict her writing as Anna Kavan in depicting the experience of disrupted reality which her experimental writing would replicate for her readers. Thus, interwar fiction had already begun to explore its own relation to the philosophy of 'subject and object and the nature of reality', as epitomised by Mr Ramsay's work in Woolf's *To the Lighthouse* (1927); as the mid-century progressed, this project became more acutely self-reflexive and its outcome more ambiguous.

Anna Kavan Rewrites Helen Ferguson: Who Are You?

The continuities and deviations between Helen Ferguson's novels and her writing as Anna Kavan can be observed explicitly in her short novel *Who Are You?* (1963), which is a rewriting of the final segment of *Let Me Alone*. Kavan's return to this autobiographically inspired episode more than three decades after the first novel was published implies that the fictional 'Anna Kavan' held some significance for the writer who had appropriated her name. The dysfunctional marriage of the earlier novel is rewritten in *Who Are You?* not once but twice; the novel's otherwise linear development is disturbed by a temporal schism when the narrative skips back to an earlier moment in the plot, repeating the previous events, an experiment with repetition that Kavan would continue to develop in *Ice*. This reiteration is a replaying rather than simply a retelling of the events; the situation is subtly altered. The novels' respective titles signpost their shift in perspective; Anna's persecuted plea of 'let me alone' is replaced by a cry of existential uncertainty 'who are you?' in the later work. Burma of *Let Me Alone* becomes an unidentified British colony in *Who Are You?* and the protagonists also lose their names, identified instead by monikers determined by their physical or psychological attributes; Matthew Kavan becomes 'Mr Dog Head', the name by which his native servants refer to him, and Anna (having sacrificed her name to her author) is simply 'the girl'. The couple's dysfunctional relationship loses its history but not its antagonism, but the girl is more emotionally detached from her husband than Anna from Matthew, demonstrating the lack of affect typical of her later characters. The feelings of unreality and division that plague Anna are diffused into the world of the text and its structure; the girl's fractured existence, already unreal and dreamlike, is ruptured more explicitly in the novel's two distinct sections.

Let Me Alone and *Who Are You?* demonstrate the characteristic narrative styles of Helen Ferguson and Anna Kavan. *Who Are You?* is substantially shorter, covering less than a fifth of the action of *Let Me Alone*, and is written in the bleak, sparse language that characterises her Kavan texts. Reading the two texts closely shows that in places Kavan directly reworked her earlier narrative, rearranging and condensing descriptive passages. In the rewriting her images become stronger, stranger and more hallucinatory but, characteristic of her narrative nonchalance, are presented more prosaically. The approach of monsoon in both texts expedites the conflation of emotional and atmospheric tension prevalent throughout Kavan's work. In *Let Me Alone* the atmospheric augmentation extends over two chapters; in *Who Are You?* it is first compressed into several pages and in the second run is summarily dealt with in a couple of sentences. In the Ferguson text the sequence opens 'By the middle of April it was almost too hot to live' (292). In *Who Are You?* the temporal setting is more immediate – 'It has now become almost too hot to live'; in the second iteration the passage becomes further condensed – 'Now it becomes almost too hot to live' (78, 110). The shift from past tense to present perfect and finally into the present marks an increasing narrative urgency, intensifying the immediacy of the rising heat. In *Who Are You?* the passages that follow gather impressions from across an entire chapter of *Let Me Alone*. On the whole, even the same images are altered in the later text but some motifs remain almost untouched in the translation from Ferguson to Kavan. In the original *Let Me Alone*:

> A curious coppery film, like a veil of electricity made visible, hung in the upper air. (306)

In *Who Are You?* the same phrase dispenses with figurative language (the 'veil of electricity'), moves from past to present tense, and is phrased more directly (subclause following, rather than breaking, main clause):

> A peculiar coppery film hangs in the upper air, as though electricity were made visible. (78–9)

Kavan rewrites the language of her earlier text to make it tighter, more urgent, less figurative and descriptive. She disrobes Ferguson's descriptive language of any explicit sense of the bizarre, often replacing simile with more complex metaphors and editing out references to aesthetic or emotional response. In *Let Me Alone*, Anna finds the Burmese landscape surreal and extraordinary:

> There was a changing, eerie beauty about the landscape. From day to day it altered, assuming gradually a strange, coppery, metallic brilliance, almost orange-coloured, like a Martian landscape. There was something unbelievable about it, really other-worldly. You could imagine yourself on some other planet. (292–3)

In the rewriting of this passage the human response is lost; both Anna's impressions and the possibility of imaginative inspiration in the second person vanish, the language is distilled, and the alien and the incredible become commonplace. The metamorphosis of the environment is signalled as being both less strange and less beautiful:

> The world is assuming a uniform coppery tinge with shades of orange, like a Martian landscape. (78)

In contrary motion, as Anna's response is edited out, the landscape itself takes on human characteristics; in *Let Me Alone*:

> Every day a little hotter than the last, with the hot sun riding up, blinding bright, into the burning sky, and the cauldron-like earth simmering below. [. . .] There was a strange electric stirring and undulating in the fiery atmosphere. (299–300)

This same sketch in *Who Are You?* animates the environment:

> Each morning the sun leaps triumphantly, unchallenged, into an empty sky [. . .] while the red-hot earth seethes like an immense cauldron in the eerie thunderlight of an eclipse, electric tremors vibrating in the breathless air. (78)

The measure of the rising sun's force is no longer its effect ('blinding'), but its mood ('leaping wilfully and triumphantly'), and the hyperbole of Ferguson's 'fiery atmosphere' works harder but achieves less than Kavan's description of the air itself struggling for breath. Bleeding Ferguson's protagonist of both affect and physical sensations, Kavan transfuses these into the landscape, redistributing the tremendous weight of Anna's feelings into the world itself. The rhetoric of emotional torment in Helen Ferguson's portrait of Anna's depression, identified by the *TLS* reviewer as 'persistently gloomy', tests rather than excites the reader's empathy; writing as Anna Kavan, her nameless protagonist is the victim not of an excess of emotion but of a world that conspires in her misery. This loss of affect, dramatically altering the reader's relationship to the world of the text and its characters, is key to the shift from Ferguson's narrative style to Kavan's, and indicative of wider trends in experimental writing.

Because Kavan's work has thwarted critical desires to fit her into established literary frameworks, her Helen Ferguson novels have become an easy category against which to define it, and her name-change has become a convenient marker of a break between writing that can be dismissed as commonplace and that which cannot. But the thematic continuities across this divide, and the variability of Kavan's writing style following her name-change, encourage reading her entire output, including her Helen Ferguson writing, as a diverse but comprehensive body of work. Thematically unconventional and, at times, thematically anti-realist, the Helen Ferguson novels already interrogate and undermine the concept and experience of reality; her nascent interest in the relationship between the real world and aesthetic representation, especially literary fiction, would develop in her later writing into a more explicit confrontation with objective reality, a move reflected more broadly across mid-century writing.[52]

Notes

1. John Berger, *Ways of Seeing* [1972] (London: Penguin, 2008), p. 41.
2. See, for example, Vivian Gornick, *The End of the Novel of Love* (London: Virago, 1999), p. 61; Carole Sweeney, 'Cadaverised Girls: The Writing of Anna Kavan', *Textual Practice*, 34:4 (April 2020), 647–68; Céline Magot, 'The Palimpsest Girl in *Ice* by Anna Kavan', *Miranda*, 12 (2016), <https://miranda.revues.org/8675> (accessed 9 September 2018).
3. Rhys Davies, 'A Lady and a Leopard', *Queen* (18–31 March 1970), 44; repeated in 'The Bazooka Girl: A Note on Anna Kavan', *London Magazine*, 1970, 13–16.
4. Rhys Davies, 'The Bazooka Girl', p. 13.
5. Anna Kavan, *The Cactus Sign*, unpublished manuscript, Anna Kavan Papers, *MFL*, p. 24. Kavan was working on this manuscript during her time travelling in the Second World War, immediately after she began publishing as Anna Kavan.
6. As noted under 'Contributors', *Harper's Magazine* (1 March 1941): 'She wrote her first book in Burma at the age of twenty'.
7. Sincere thanks to Clara Jones for drawing these stories to my attention. 'Martin's Wife', *Home and Country* (July 1937), 365–7; 'Christmas Afternoon in Burma', *Home and Country* (December 1937), 629–31; 'Wives' Encounter', *Home and Country* (October 1938), 407–8.
8. Records show Helen Ferguson held a lending card for Shakespeare and Company in Paris for the years 1929 and 1932. See Joshua Kotin, Rebecca Sutton Koeser et al., *Shakespeare and Company Project*, version 1.5.2. Center for Digital Humanities, Princeton University, 2021, <https://shakespeareandco.princeton.edu> (accessed 1 September 2021).
9. Helen Ferguson to Jonathan Cape, 13 October 1930, *JC*.
10. Helen Ferguson to W. A. Bradley, 21 April 1933, William A. Bradley Literary Agency Records, *HRC*.
11. Aorewa McLeod Interview with Ian Hamilton, Auckland, 1981, transcribed in Raewyn Glynn, 'Anna Kavan on Ice: An Encounter with Anna Kavan's Wartime Writing Via New Zealand and the Arctic Imaginary' (unpublished MA thesis: University of Auckland, 1997).
12. Betty Walker, 'New Novels: *Let Me Alone*', *Times Literary Supplement* (4 December 1930), p. 1036.
13. Walter Benjamin, 'On Some Motifs in Baudelaire', *Illuminations*, trans. by Harry Zorn (London: Pimlico, 1999), p. 184.
14. Benjamin, p. 184.
15. Kavan's own visual art is even less well-known than her writing. She studied at the London Central School of Arts and Crafts in the mid-1920s and exhibited at the Wertheim Gallery in London during the 1930s (as Helen Ferguson) and later at the Redfern Galleries (see Lorraine Toeg to Richard R. Centing, 1971: 'she exhibited twice at the Redfern Galleries', *UT*). Her surviving paintings, which include her landscapes from the 1930s as well as dark, expressionistic images of execution, are mostly in private ownership or held in the McFarlin Library collections. See Natalie Ferris, 'The Double Play of Mirrors: Anna Kavan, Autobiography and Self-Portraiture', *Women: A Cultural Review*, 28:4 (Winter 2017), 285–94.

16. Janet Wilson, 'A Pacific Sojourn: Anna Kavan and the New Zealand Connection, 1941–2', *Women: A Cultural Review*, 28:4 (Winter 2017), 343–57, p. 347.
17. David Callard, *The Case of Anna Kavan: A Biography* (London: Peter Owen, 1992) p. 23, p. 84.
18. Helen Ferguson to W. A. Bradley, 21 April 1933, *HRC*.
19. Clara Jones, "Mystery at the Lilacs': Elizabeth Bowen's Thriller Serial for Home and Country Magazine', *Literature and History*, 27:1 (2018), 3–27.
20. Helen Ferguson, 'Martin's Wife', p. 366.
21. Helen Ferguson, 'Wives' Encounter', p. 407.
22. Valentine Cunningham, *British Writers of the Thirties* (Oxford: Oxford University Press, 1988), pp. 44, 45.
23. Tyrus Miller, *Late Modernism: Politics, Fiction, and the Arts Between the Wars* (Berkeley: University of California Press, 1999), p. 24.
24. Miller, p. 24.
25. Marina MacKay, 'The Literary Novel', in *The Cambridge Companion to British Literature of the 1930s*, ed. by James Smith (Cambridge: Cambridge University Press, 2019), p. 44.
26. Anna Kavan, 'Two New Zealand Pieces', in *Choice: Some New Stories and Prose*, ed. by William Sansom (London: Progress Publishing, 1946), 66–73, p. 66.
27. See especially Wilson, 'A Pacific Sojourn', 285–94; Kate Houlden, 'Queering the World or Worlding the Queer? New Readings of Anna Kavan's *Who Are You?*', *Women: A Cultural Review*, 28:4 (Winter 2017), 295–311.
28. George Orwell, *Burmese Days* [1934] (London: Secker & Warburg, 1949), p. 69.
29. Lara Vetter, 'Journeys without Maps: Literature and Spiritual Experience', in *British Literature in Transition, 1920–1940: Futility and Anarchy*, ed. by Charles Ferrall and Dougal McNeill (Cambridge: Cambridge University Press, 2018), 68–83, p. 81.
30. Anna Kavan, 'Annunciation', in *A Bright Green Field* (London: Peter Owen, 1958).
31. Anna Kavan to Raymond Marriott, 21 January 1948, quoted in David Callard, p. 94.
32. Kavan, 'The man with two faces', *Anna Kavan's New Zealand: A Pacific Interlude in a Turbulent Life*, ed. by Jennifer Sturm (Auckland: Vintage, Random House New Zealand, 2009), pp. 84, 85.
33. Erica L. Johnson and Patricia Moran (eds), 'Introduction: The Haunting of Jean Rhys', in *Jean Rhys: Twenty-First-Century Approaches* (Edinburgh: Edinburgh University Press, 2015), p. 10.
34. Mary L. Emery, *Jean Rhys at World's End: Novels of Colonial and Sexual Exile* (Austin: University of Texas Press, 1990), p. 123.
35. Johnson and Moran, p. 10.
36. Jean Rhys, *After Leaving Mr Mackenzie* [1930] (London: Penguin, 2000), p. 38.
37. Julia Martin must 'pull herself together' in *After Leaving Mr Mackenzie*, p. 31, and Sasha Jansen is told repeatedly to 'pull yourself together' in *Good Morning, Midnight*, p. 18, 27.

38. Anna Kavan to Ian Hamilton, 11 November 1940, *NLNZ*; Jean Rhys, *Good Morning, Midnight* [1939] (London: Penguin, 2000), p. 11.
39. Eleonora Rao, 'The "Black Sun": Anna Kavan's Narratives of Abjection', *Textus*, 9 (1991), 119–46, p. 136.
40. Anna Kavan, 'Selected Notices: Back to Victoria', *Horizon*, 13:73 (January 1946), p. 63.
41. Kavan, *Horizon*, 13:73, p. 65.
42. Anna Kavan to Raymond Marriott, September 1964, Anna Kavan Papers, *MFL*.
43. See Walter Benjamin, 'The Work of Art in the Age of Mechanical Reproduction', *Illuminations*, trans. by Harry Zorn (London: Pimlico, 1999).
44. Raymond Williams, 'Realism and the Contemporary Novel', *Universities and Left Review*, 4, Summer 1958, 22–5, p. 22. See, for example, Georg Lukács, *The Meaning of Contemporary Realism* [1957], trans. by John and Necke Mander (London: Merlin Press, 1963).
45. Zola, Émile, 'The Experimental Novel', in *The Experimental Novel and Other Essays*, trans. by Belle M. Sherman (New York: The Cassell Publishing Co., 1893), p. 11.
46. Alain Robbe-Grillet, 'From Realism to Reality' [1955 and 1963], *Snapshots and Towards a New Novel*, trans. by Barbara Wright (London: Calder and Boyars, 1965), 153–61, p. 153.
47. For detailed study of the influence of the *nouveau roman* on British writing see Adam Guy, *The nouveau roman and Writing in Britain after Modernism* (Oxford: Oxford University Press, 2019).
48. Dominic Head, *The Cambridge Introduction to Modern British Fiction, 1950–2000* (Cambridge: Cambridge University Press, 2002), p. 226.
49. Carole Sweeney, *Vagabond Fictions: Gender and Experiment in British Women's Writing, 1945–1970* (Edinburgh: Edinburgh University Press, 2020), p. 4.
50. Christine Brooke-Rose, *A Rhetoric of the Unreal: Studies in Narrative and Structure, Especially of the Fantastic* (Cambridge: Cambridge University Press, 1981).
51. Julia Jordan, *Late Modernism and the Avant-Garde British Novel: Oblique Strategies* (Oxford: Oxford University Press, 2020), pp. 26–7.

Chapter 2

Psychiatry, Anti-Psychiatry and the Asylum at Mid-Century

Kavan's narrative experiment under her new name began with *Asylum Piece* (1940). Writing in the first person for the first time and introducing the characteristically sparse style that would continue in much of her later work, her elusive and deeply unreliable narrator in these stories (like many of her characters from this time forward) has no history or name; their identity is defined only by negative experiences of emptiness, hopelessness, guilt and persecution. This anonymous but distinctive narrative voice, in turns despairing and affectless, is interspersed with more realist third-person narratives, a combination that would characterise her later fiction. The asylum experience would continue to be a central feature of Kavan's writing throughout the 1940s in stories collected in *I Am Lazarus* (1945) and in the satirical novel *The Horse's Tale* (1949). These writings represented and responded to mid-century advances in psychiatric treatment (particularly drug and talking therapies), along with a growing critique of psychiatry and asylum incarceration. But these developments were at the sharp end of broader cultural changes in perceptions of subjectivity and human relations, and Kavan's experimental strategies to disturb the reader's relationship with the text would become a wider feature of mid-century writing. The barriers to communication and understanding between the depressed subject and others, and between patient and psychiatrist, touched the same issues of human relations and literary representations addressed by Virginia Woolf and Nathalie Sarraute, as outlined in the introduction to this book, necessitating new ways of writing character. Kavan's experiment in *Asylum Piece* suggests that the experience of the psychiatric patient, seemingly so outside of normal life, shows *in extremis* a disrupted relationship to self, others and objective reality that would increase and intensify across the literature of the mid-century.

Notwithstanding the continuities noted in the previous chapter, the shift from Helen Ferguson's psychological realism to the bleak and haunted narratives of her first publication as Anna Kavan is striking. Freed from the constraints of realist plot and character development, much of the narrative work in *Asylum Piece* is done by ambiguity and inference. Sketched out in language as spare and unornamented as the stark reality it describes, this more experimental mode of writing formalised the representation of profound depression and psychic division experienced by Helen Ferguson's characters. The protagonists of Kavan's asylum stories, whether patients in the institution or narrators in a hostile world, internalise their confinement and simultaneously project their despair onto their surroundings. Augmenting the gothic elements of her earlier novels and leaving the reader uncertain of where delusion ends and real-life surveillance and confinement begin, her asylum writing shows, as well as tells, the enmeshed experiences of severe depression, psychiatric intervention and confinement.

The brief, fragmentary and disjointed tales in *Asylum Piece* bear out Helen Ferguson's description of her earlier stories as 'not quite conventional' in type and length. Their singular title encourages reading them as a cohesive text which constitutes a single 'piece' of a larger whole or series of fragments. The stories are loosely but intricately connected; shifts in tense, mood and situation trouble the stability of the first-person voice, there are few clues as to whether the narrator of one story is the same as the next and any sense of progressive linearity repeatedly slips away. The narrator's gender is seldom indicated; only in some stories, and at rare moments, is the voice definitely female. Minor characters, identified by initials, reappear in subtly altered incarnations as the world of the text and its inhabitants shift and mutate. Any distinction between dream, reality and delusion is impossible to pin down. The collection opens with three gothic tales, which are the overtly sensational prelude to the more ambiguous interior narrative of the collection, but their themes of unjust condemnation, confinement and surveillance anticipate the later stories. The oblique and persecuted first-person voice then begins its narration, broken by a sequence of eight numbered 'Asylum Pieces' (all but one in the third person) before the first person returns in the final two stories.

Written in the immediate aftermath of her psychiatric breakdown and internment in the late 1930s, *Asylum Piece* was undoubtedly influenced by Kavan's experiences but, transmuted into fiction, this portrait of an unidentified and disembodied narrator reflects the world outside the asylum. Desmond MacCarthy observed the 'beauty about these stories which has nothing to do with their pathological interest, and is the result of art', while Edwin Muir described how: 'The fears and suspicions are a little more articulate, the conviction of oncoming disaster a little more definite; but they are all recognizable, they are all things which we have felt.'[1]

Published in the opening months of the Second World War, Muir's comments suggest that for their first readers, the atmosphere of anxiety and authoritarianism in the stories reflected contemporary life. Many of the features of Kavan's asylum writing – sparse description and characterisation; shifts between first- and third-person voice; uncertain reality and unreliable narrators; disrupted experience of time and themes of guilt, persecution and trial – would continue across her later writing. The fictional asylum was thus fertile ground for her experimental strategies, including her reworking of the relationship between narrator and reader and metafictional engagement with issues of literary representation.

Kavan's newly experimental style in *Asylum Piece* introduced Kafkaesque motifs that would continue throughout her writing, including initialised names and what she herself described in relation to Ruthven Todd as a 'Kafka atmosphere of horror, the sense of impending doom and of incalculable, merciless forces at work'.[2] Navigating arbitrary persecution by unassailable authorities, Kavan's abstract but disarmingly intimate first-person narrators invoke those of Kafka's stories, whose eerily familiar vacancy was captured in W. H. Auden's statement that 'nobody ever met a Kafka character' but 'one can have experiences which one recognizes as Kafkaesque'.[3] The proliferation of human/non-human hybrids in Kavan's writing (both human/animal and animate/inanimate) also chime with Kafka's fiction. Her admiration for Kafka is stated in her journalism and correspondence, and in *The Horse's Tale* the eponymous horse Kathbar's famed dance interpretation of *The Metamorphosis* is a clear tribute to Kafka's absurdist humour. Resonances with Kafka have been a mainstay of Kavan's critical reception. As Kafka's first English translator along with his wife Willa Muir, Edwin Muir immediately identified similarities between Kavan's writing and Kafka's, and Brian Aldiss's description of Kavan as 'Kafka's sister' has been often repeated.[4] Leigh Wilson has examined in detail how comparisons to Kafka have been used in the critical and paratextual literature surrounding Kavan's work with troublingly gendered inflections, reflecting how issues of stereotype have directed and obstructed the publication of women's experimental writing. Taking Kavan's own descriptions of Kafka's writing as more illuminating on this point, Wilson identifies the affinities between their work as being 'clear-eyed without being cold' and 'vulnerable without being ethereal'.[5]

In *Asylum Piece*, Kavan engages directly with Kafka's *The Trial* (1925), which Ian Hamilton described as 'her bible', but the horror of Josef K's situation is that he is a sane protagonist in a world gone mad; the first-person narrator of *Asylum Piece* gives the reader ample reason to doubt their sanity, and both world and protagonist are implicated in the madness of the text.⁶ In a letter describing her encounters with British wartime bureaucracy, Kavan wryly observed: 'At times when I'm in one or another of these enormous buildings waiting for an interview with some new authority, I feel as if I were the victim of a private madness induced by too much reading of *The Trial* and *The Castle*'.⁷ This remark reflects the influence of Kafka on her outlook, but also illuminates one distinction between her writing and his, as Kafka's dystopias become internalised in Kavan's fictional worlds as 'private madness'. The arbitrary and overwhelming force of the law in Kafka's writing becomes actively hostile and personal in Kavan's, and her protagonists' unwarranted persecution is often matched by their feelings of guilt. K's dawn execution in 'The End', the final chapter of *The Trial*, is simultaneously evoked and denied in the concluding episode of *Asylum Piece*, 'There is No End', as Kavan's narrator finds themselves condemned to 'innumerable lifetimes' (211) of imprisonment.

Gregory Ariail has traced in detail Kavan's intertextual engagement with Kafka's fables in a study that groups her with Leonora Carrington, Rex Warner and William Sansom. Ariail's analysis demonstrates the profound thematic and narrative influence of Kafka's short prose on diverse mid-century Anglophone writers, identifying how a 'widespread disdain for imitative writing' has hindered previous study of Kafka's impact, while Ariail's own project 'considers repetitions, mimicries, and even plagiarisms as luminous fields of inquiry'.⁸ Such thinking suggests a useful approach to the imitative nature of some of Kavan's writing, including and beyond the influence of Kafka, and her direct borrowings from other writers. Most explicit is the posthumous story 'A Visit' which reworks German writer Christoph Meckel's story 'The Lion' (1962); Kavan changes Meckel's lion for a leopard and develops and expands his narrative, but the debt to his original text is immense.⁹ Leigh Wilson has demonstrated that Kavan's *Ice* was in dialogue with Alan Burns's *Europe After the Rain* (1965), which she describes as a 'riposte' to Burns's novel.¹⁰ Such examples intimate that direct engagement with other texts went further than literary influence for Kavan and that it was central to her experimental writing practice. The reworking of her own Helen Ferguson novel, *Let Me Alone*, is therefore only one instance of the type of return, repetition or response identified by Ariail and Wilson in her writing.

Kavan, Psychiatry and Anti-Psychiatry

In *Asylum Piece*, the encounter with psychiatry, as much as the experience of mental breakdown itself, shapes the narrator's apprehension of unreliable reality and identity, and unstable interface between self and world. Kavan's own relationship with psychiatry was complex and conflicted, combining necessary engagement with political suspicion. Her experiences of psychiatric and psychoanalytic treatment are remarkable for the range of influential and innovative practitioners with whom she came into contact, either as a patient or through her writing. Her diverse interactions with the rapidly changing and largely unregulated field of psychiatry in the mid-twentieth century would profoundly shape both her politics and the experimental form of her fiction. Little is known of Kavan's psychiatric history before her admission to a Swiss clinic in the late 1930s, and even this (like much in the published biographies) is anecdotal rather than evidenced fact. Certainly, her social and economic advantage influenced her experiences of psychiatric care; her internments were in private institutions and paid for by the income she received from her mother, whose third husband was extremely wealthy. Carole Sweeney has suggested that Kavan's heroin use, which began in the late 1920s, may have begun as a prescription 'to alleviate the severe, often suicidal, depression from which she suffered' and there is clear evidence that Kavan considered the drug to be treatment for her psychiatric illness.[11] When she returned from Switzerland she was treated in London by Henry Dicks, then Director of the Tavistock Clinic, either at the clinic or in his consulting rooms in Wimpole Street.[12] Later, she would be treated at the Tavistock for a 'very sticky patch of depression' in early 1943.[13]

During the war, Kavan became a patient of psychiatrist Karl Bluth, a German émigré who would remain both her doctor and intimate friend until his death in 1964; they co-authored a book, *The Horse's Tale*, in 1949. Bluth had been a poet and playwright as well as psychiatrist in Germany; his anti-fascist views resulted in his medical licence being revoked and his books being included in the Nazi book burnings. He fled with his Jewish wife to South America in 1934, arriving in Britain two years later, and eventually established a practice in London where he treated a coterie of artistic patients.[14] Little definite is known of Bluth's unconventional methods; certainly, he prescribed heroin for Kavan and anecdotal evidence suggests that he routinely administered amphetamines to his patients.[15] He was strongly influenced by Ludwig Binswanger's existential psychoanalysis, referring patients, including Kavan, for treatment at Binswanger's Swiss clinic.

Kavan met Dr Maxwell Jones during the four months she spent working at the Mill Hill Emergency Hospital in 1943, where she also studied for the Diploma in Psychological Medicine.[16] The two would later collaborate on the *Horizon* article 'The Case of Bill Williams' (1944).

Presented as a case study of a patient in a military psychiatric hospital (the fictional Bill Williams), Kavan uses the article to mount an attack on the prescriptive standards of both the psychiatric profession and modern society as a whole:

> Private Williams is a neurotic case. Society doesn't approve of Private Williams. The hospital staff takes a very poor view of him . . . in spite of pep talks and electrical treatment and benzidrene tablets, he persists in being resentful and unfriendly, apathetic and slovenly, unco-operative and bad-tempered, rebellious and disintegrated. (96–7)

Although the Second World War is the conspicuous backdrop of the piece, Kavan presents Bill Williams as a soldier in another conflict entirely:

> Inevitably, right from the start, the social machine is the enemy of the individual Bill Williams. [. . .] Every door closing, every form filled in, every official, every broadcast, every regulation, every propaganda slogan, is a munition in the war; Society versus Bill Williams. (97)

Thus, 'The Case of Bill Williams' is a war cry for the individual, but it is no coincidence that he is a neurotic case; Kavan proposes an intimate relationship between his 'individualism' and behaviours classified as symptoms of mental illness. If he chooses to, Bill Williams could decide to 'co-operate and discard his neurosis and be secure and passive and numbered and nullified' (98), making his neurosis a conscious resistance to totalitarian models of normalcy and conformity. Kavan's passionate defence of the neurotic case in the article does not simply call for an end to the stigma of mental illness and its persistent associations of immorality and degeneracy; it champions the condition itself. She predicts that the fate of mankind is in peril unless 'a tonic epidemic of madness blazes across the world' (98); madness is therefore not a disease but humanity's cure. However, Kavan's portrayal of psychiatry as invasive and normalising was synchronous with the treatment she sought to alleviate her own debilitating depressive symptoms.

Maxwell Jones and the psychoanalyst Edward Glover follow Kavan's contribution, giving their professional opinion of Bill Williams as though he were a real patient. In his editorial introduction to the piece, Cyril Connolly introduced Kavan as 'an expert on psychiatric methods', an ambiguous description referencing any or all of her Mill Hill work, associated studies, asylum writing and personal experiences of psychiatric breakdown and treatment (which were common knowledge in the *Horizon* offices).[17] 'Bill Williams' comprehensively demonstrates that Kavan's asylum writing goes beyond subjective testimony of her own experiences to support a radical political commentary on psychiatric diagnosis, treatment and institutions. Its relationship with her fiction is made most explicit when Bill Williams appears as a minor character in the story 'Face of My People' (1944), published in *Horizon* two months later, demonstrating her increasing disruption of the divide between life and fiction. The response from *Horizon* readers to the article reveals that they were comfortable in colluding with Kavan's destabilisation of fact and fiction. Letters in the correspondence pages of the next edition follow Maxwell Jones in commenting on the case as though Williams were a living person; he provokes their sympathy and, in a gesture of solidarity, one reader goes so far as to claim that 'I am Bill Williams'.[18]

Privately, Kavan referred to the article as her '"Bill Williams" outburst' and predicted that the 'result should be provocative if nothing else'.[19] Despite her evident respect for Maxwell Jones and his work, they had arranged that he should respond with 'the orthodox state-employed psychiatrist's attitude', and neither holds back criticism of the other.[20] Kavan describes the psychiatrist as 'the authorized voice of the social order, the man who knows all the answers' and Jones responds by suggesting that Kavan is not qualified to speak on psychiatric matters, conceding that she 'has a remarkable knack of stimulating thought' but maintaining that her attitude 'seems unthought-out and over-emotional'.[21] Edward Glover, a considerable force in the British Psycho-Analytic Society at the time, was the last to respond. Avoiding the trap of attempting to analyse Bill Williams, Glover evaluates the debate so far, calling attention to gaps in Kavan's argument and identifying Jones's primary error of engaging with her on her own terms. He finds that Kavan's description of the inherent conflict between individual and society fits well with psychoanalytic premises, agreeing with her diagnosis of society's pathology and following her lead in rubbishing the British psychiatric system. His message is vitriolic, predicting disaster for a State Mental Service after the war, and his prescription for these ills is not Kavan's tonic of neurosis for humankind, but a course of forced psychiatric treatment for all psychiatrists.

Contributing to a nascent criticism of the psychiatric institution dated by Michel Foucault to 1930–40, 'The Case of Bill Williams' demonstrates that Kavan's writing of madness and asylum treatment was underpinned by a conscious critique of both psychiatry and normative social standards.[22] In its explicit engagement with the political and ethical implications of psychiatric practice and diagnoses, the article directly anticipates the trend of psychiatric critique which accompanied the rapid developments in psychiatric care in the mid-twentieth century, and which would come to be described as the anti-psychiatry movement.

Developing simultaneously across Europe and the United States in the 1960s, this thinking emerged from the joint concerns of existential philosophy, humanistic psychology and political reform around the mid-century and encompassed criticism of the psychiatric institution, invasive treatments and psychiatric diagnosis. R. D. Laing's *The Divided Self* (1960) had profound impact beyond the field of psychiatry. A year later, Foucault's *Madness and Civilization* (1961), Erving Goffman's sociological critique of the American psychiatric hospital, *Asylums* (1961) and Thomas Szasz's *The Myth of Mental Illness* (1961) were all published. Franco Basaglia's work in the 1960s and 1970s influenced major reform of the psychiatric institution in Italy, and Gilles Deleuze and Félix Guattari would take up the call for 'an effective politicization of psychiatry' in *Anti-Oedipus* (1972).[23] 'Anti-psychiatry', coined by David Cooper in 1967, was never a cohesive movement; its proponents were often inimical to one another and the term was rarely self-applied. One clear divide in this category of thinkers can be drawn between those who worked with patients in a clinical or practical environment and those whose work was exclusively theoretical. Despite their diversity of thought, they were exclusively male and, as stressed by later feminist critique of the movement, often blind to issues of gender. Several of the practitioners with whom Kavan came into contact would influence the development of anti-psychiatry in Europe; Maxwell Jones would go on to pioneer the therapeutic community which would influence R. D. Laing's project at Kingley Hall, and both Foucault and Laing acknowledged the significance of Ludwig Binswanger's existential analysis to their thinking.[24] 'Bill Williams' brings Kavan's representations of isolated and marginalised individuals into sharper political focus, and emphasises the significance of fictional character to her experiment.

Writing Madness, Writing the Asylum

The 'nameless place' described by a nameless narrator in the final story of *Asylum Piece* formalises the inadequacy of words to represent the experience it portrays:

> For, strangely enough, there are windows without bars in this place and doors which are not even locked. Apparently there is nothing to prevent me from walking out whenever I feel inclined. Yet though there is no visible barrier I know only too well that I am surrounded by unseen and impassable walls which tower into the highest domes of the zenith and sink many miles below the surface of the earth...

> Already it seems to me that I have spent a lifetime in this narrow room whose walls will continue to regard me with secrecy through innumerable lifetimes to come. Is it life, then, or death, stretching like an uncoloured stream behind and in front of me? There is no love here, nor hate, nor any point where feeling accumulates. In this nameless place nothing appears animate, nothing is close, nothing is real. (211)

Identity and coordinates are unfixed in this liminal zone which is neither life nor death; in a room both narrow and without spatial horizon, with walls that surveil and confine, the view from the window is equally barren, there is nowhere beyond. This portrait of the asylum can only be defined by absence; all is colourless, lifeless, affectless and unreal. Even the promise of death that hangs over this collection is here, at the last, denied; this is an 'end without end' (211) and the emptiness of despair becomes interminable. In these stories, inner and outer worlds are indistinguishable, bodily confinement mirrors mental restriction, the psyche and the asylum are one, making the 'unseen and impassable walls' those of both the institution and the glass bell jar of depression.

In 'A Certain Experience' from the *I Am Lazarus* collection, another nameless first-person narrator wrestles with the challenge of representing their experience of incarceration:

> I can describe the peep-hole in the hookless door, the hard, unsleeping eye-bulb in its cage. I can describe the smells in corridors, the sounds ambiguously interpreted, the sights from which eyes were averted hastily. I can describe the hands under which I suffered [. . .]
>
> But all these descriptions, no matter how detailed, give only the bare shell of the experience, the true significance of which beats within them like a heart that can never die. The objective side of the matter does in fact die; or at least it can be said to grow old and frail (*Lazarus*, 107)

This 'certain experience', again too raw to be named, is evoked by an overload of sensory evidence and the sensation of being under constant surveillance. Yet the narrator disavows their own description of the 'objective side of the matter' as only a husk that withers away, maintaining that it is 'the personal nature of the experience which is incommunicable and which gives it its supreme value' (107). Evoking the 'uncompromising, personal, true' 'reality' that Kavan would describe as characteristic of the work of great writers, and directly confronting the gulf between description and understanding which is vital to her asylum writing, her narrator self-consciously identifies the possibilities and limitations of narrative representation.[25]

The self-reflexive tendencies of Kavan's asylum fiction are evident in other asylum narratives of the mid-century such as Antonia White's

'The House of Clouds' (1930); Leonora Carrington's *Down Below* (1944); Jennifer Dawson's *The Ha Ha* (1961); Janet Frame's *Faces in the Water* (1961); Sylvia Plath's *The Bell Jar* (1963) and stories in Ann Quin's posthumously published *The Unmapped Country* (1973). These first-person asylum fictions, influenced by their authors' experiences, have often been interpreted as autobiographical, and their value as testimony of the brutal confinement and abuses involved in the 'care' of the twentieth-century psychiatric institution is indisputable. However, for their writers, these were creative rather than confessional texts and one of their common features is their subtle and self-conscious attention to the meeting point of madness, asylum treatment and fiction. In these writings, the encounter with psychiatry and the asylum reflects, and becomes indistinguishable from, mental breakdown itself, and their first-person narrators invite and engage in self-reflexive consideration of the relationship between narrative and madness.

Nonia Williams has examined how Ann Quin's stories of madness and the psychiatric institution in *The Unmapped Country* are concerned with 'questions of narrative representation' and 'probing the possibility of writing madness', demonstrating how 'Quin's writing works to activate (rather than describe) madness at the level of the text itself'.[26] Likewise, Sylvie Gambaudo describes how in Janet Frame's *Faces in the Water* 'the narrator creates a tension between realism and fiction by situating herself at once in and out of the asylum experience, at once the mad woman and the observer of the mad'.[27] Thus, like Kavan, these writers use first-person fictional narrative to acknowledge and engage with philosophical questions around the possibility of authentically writing madness, exemplified in the Foucault/Derrida debate.[28] Such issues of truth and representation apply to both fictional and historical narratives of madness and psychiatry, and have implications beyond. As Roy Porter described it: 'The delusions of the mad, the myths of psychiatry and the ideologies of society at large all form part of a common ideological fabric.'[29] Porter's schema for a comprehensive history of madness is one that always reflects social and historical context, for '[e]ven the mad are men of their times' (5). These lessons can be applied to readings of Kavan's asylum fiction, emphasising its value not only as personal testimony of her experiences of mental ill-health and psychiatric treatment, nor even of her political 'anti-psychiatric' views, but also in reflecting their historical and cultural context, and the common ways in which narrative functions in each of these spheres. The experimental narrative strategies and metafictional tendencies of Kavan's asylum writing are thus features of other asylum fictions, but also reflect more widely the mid-century's increasing ontological and epistemological uncertainty in real-world scenarios and fictional encounters.

Asylum incarceration, psychiatric treatment, the existential experience of depression and the category of 'madness' intersect and overlap in *Asylum Piece*. The tension between the objective and subjective representation of these experiences is complex; the combination of third- and first-person narratives, which Kavan would carry forward into her later writing, does not demarcate a clear divide between the two. In *Sleep Has His House*, she would use the third- rather than first-person passages to represent the subjectivity of the unconscious and in *Asylum Piece*, the first-person narratives often give a detached and affectless account of the experiences they present. In the sequence of eight narratives titled 'Asylum Piece I – VIII', predominantly in the third person, both the asylum and its patients are named and more clearly defined. Viewed from the outside, the handsome building and lakeside grounds of this Swiss clinic make it indistinguishable from an expensive hotel; its occupants wander in despair through its incongruously sunny days. Workshops for occupational therapy and a communal staff and patient dining room mark this as a liberal institution for the privileged few, distinct from the indignities and discomforts of the early twentieth-century state asylum, but it offers no more comfort or respite to its patients than the perpetual winter of the first-person narrator's anguished existence. The staff at the clinic have little contact with the patients whose distress originates more from their enforced incarceration and separation from loved ones than from any obvious psychiatric affliction. In 'Asylum Piece I', Kavan sets the scene 'exactly like a stage' (123), with the patients as puppets controlled by the psychiatrist. Each of the following 'pieces' presents a tableaux showing one patient's vexed relationship to the asylum and to their loved ones outside it; Hans fears he will be forced to leave the clinic because of financial difficulties; Zelie discovers that her parents have been sent away without seeing her; a nameless woman is abandoned by her husband and another, or the same, is comforted by a maid; Marcel's attempt to escape is thwarted by his own institutionalisation; Miss Swanson comforts fellow-patient Frieda when her husband refuses to take her home. These patients are affected both by their physical incarceration and by the asylum's insidious incursion into their minds; they cannot escape from it, literally or otherwise. Zelie's mother finds that her child has been 'hidden away' from her behind 'invisible barriers of medical authority and discipline' (144); despite its seemingly liberal regime, the clinic is a gilded cage in which psychiatric control holds sway. Kavan's text thus demonstrates lucidly what Foucault identifies as the disciplinary power of the asylum, where 'psychiatric knowledge' becomes 'converted into something else in real practice', a force to maintain order within both institution and society.[30]

Psychiatric Drugs and Interventions: 'locked doors *inside* the patient'

In keeping with the lack of descriptive detail in Kavan's experimental texts, references to the treatment administered in the asylum are often oblique. Most notably absent in *Asylum Piece* are depictions of the brutal physical restraints painfully detailed by Leonora Carrington and Antonia White; instead, Kavan's fictional patients are frequently subject to the influence of psychotropic drugs. In this way, her writing reflects the increasing medicalisation of twentieth-century psychiatry, which reconceived madness as mental illness and developed pharmaceutical and surgical treatments to address psychiatric problems as they would physical ailments. By 1964, R. D. Laing would observe that: 'In the best places, where straitjackets are abolished, doors are unlocked, leucotomies largely forgone, these can be replaced by more subtle lobotomies and tranquilizers that place the bars of Bedlam and the locked doors *inside* the patient.'[31] Kavan's own experiences of asylum treatment took place in private clinics that might well be described as 'the best places', the expense of which often limited her time there, despite the support of her mother's money.[32] Laing's remark can be seen illustrated in the *Asylum Piece* narrator's observation of 'windows without bars' 'and doors which are not even locked' (211) and the internalisation of psychiatric confinement in these stories reflects the way in which drugs and other interventions were forced onto and into the body of the patient. Thus, the asylum of *Asylum Piece* is not only a physical location but a set of practices and a state of mind, the template for Kavan's later writing of conflated inner and outer worlds.

The regulatory role of the psychiatrist, whom Kavan describes as 'the authorized voice of the social order' (98) in 'Bill Williams', makes psychiatry the mouthpiece of social control, and psychotropic drugs tools for enforcing conformity. In 'An Unpleasant Reminder', the narrator's long-awaited judgement is delivered in the form of tablets which she is instructed to swallow in what she interprets as an enforced suicide:

> holding the four pills on the palm of my hand; I lifted them to my mouth. And then the most ridiculous contretemps occurred – there was no drinking glass in the bathroom [. . .] In despair I filled the soapdish with water and swallowed them down somehow. I hadn't even waited to wash out the slimy layer of soap at the bottom and the taste nearly made me sick. (110–11)

In this execution gilded with indignity, the narrator must act with decorum and avoid the embarrassment of requesting a glass of water; but choking down the tablets turns out to be only 'a cruel hoax, just a reminder of what is in store' (111), another frightening uncertainty in a hostile world. Administered by impenetrable authority, with unknown but potentially devastating consequences, the scene plays out a metaphor of forced medication.

Later in the 1940s, Kavan's fiction depicts more specific psychiatric treatments: drug-induced narcosis, electroconvulsive therapy (ECT), narco-analysis under sodium amytal, and the stimulant benzedrine (amphetamine). Some of the most explicit references to treatment occur in the novel on which she collaborated with her psychiatrist Karl Bluth, *The Horse's Tale* (1949). This allegorical satire in the manner of Orwell's *Animal Farm* (1945) parodies postwar British culture and intellectualism and testifies to Bluth and Kavan's shared sense of humour. Its wry disclaimer: 'All characters in this story are fictitious, even the horse' is disingenuous, for it is as autobiographical as any of Kavan's works. Although the horse's name, Kathbar, amalgamates the initials of Karl Theodor Bluth, his experiences mirror many of Kavan's, and Bluth appears fictionalised as the benefactor Mr Patronage. Kathbar is an old circus horse who has lost his memory and is displaced and homeless in a wartorn country; he has an artistic nature, reads, recites poetry and dances beautifully (most notably in a performance of Kafka's *Metamorphosis*). The horse founds a successful school of art which he names 'Hoofism' (44), but later becomes depressed and is diagnosed by a psychiatrist as 'a psychopath, unbalanced, autistic and somewhat degenerate' (54). After falling down drunk at an intellectual party, Kathbar is sent to a public asylum where his experiences recall the descriptive language and anti-psychiatric message of *Asylum Piece*: 'The days in this place were utterly vacant, devoted to a routine of emptiness which seemed as if it might have been devised to deprive sane people of their wits rather than for the purpose of curing those who'd already lost them' (88). Kathbar's friends rescue him and pay for his treatment at 'the establishment of a foreign expert who had recently been successful in treating a famous dancer' (99). This expert, Dr Hieronymous, clearly references Ludwig Binswanger and his treatment of Vaslav Nijinski, and he discusses 'art and its symbolism' with Kathbar, explaining the 'principles of "existential psychology" of which he was one of the founders' (103).

Kavan was referred by Bluth to Binswanger at his Bellevue clinic the year before *The Horse's Tale* was published. She was pleased to find that he 'really has read *Asylum Piece* and *Lazarus* and knows them well' and the friendly relations between Kathbar and Dr Hieronymous clearly reflect Kavan's belief that Binswanger behaved 'as if one were an equal cooperating with him in one's own treatment'.[33] Dr Hieronymous deduces from a Rorschach test that the horse's depression is 'due to a constitutional abnormality' (102) and prescribes electric shocks and narco-analysis under the influence of sodium amytal. Kathbar responds badly to ECT, but Dr Hieronymous establishes contact with his unconscious through narco-analysis, retrieving information about the horse's forgotten former life, eventually allowing him to find his way home. Dr Bluth sent Binswanger a copy of the book and he replied wishing it success and sending his regards to 'unserer gemeinsamen Freundin' [our mutual friend] the horse.[34] The absurdism of *The Horse's Tale* shows the humour in Kavan's writing at its most explicit, an element of her work often overlooked by readings founded on the expectation of earnest accounts of personal pain and tragedy. But her fiction is frequently arch and satirical, even in its portrayals of injustice and despair; Geoff Ward has highlighted the sardonic and parodic elements of Kavan's postwar prose and Angelos Evangelou has observed 'the intricacy with which Kavan blends irony and parody with truth' in her asylum writing.[35]

Kavan's writing of psychiatric treatment, like that of many of her mid-century contemporaries, is intertwined with her writing of psychiatric symptoms. The sensations of guilt and worthlessness associated with depression and which saturate her fiction are further augmented by brutal asylum treatments which, especially unaccompanied by adequate explanation, appear punitive rather than palliative to the patient. ECT, which would later become emblematic of the abuses of psychiatry in part through its depiction in Ken Kesey's *One Flew Over the Cuckoo's Nest* (1962) and its film adaptation (1975), is frequently depicted in mid-century literature as punishment or torture. In *The Bell Jar*, Esther Greenwood's horror at the electrocution of the Rosenbergs is echoed in her first experience of ECT, which leads her to wonder 'what terrible thing it was that I had done'.[36] Likewise, Estina Mavet in Janet Frame's *Faces in the Water* believes shock treatment to be a 'punishment' for her difficult behaviour on the ward and her fear of the treatment fuels her delusion that the hospital staff are 'planning to murder me with electricity'.[37] Kavan's only direct portrayal of ECT in *The Horse's Tale* is unusual in that Kathbar's close relationship with his psychiatrist allows him to beg off further shocks when the experience leads him to 'despair' (106).

The drug treatments Kavan represents in her fiction were designed to either subdue consciousness for an extended period or encourage the patient to reveal truths during analysis. Narco-analysis, which features in both in *The Horse's Tale* and in 'Face of My People' (first published in *Horizon* and collected in *I Am Lazarus*), was a barbiturate therapy used to encourage a patient to reach a crisis or relive a repressed memory, bringing together early twentieth-century advances in medicinal and talking therapies.[38] But what is a 'talking cure' for Kathbar, restoring his lost memories, is alarming and invasive to Kling, the protagonist of the earlier story. In Kavan's fiction, the administering doctor is the deciding factor in whether such treatment is therapeutic or intrusive. Two of the stories from the *Lazarus* collection, 'I Am Lazarus' and 'Palace of Sleep', feature patients treated with paraldehyde-induced prolonged narcosis, during which sleep was induced for a period of days or even weeks. Kavan puts to use its potential as a gothic device in invoking the uncanniness of sleepwalking and life without free will. In 'Palace of Sleep' a visiting doctor watches the face of a female patient, lying 'absolutely lifeless' until 'slowly, with intolerable, incalculable effort, the drugged eyes opened and stared straight into his' (20). He perceives 'a look of terror, of wild suspicion, of frantic, abysmal appeal' and feels 'almost ashamed' at the sight of this sleeping beauty, whom he cannot rescue from the prison of her own unconscious body (20).

If the artificially induced sleeping body confines the waking mind during treatment, the longer-term consequences of narcosis are invoked in the title story of the collection 'I Am Lazarus'. Thomas Bow, a patient with a diagnosis of 'dementia praecox', who was once 'hopelessly insane' and 'an imbecile', has been treated with prolonged narcosis, revealed by his fear of the doctor who 'for many months had put him into a hideous sleep with his poisoned needle' (15). The psychiatrist who administered the treatment boasts that he has performed a resurrection: 'We've pulled him back literally from a living death' (16), but to the nurses, there is something unnerving about Mr Bow: 'He gives me the creeps' . . . 'Like an automaton walking about. Like a robot' (13). Always maintaining distance from Mr Bow by using his formal title, the narrative nonetheless allows the reader to see through his eyes: 'All around the table were different coloured shapes whose mouths opened and closed and emitted sounds that meant nothing to him' (10). Echoing the character Anna Kavan's perception of a world 'made up of shapes and noises, without reality of consequence' (*Let Me Alone*, 286), for Mr Bow, the human world is abstract and drained of meaning. Conversely, his response to physical objects is highly sensitive; he feels deep suspicion towards a row of hanging coats, keeping half an eye on them 'to make sure they did not get up to anything', and the 'yellow eyes' of moon daisies watch him with a 'base and knowing expression' (12). Sensing the reaction of the inanimate world to him, he touches the heads of grasses, 'like thin sensitive cats they arched themselves to receive the caress of his finger-tips' (11), and he thinks of the leather belt he has been working on and feels it 'lonely for him as he was for it' (15). His emotional intimacy with the physical world is the inverse of his alienation from other people, a relationship that reflects the lack of emotional care offered to him in the asylum, for it 'was not the fashion at the clinic to listen to what patients said. There was not enough time' (10). Borrowing from a line of Eliot's *Prufrock* for its title – 'I am Lazarus, come from the dead' – this story interrogates what it means to be alive and how the 'success' of psychiatric treatment can be measured. The asylum has made Thomas Bow into the 'machine-part' (97) that Kavan predicts is the intended outcome of psychiatric intervention in 'Bill Williams', but he is not the 'contented cog' (98) the psychiatrist believes him to be, but an uncanny automaton operating outside of human meaning and interaction.

These stories show explicitly how Kavan's newly experimental style continued to draw on the gothic influences that had inflected her Helen Ferguson novels and which would endure throughout her oeuvre.[39] As Thomas S. Davis notes, gothic features 'accrue power only in relation to their historical situation', and Kavan transposes its motifs – madness and incarceration, sinister locations, uncanny coincidences, doubling and images of self and anti-self – into the contexts of her interwar, wartime and asylum writings.[40] In her asylum stories, the gothic shapes both the content and structure of her representations of psychiatric illness and treatment. Scott Brewster has captured the aptness of gothic form for representing madness, describing how 'its narrative structures and voices are interwoven with and intensify the apparent madness they represent'.[41] Brewster observes how the reader's desire to interpret the ambiguity of the narrator/character's madness or sanity in such texts is thwarted not by a paucity of interpretation (that is, by the lack of certainty it presents) but rather by 'an excess or overabundance of interpretation' (486). Thus, the reading process becomes an exercise that brings the reader close to delirium, and for Brewster 'madness in Gothic lies in the reading' (493). This model is fitting to the reticulation of meaning arising from the multiple narrative ambiguities of the *Asylum Piece* stories, and to Kavan's method of involving the reader in the existential experience of mental breakdown.

Depression, the Reader and Experimental Form

In her personal correspondence, Kavan describes 'the horrible depression which hangs over me' as 'a great oppressive amorphous mass; something heavy and unresolved that prevents me from working, from making contact with anybody, even from seeing the sky', with 'the quality of eternity'.[42] She remembers the 'inexplicable glooms' of her 'unhappy school days' and these feelings, along with associated suicide attempts, stayed with her throughout her life, especially when she was withdrawing from, or unable to access, heroin.[43] Eleonora Rao has described how the 'lack of geographical and, at times, temporal coordinates' keeps Kavan's 'melancholic outsiders' 'literally outside the circle of ordinary human life'.[44] Likewise, Carole Sweeney observes in her writing: 'a profound *weirdness* in which protagonists are aliens; outcasts from warmth, intimacy, kinship and, above all, from any sense or promise of love'.[45] This 'weirdness', beyond 'ordinary human life', is the alienated and dissociated worldview of severe depression, the 'living death' that Julia Kristeva describes in *Black Sun*, in which 'time has been erased or bloated, absorbed into sorrow', one becomes '[a]bsent from other people's meaning, alien', and is excluded from the 'normal category of normal people'.[46] This extraordinary relationship to world and others is one that Kavan's experimental strategies would work to replicate in the relationship between narrator and reader.

Since Kavan's death, the incidence of depression has increased to epidemic proportions, but medical understanding of its causes is still evolving, being variously traced to genetic or biological basis, experience of personal trauma or, more recently, as an inevitable response to the social forces of modern life.[47] Its dual status as common human emotion and psychiatric disorder has made it integral to ongoing debate over the ethics of diagnosing and medicating mental illness. The first-person narrator of *Asylum Piece* never openly refers to psychiatric diagnosis or treatment, but their disturbed state of mind is indicated by sleeplessness, suicidal thoughts, sensations of isolation, hopelessness, persecution and their description of the way a 'human being can only endure depression up to a certain point' (47):

> One loses sleep, it becomes harder and harder to take any interest in conversation, books, music, plays, eating and drinking, love-making, even in one's personal appearance. Ultimately one becomes completely cut off from reality, alone in a world in which there is nothing to do but wait, day after day, for some fate at which one can only guess. (45)

The formal detachment of the indefinite pronoun makes this a text-book description of symptoms, outlining the 'objective side' of the experience of depression. The narrator's nosology anticipates the current diagnostic criteria for major or recurrent depressive disorder as set forth in both the American Psychiatric Association's *Diagnostic and Statistical Manual of Mental Disorders* (DSM-5) and the World Health Organization's

International Statistical Classification of Diseases and Related Health Problems (ICD-11). According to these, major depression occurs when five or more of the following symptoms are present nearly every day over at least two weeks: a depressed mood (e.g. feeling sad, empty or hopeless); markedly diminished interest and pleasure in all, or almost all, activities; significant decrease or increase in appetite or weight; insomnia or hypersomnia; psychomotor agitation or retardation; fatigue; feelings of worthlessness or excessive or inappropriate guilt (which may be delusional); inability to concentrate; recurrent thoughts of death or suicide.[48]

Rather than establishing an increased intimacy and trust between her narrator and the reader, Kavan's shift into the first person with *Asylum Piece* is often used to the converse effect of making her narrator appear deeply unreliable, thus holding them at a distance. The affectless quality of many of Kavan's narratives from this time forward, described by Leigh Wilson as 'flat, amnesiac voices', is instrumental in this.[49] Her first-person narrators, often unreliable or delusional, are always scrupulously polite, juxtaposing conventionally courteous expression with dark and disturbing content. In *Asylum Piece*, the narrator's breezy introduction to the persecutor that stalks them throughout the collection is exemplative of this:

> Somewhere in the world I have an implacable enemy although I do not know his name. I do not know what he looks like, either. In fact, if he were to walk into the room at this moment, while I am writing, I shouldn't be any the wiser (31).

Treading a fine line between diffidence and desperate appeal, the narrator makes small talk with the reader in what Geoff Ward has described as Kavan's 'so-do-I parodies of formal speech', while simultaneously confiding dark secrets.[50] In her asylum writing, this formality of language deadens the affect of the painful experiences described. At one moment, the narrator's despair leads them to fear they will 'suddenly become mad, scream, perpetrate some shocking act of violence in the open street' (78) but this is superseded by the absolute knowledge that they are 'inexorably imprisoned behind' their 'determination to display no emotion whatever' (79). This restraint under duress, exemplary of both British upper-class stoicism and a pathological lack of affect, reflects what the DSM describes as the 'empty' sensations of depression, holding the reader at a distance from the narrator's felt experience and replicating their sense that there is no 'point where feeling accumulates' (212).

Angelos Evangelou has examined how the inhumanity of the psychiatric profession leads Kavan's protagonists to seek interaction with non-human subjectivities in *Asylum Piece* and describes how the narrator 'finds in human interaction the potential for a devastating intrusion – almost a threatening and hostile penetration – into her fragile mental and emotional space'.[51] This fear of intimacy is one the narrator carries over into their relationship with the reader, reproducing the deficiency in emotional connection, alienation and suspicion they experience in the world of the text. The challenge that mental illness poses to empathy is one that the protagonist of Kavan's later story 'The Heavenly Adversary' tackles head-on: 'I have never heard of anybody who loved a mad person. I should think it would be impossible to do so. Pity or aversion one would feel, but not love'.[52] The discomfort and uncertainty that the *Asylum Piece* narrator insistently invites makes this challenge to empathy one that the reader shares. By holding the reader at a distance, their deep distrust of even those closest to them is reflected back in an infinite regress of doubt and suspicion, echoing the intrinsically isolated and solipsistic position of the depressed subject. But despite persistent misgivings about their sanity and reliability, as Evangelou concludes, the pain and fear of Kavan's narrator is real and their humanity endures.

As the narrator attempts negotiations with the authorities via their 'official advisor', it remains unclear whether their 'case' is legal or psychiatric, an ambiguity that draws on the likeness of practice between penal and psychiatric institutions in the early to mid-twentieth century. They confide that 'the time can't be far off when I shall be taken away' and the officials who will escort them will be 'two or three men in uniform, or white jackets, and one of them will carry a hypodermic syringe' (33–4). Later, lying in bed 'like a well-drilled prisoner' (99), they are under internal surveillance:

> An iron band has been clamped round my head, and just at this moment the jailer strikes the cold metal a ringing blow which sends needles of pain into my eye sockets. He is showing his disapproval of my inquiring thoughts; or perhaps he merely wishes to assert his authority over me. (100)

Playing out delusions common to depression, described by Aaron T. Beck in his detailed clinical analysis as 'the patient's belief that they will experience severe and imminent punishment or that they have committed a terrible crime', the narrator believes they have been 'tried and condemned' to 'a heavy sentence' (102).[53] As delusions of guilt meet the reality of stigma and confinement, the experiences of depression and psychiatric treatment are coincident. In a direct appeal to the reader, the narrator confides: 'I know that I'm doomed and I'm not going to struggle against my fate. I am only writing this down so that when you do not see me any more you will know that my enemy has finally triumphed' (34).

The reader becomes the narrator's only confidant, a helpless witness to persecution or madness.

The more fantastic and experimental of the *Asylum Piece* stories allow Kavan to make the subjective experience of depression and incarceration manifest. Reflecting a lack of bodily autonomy and freedom indicative of psychiatric incarceration and intervention, and the self-alienation and suicidal tendencies of depression, the narrator is confined and tortured by mysterious and unseen enemies and authorities. In a dreadful conspiracy of biology and technology, the voice of 'Machines in the Head' is controlled from within by 'the wheels, my masters' (115), making them the 'dispirited slave' of a 'monotonous, hateful functioning' (115). The 'intolerable and inescapable' working of the mechanism's cogs and engines is 'a sickness inside the blood' and any bid for freedom can only be achieved through an impulse of monstrous self-harm: 'it drives me to rebellion, to madness; I want to batter my head on the walls, to shatter my head with bullets, to beat the machines into pulp, into powder, along with my skull' (116). The hopeless contemplation of suicide in the earlier story, 'Just Another Failure', in which the narrator finds that although it is 'difficult to live with so much unhappiness and so many failures, to die seems to be harder still' (81), is here overcome by an intense urge towards self-destruction. The story's association of mental breakdown and mechanisation develops a theme introduced in Helen Ferguson's *A Stranger Still*, in which chauffeur George West grows increasingly like his car and becomes an automaton, and would continue in the *I Am Lazarus* stories in the automised existence of patients Lennie and Thomas Bow. The horror of the soulless 'social machine' expounded in 'The Case of Bill Williams' carries Helen Ferguson's preoccupation with the uncanny qualities of modernity into her representations of the loss of selfhood in depression and neurosis.

Andrew Gaedtke's sophisticated reading of 'Machines in the Head' returns to the opposition of objective and subjective representation of mental illness and its treatment, suggesting that the narrator's self-experience 'reflects the discourse of mechanistic "explanation" that Karl Jaspers distinguishes from phenomenological understanding in which the doctor might inquire more fully into the first-person experiences of the patient' (114). Thus, in what Gaedtke describes as 'a mirroring or looping effect between the discourses of the mind sciences and their patients' (114), Kavan's story replicates the violence of psychiatric diagnosis as much as psychiatric breakdown itself. This interpretation can be applied more broadly to the *Asylum Piece* stories which consistently demonstrate that when asylum treatment comprises confinement, constant surveillance and lack of human empathy, it only reflects and augments the experience of depression itself. Kavan's narrative technique thus formally represents both an existential mode of being and a relationship to the psychiatric institution. Gaedtke identifies the implications of Kavan's ongoing attention to reality and unreality in representing the existential experience of mental illness:

> If one power of fiction is to produce a 'reality effect' in which characters are experienced by readers as virtually real personalities, an obverse power may be described as an 'unreality effect.' This does not indicate a deficit in a narrative's capacity to persuade the reader; instead, it is a capacity to represent a felt lack of personhood. (120)

Highlighting the 'formal capacity' of *Asylum Piece* 'to reproduce for its readers the phenomenology of mental illness' (120), Gaedtke's analysis pinpoints the importance of the relationship between reader and character to Kavan's newly experimental style. Her descriptions of the feelings of unreality experienced by Anna in *Let Me Alone* give an objective account of the matter; her representation of a nameless individual, persecuted and tortured, captures the felt experience of depression along with asylum incarceration and treatment. Thus, *Asylum Piece* shows rather than tells the reader what it is to experience depression by formally replicating for them the depressed subject's experience of claustrophobia, de-realisation, alienation and profound mistrust in an empty and colourless world in which all is 'dangerous, hostile and liable to inflict pain' (47). This was the beginning of Kavan's experimental negotiations with reality, which would continue for the rest of her writing career.

The experience and politics of madness and its treatment, disrupting and confusing binaries of madness and sanity, self and world, life and death, reality and fiction, underpinned Kavan's newly experimental approach, and the difficulties inherent in representing these experiences, which she explicitly foregrounds, tested the relationship between reality and fiction. Like the mid-century reader Nathalie Sarraute would describe as 'wary of practically everything', Kavan's narrator in *Asylum Piece* trusts no one.[54] The mistrustful relationship between the depressed subject and others, which Kavan's text replicates for the reader, thus anticipates an increasingly uncertain and troubled relationship between reader and author across mid-century writing.

Notes

1. Desmond MacCarthy, 'Madness and Art', Review of *Asylum Piece*, *The Times*, 10 March 1940, 4; Edwin Muir, Review of *Asylum Piece*, *The Listener*, 21 March 1940, 597.

2. Anna Kavan, reviewing Ruthven Todd's *The Lost Traveler*, *Horizon*, 50, Febuary 1944, p. 141.
3. W. H. Auden, 'The I Without a Self', in *The Dyer's Hand and Other Essays* (London: Faber and Faber, 1962), 159–67, p. 160.
4. See Edwin Muir, *The Listener*, and Brian Aldiss, 'Kafka's Sister', *Journal of the Fantastic in the Arts*, 3:2 (1991). For a discussion of the gendered implications of this accolade see Leigh Wilson, 'Whose Sister? "Convenient Pigeonholes", Peter Owen and the Publishing of Anna Kavan', in Andrew Radford and Hannah Van Hove (eds), *British Experimental Women's Fiction, 1945–1975: Slipping Through the Labels* (Basingstoke: Palgrave Macmillan, 2021), 83–101.
5. Wilson, 'Whose Sister?', p. 98.
6. Ian Hamilton interviewed by Aorewa McLeod, transcribed in Glynn, p. 99.
7. Anna Kavan to Ian Hamilton, 7 March 1943, *NLNZ*. See also 'Rather Kafka', in *Anna Kavan's New Zealand: A Pacific Interlude in a Turbulent Life (Stories)*, ed. by Jennifer Sturm (Auckland: Vintage, Random House New Zealand, 2009).
8. Gregory Ariail, 'Kafka's Copycats: Imitation, Fabulism, and Late Modernism' (unpublished doctoral dissertation, University of Michigan, 2018), p. 3.
9. Christoph Meckel, 'The Lion', trans. by Christopher Middleton, in *The Figure on the Boundary Line: Selected Prose*, ed. by Christopher Middleton (Manchester: Carcanet Press, 1983), 43–7. Meckel's own Kafkaesque style throughout his short prose displays many similarities with Kavan's earlier writing; it is possible, perhaps likely, that she was introduced to his work in German via Dr Bluth.
10. Leigh Wilson, 'Anna Kavan's *Ice* and Alan Burns' *Europe After the Rain*: Repetition with a Difference', *Women: A Cultural Review*, 28:4 (Winter 2017), 327–42, p. 332.
11. Carole Sweeney, '"Keeping the Ruins Private": Anna Kavan and Heroin Addiction', *Women: A Cultural Review*, 28:4 (Winter 2017), 312–26, p. 315.
12. Raewyn Glynn's unpublished MA thesis 'Anna Kavan on Ice: An Encounter with Anna Kavan's Wartime Writing Via New Zealand and the Arctic Imaginary' (University of Auckland, 1997) contains a transcript of an interview between Aorewa McLeod and Ian Hamilton, Auckland, 1981, in which he refers to the psychiatrist treating Kavan in the late 1930s. Her treatment at the Tavistock Clinic three years later strongly implies that the name transcribed as 'Dix' was actually Dicks, and her contacts with the psychoanalytic community in London continued when Edward Glover collaborated in 'The Case of Bill Williams'. For details of Henry Dick's work and career, see Daniel Pick, *The Pursuit of the Nazi Mind* (Oxford: Oxford University Press, 2012).
13. Anna Kavan to Ian Hamilton, 12 October 1943, *NLNZ*. For details of the history of the clinic see Henry Dicks, *Fifty Years of the Tavistock Clinic* (London: Routledge & Kegan Paul, 1970).
14. Jeremy Reed reports that Bluth treated the poets David Gascoyne and George Barker and the artist Julian Trevelyan. See Jeremy Reed, *A Stranger on Earth: The Life and Work of Anna Kavan* (London: Peter Owen, 2006), p. 107.

15. See Peter Owen and James Nye, *Peter Owen, Not a Nice Jewish Boy: Memoirs of a Maverick Publisher* (London: Fonthill, 2021), p. 102.
16. For details of Kavan's time at Mill Hill, see Anna Kavan letters to Ian Hamilton, *NLNZ*.
17. Cyril Connolly, 'Introduction', *Horizon*, 9:50 (February 1944); see Arthur Koestler to Cyril Connolly, 28 June 1944, Cyril Vernon Connolly Papers, *MFL*.
18. See 'Correspondence: The Case of Bill Williams', *Horizon*, 9:51 (March 1944), pp. 286–8.
19. Anna Kavan to Ian Hamilton, 14 November 1943, *NLNZ*.
20. Anna Kavan to Ian Hamilton, 14 November 1943, *NLNZ*.
21. Anna Kavan, 'The Case of Bill Williams', pp. 98, 103.
22. Michel Foucault, *Psychiatric Power: Lectures at the Collège De France, 1973–4* (Basingstoke: Palgrave Macmillan, 2003), p. 39.
23. Gilles Deleuze and Félix Guattari, *Anti-Oedipus: Capitalism and Schizophrenia*, trans. by Robert Hurley, Mark Seem and Helen R. Lane (London: Continuum, 2004), p. 352.
24. See Michel Foucault, 'Dream, Imagination and Existence', *Dream and Existence*, trans. by Forrest Williams and Jacob Needleman, ed. by Keith Hoeller (Seattle, WA: Review of Existential Psychology and Psychiatry, 1986), 31–80; R. D. Laing in Bob Mullan, *Mad to Be Normal: Conversations with R. D. Laing* (London: Free Association Books, 1995), p. 159.
25. Anna Kavan, 'Selected Notices: Back to Victoria', *Horizon*, 13:73 (January 1946), p. 65.
26. Nonia Williams, 'About/of Madness: Ann Quin's *The Unmapped Country*', *Textual Practice*, 34:6 (2020), 903–20, pp. 904, 906.
27. Sylvie Gambaudo, 'Melancholia in Janet Frame's *Faces in the Water*', *Literature and Medicine*, 30:1 (Spring 2012), 42–60, p. 42.
28. See, for the beginnings of this debate, Michel Foucault, *Madness and Civilization*, trans. by Richard Howard (London and New York: Routledge, 2001) and Jacques Derrida, 'Cogito and the History of Madness', *Writing and Difference*, trans. by Alan Bass (London: Routledge, 2001).
29. Roy Porter, *A Social History of Madness: The World Through the Eyes of the Insane* (London: Weidenfeld & Nicolson, 1987), p. 4.
30. Michel Foucault, *Psychiatric Power: Lectures at the Collège De France, 1973–4* (Basingstoke: Palgrave Macmillan, 2003), p. 181.
31. R. D. Laing, 'Preface', *The Divided Self* (London: Pelican, 1964), p. 12.
32. See Anna Kavan letters to George Bullock from Bellevue and Fellowes Rd, Anna Kavan Papers, *MFL*.
33. Anna Kavan to George Bullock, undated, *MFL*.
34. Ludwig Binswanger to Karl Theodor Bluth, 10 January 1950, *EKUT*.
35. Geoff Ward, 'The Wibberlee Wobberlee Walk: Lowry, Hamilton, Kavan and the Addictions of 1940s Fiction', in *The Fiction of the 1940s: Stories of Survival*, ed. by Rod Mengham and N. H. Reeve (Basingstoke: Palgrave Macmillan, 2001), 26–45, p. 42; Angelos Evangelou, '"In fact I am an animal": Mental Illness, Vulnerability and the Problem of Empathy in Anna Kavan's *Asylum Piece*', *English Studies*, 2021, p. 19.
36. Sylvia Plath, *The Bell Jar* [1963] (London: Faber and Faber, 1966), p. 138.

37. Janet Frame, *Faces in the Water* [1961] (London: Virago, 2009), pp. 99, 100.
38. See Stephen J. Horsley, *Narco-Analysis: A New Technique in Short-Cut Psychotherapy: A Comparison with Other Methods: And Notes on the Barbiturates* (London: Oxford University Press, 1943); Ben Shephard, *A War of Nerves: Soldiers and Psychiatrists 1914–1994* (London: Jonathan Cape, 2000), 207–8.
39. For the most detailed study of Kavan's writing and the gothic to date, see Sara Wasson, *Urban Gothic of the Second World War: Dark London* (Basingstoke: Palgrave Macmillan, 2010).
40. Thomas S. Davis, *The Extinct Scene: Late Modernism and Everyday Life* (New York: Columbia University Press, 2016), p. 145.
41. Scott Brewster, 'Seeing Things: Gothic and the Madness of Interpretation', in *A New Companion to the Gothic*, ed. by David Punter (Chichester: Wiley-Blackwell, 2012), 481–95, p. 482.
42. Anna Kavan to George Bullock from Bellevue, Kreuzlingen, 'Saturday' [March 1947], Anna Kavan Papers, *MFL*.
43. Anna Kavan to George Bullock, 'Monday night' [Easter Monday, 7 April 1947], *MFL*.
44. Eleonora Rao, 'The "Black Sun": Anna Kavan's Narratives of Abjection', *Textus*, IV (1991), 119–46, p. 122.
45. Sweeney, '"Keeping the Ruins Private"', p. 323.
46. Julia Kristeva, *Black Sun: Depression and Melancholia*, trans. by Leon S. Roudiez (New York: Columbia University Press, 1989), p. 4.
47. See, for example, Ann Cvetkovich's *Depression: A Public Feeling* (Durham, NC: Duke University Press, 2012) and Barbara Dowds's *Depression and the Erosion of the Self in Late Modernity: The Lesson of Icarus* (London and New York: Routledge, 2018).
48. See American Psychiatric Association, *Diagnostic and Statistical Manual of Mental Disorders, Fifth Edition (DSM-5)* (Washington DC: American Psychiatric Publishing, 2013), pp. 160–1 and World Health Organization, International Statistical Classification of Diseases and Related Health Problems (ICD-11): 6A71 Recurrent depressive disorder *Foundation URI* <https://icd.who.int/browse11/l-m/en#/http%3a%2f%2fid.who.int%2ficd%2fentity%2f1194756772> (accessed 6 November 2022).
49. Wilson, 'Whose Sister?', p. 94.
50. Geoff Ward, 'The Wibberlee Wobberlee Walk', p. 42.
51. Angelos Evangelou, '"In fact I am an animal"', pp. 11–12.
52. Anna Kavan, 'The Heavenly Adversary', *I Am Lazarus*, p. 67.
53. Aaron T. Beck and Brad A. Alford, *Depression: Causes and Treatment, Second Edition* (Philadelphia: University of Pennsylvania Press, 2009), pp. 36–7.
54. Nathalie Sarraute, 'The Age of Suspicion' [1950], in *The Age of Suspicion: Essays on the Novel*, trans. by Maria Jolas (New York: George Braziller, 1963), p. 61.

Chapter 3

Blackout: Hearts and Minds Under Aerial Bombardment

Kavan's second collection of stories, *I Am Lazarus*, was published in March 1945; she described an advance copy as looking 'rather a mean and insignificant little starved war baby of a book'.[1] Continuing the experimental style of *Asylum Piece* in their hybrid of realism and fantasy, these stories assimilate the atmosphere and incidents of the Second World War into the dystopian world she introduced in the earlier collection, presenting tales of psychiatric patients in the third person alongside nameless, misanthropic first-person narrators. Bringing together stories of psychiatric internment with those of bombing in wartime London, the collection shows how these extreme situations touch and resonate with one another. The global conflict heightens her characters' sense of inevitable doom, but the crisis of representation with which Kavan grappled was the same; if profound depression and the asylum experience necessitated new and experimental representations of reality, so too did life under aerial bombardment. These aesthetic challenges were shared by many other British writers and this phase of Kavan's career aligns her writing with that of her contemporaries who likewise drew on hallucinatory imagery, gothic trope and experimental narrative temporality in their war writing, especially Elizabeth Bowen, William Sansom and James Hanley. The intensity of the aesthetic struggle to adequately represent total war carried an associated burden of ethical and political responsibility, exemplified by Cyril Connolly's statement in *Horizon* (contradicting his position early in the conflict) that the 'role of writers today, when every free nation and every free man and woman is threatened by the Nazi war-machine, is a matter of supreme importance'.[2]

For Kavan, the political impetus of her writing of madness and its treatment became more explicit and was further inflected by her pacifist views. Her continuing focus on marginalised individuals, running counter to narratives of wartime camaraderie, framed madness as a form of political resistance.

The literal and metaphorical darkness and the disrupted experience of time experienced by the depressed narrator of the *Asylum Piece* stories recrudesce in the enforced wartime blackout of the *Lazarus* stories and, as elsewhere in Blitz writing, the blackout is both a physical reality and a metaphor for a restricted relationship with time. As Angela Lyne remarks in Evelyn Waugh's *Put Out More Flags*: 'The only thing in war-time is not to think ahead. It's like walking in the blackout with a shaded torch. You can just see as far as the step you're taking.'[3] If thinking ahead in wartime is treacherous, thinking back becomes increasingly important and problematic in Kavan's stories. The end that could not be foreseen at the close of *Asylum Piece* is now on the horizon; apocalypse approaches, anticipating 'the ceaselessly shrinking fragment of time called "now"' (153) in the final pages of *Ice*. This intense anxiety and limited experience of time combine into what Paul K. Saint-Amour has described as the 'perpetual suspense' of total war.[4] With no scope to move temporally forward, there is a contrary move backwards in the minds of Kavan's protagonists and memory becomes invasive, uncontrollable, elusive or confused, manifest as a 'thing' to be preserved or avoided. Beryl Pong's study of Second World wartime observes a proliferation of literary and cultural 'temporal strategies and apprehensions of time: above all, forms of anticipation and retrospection, and how these relate to one another, to dread and anxiety, to modernist and postwar aesthetics, and to modern wartime'.[5] Kavan's temporal strategies in her war writing intersect with the already disrupted temporality in the *Asylum Piece* stories, in which time was simultaneously interminable and imminently ending; thus, asylum time and war time share affinities. *I Am Lazarus* features several psychiatric patients suffering from partial amnesia and haunted by traumatic events; their failures of recollection are acts of self-preservation. Pong's emphasis on the relation between anticipation and retrospection in wartime is borne out in the increasing importance of past and childhood events to the fates of Kavan's characters from this time forward.

The erosion of discrete categories of sanity and madness, so central to Kavan's writing, emerges as a theme across the body of Blitz writing; in a world gone mad, any stable relationship with objective reality becomes impossible, and no one is fully exempt from the suspicion that they are losing their minds. This ambiguous state affects characters across British war writing to varying degrees: Cousin Nettie in Elizabeth Bowen's *The Heat of the Day* (1948) has 'gone not quite mad';[6] Miss Roach in Patrick Hamilton's *The Slaves of Solitude* (1947) suspects that: 'Any sane person [. . .] would see that she was out of her mind';[7] Pye's mentally unstable sister in Henry Green's *Caught* (1943) anticipates the psychological breakdown of both her brother and his antagonist, Roe.

Kavan's descriptions of her own psychic responses to the war in her letters, and her time working with soldiers suffering from war neurosis, can be seen shaping her narrative experiments with time and reality in her *Lazarus* stories. Other British writers can be observed engaging with similar concerns as the realities of wartime directed a departure from more traditionally realist modes of writing.

The nameless, unreliable and uncomfortably intimate first-person narrator that emerged in *Asylum Piece* reappears in several of the *Lazarus* stories. Just as the paranoias of Kavan's earlier narrator revealed truths about the authoritarianism of the psychiatric profession and the asylum, the often-fantastical narratives of her wartime stories illuminate genuinely restrictive wartime bureaucracy and social control. Sara Wasson has described how Kavan's wartime writing 'can be read as a hallucinatory refraction of some of the authoritarian pressures that convulsed the home front', citing the arbitrary and secretive nature of wartime administration to which Kavan, newly returned to the country, was subject.[8] Observing that Kavan's protagonists are 'outsiders rendered "other" by national position, by madness, or by falling prey to callous bureaucracy' (60), Wasson's study demonstrates that 'Kavan's work of fantastical persecution renders wartime oppressions visible' (74). Kavan's description of sensations of 'madness induced by too much reading of *The Trial* and *The Castle*'[9] in her encounters with British wartime bureaucracy illustrates Mark Rawlinson's observation of the way in which 'formal components of Kafka's fiction, the protagonist interpellated by obscure compulsions, and an occluded, para-state organisation', 'helped make *The Trial* a master-narrative for imagining aspects of life under totalitarianism'.[10] Thus, the totalitarian atmosphere of the asylum in the Kafkaesque dystopias of *Asylum Piece* is fitting to wartime and further augmented in Kavan's *Lazarus* stories.

Kavan travelled widely early in the war years, journeying over four continents and returning to England by boat in late 1942 as German submarine power reached the pinnacle of its destructive strength.[11] She gave a strikingly composed account of her journey:

> . . . it wasn't bad really. The ship just beside us was torpedoed in daylight and that was an extraordinary thing to watch. Her back was broken and she seemed to be almost in two, with a very tall, black, evil looking smoke standing over her like a demon. It was extraordinary, but not really shattering at all. Of course, everything that happens always seems slightly familiar because of the movies.[12]

This sensation of cinematic spectatorship in the face of extreme danger is echoed across accounts of wartime bombing. In one of her *New Yorker* 'letters from London', Mollie Panter-Downes described how such scenes of destruction were 'new enough to seem both shocking and unreal', making 'one feel that one must have strayed onto a Hollywood set'.[13] These references to the fictional atmosphere of 'the movies' indicate a shared sensation of de-realisation, and the need for an aesthetic reference point in describing the 'extraordinary' and 'unreal' effects of aerial bombardment, as writers attempted to explore how known modes of representation might be capable of communicating the unfamiliar scenes and experience of total war. Kavan's personal reflections can be seen mirrored in both the form and content of her wartime fiction.

By the time *Asylum Piece* (1940) was published in Britain, Kavan had been out of the country for several months, and she continued to use her married name during her years abroad.[14] But the critical success of the collection followed her, granting access to literary circles in New Zealand and New York. Stopping off in New York on the way back to England she took the decision to claim her penname, writing to her lover Ian Hamilton: 'Only call me Anna Kavan. I use it always now' (14 November) and after her arrival explained: 'As Anna Kavan I want to get right away from Helen Edmonds and all her associations.'[15] Back in London, she took a job at *Horizon*, providing secretarial support and contributing articles, literary reviews and stories to the journal until serious illness prevented her from working.[16] Kavan's time at *Horizon* from 1943–1944, like many episodes in her life, has been presented in sensational fashion in standard histories of the journal, emphasising her drug use and downplaying her role as a serious contributor and staff member.[17] Arthur Koestler would accuse Cyril Connolly of encouraging this narrative, citing 'after-dinner stories in which you told with gusto about her last suicides' [sic].[18] Although her association with Connolly was variable (at their first meeting she found him 'pretentious and rude'), and did not endure beyond the war, there are clear correspondences in their wartime writing.[19] Connolly's *The Unquiet Grave* (1944) echoes the polemical style of Kavan's journalism and his irreverent and provocative dismissal of Christianity and frequent quotations from Chinese philosophy can be seen too in Kavan's *Lazarus* stories.

Kavan lived with Ian Hamilton in New Zealand from early 1941 to late 1942 and the impact of this time on her writing has been explored in Jennifer Sturm's edition of Kavan's previously unpublished stories written during her time living in a small community not far from Auckland.[20] Several of the *Lazarus* stories were also written in New Zealand and, as Janet Wilson has demonstrated, look back to her time in the country.[21] Kavan's first article for *Horizon*, 'New Zealand: Answer to an Inquiry' (1943), gives an awed and bitter account of the country from which she had recently returned. She describes the landscape as 'weird, unearthly', 'full of splendour and strangeness', a '[s]trange lonely dream scene full of lovely sadness', a 'dream without a dreamer'.[22] Her representation of the islands' society and inhabitants is provocatively condescending and might have been calculated to offend; she portrays a nation of insular, defensive and dissatisfied people and alludes to inherent sexism, alcoholism and corruption. As Sturm has noted, Kavan's fictional representations of New Zealand, in which the country is associated with peace and freedom, are incommensurate with her *Horizon* article. Her negativity is likely to have been shaped in part by Ian Hamilton's experiences as a conscientious objector; he was a committed pacifist, and Kavan left the country as it appeared increasingly likely that he would be incarcerated for refusing to contribute to the war effort. The article refers to 'the man with hate-sharpened features writing anonymous letters' and 'the conscientious objectors of the last war' bringing 'conscription to their homeland the first of all the dominions'.[23] Hamilton would later publish an account of the harsh treatment to which he was subjected in prisons and the detention camp, including periods of solitary confinement.[24] His experiences undoubtedly influenced the paradox Kavan would set out in 'The Case of Bill Williams', that to be pacifist necessitates conflict with society and to be deemed guilty is not necessarily to have committed a crime.[25]

The polemical narrative of 'New Zealand' is framed as the 'answer to an inquiry', in the style of Woolf's *Three Guineas* (1938), and Kavan's narrator addresses an unknown interlocutor 'John'. In a forum in which she might be expected to write with journalistic authority, she felt the need to set out her position: 'The transmission of information is not my department. The only job for which I am qualified as an individualist and a subjective writer is the recording of my personal reactions' (153). She refuses all claims to objectivity in this piece of non-fiction, promising only 'a vague account of my own impressions' and a 'private picture of New Zealand' which will be 'biased, inaccurate and fragmentary' (154). Kavan's journalism, like her fiction, makes claims for the value of subjectivity in its power to describe 'something very much alive' (154).

War Neurosis, the Politics of Madness and Anna Kavan's Broken Heart

In 1943, Kavan took a job at the Mill Hill Emergency Hospital in London, one of the two neurosis centres into which the Maudsley Hospital split during the war. The 100-bed unit at Mill Hill treated soldiers suffering from effort syndrome.[26] This condition was first diagnosed as early as

1863 and was initially identified as a cardiac disorder affecting soldiers. Since then, it has been known under various names, including Da Costa's syndrome, disordered action of the heart, neurocirculatory asthenia and, more colloquially, 'soldier's heart'. Symptoms included fatigue, shortness of breath on exertion and chest pains, but by the Second World War these physiological indications were deemed to be without physical cause, and effort syndrome had been identified as a psychosomatic disorder – a type of war neurosis.[27] Its typological shift from cardiac disorder to neurosis highlights the contingency of psychiatric diagnosis in the early twentieth century, and its symptoms would be significant to Kavan's wartime witing.

Kavan spent four months at Mill Hill, working directly for Maxwell Jones; it was here that Jones first began to pioneer the method of community therapy that he would go on to develop throughout his career. The offer of a job at *Horizon*, which would allow her more time to write, prompted Kavan to leave Mill Hill after only four months, but her association with Jones continued when they jointly contributed to 'The Case of Bill Williams'. Reflecting on his time at the hospital, Jones characterises the conscripted nurses there as 'educated mature women from the professions who chose to do nursing as their war work', noting that 'such people expected and deserved an active role in the treatment programme'.[28] Jones describes a move away from traditionally hierarchical roles and a trend towards 'the tutorial system and integration of the work of the doctors and nurses' (2) at Mill Hill, a progressive inclusivity that enabled Kavan to become directly involved in the work of the centre. Her relationship to the men she worked with, and to the permanent hospital staff, was filtered through her own previous experience of psychiatric treatment and internment. At a time when she was struggling to adjust to life in wartime London and recovering from a bout of severe depression, the job clearly had therapeutic benefits for her. She believed that it had 'about saved my life', describing 'interviewing the patients one at a time and putting them through a sort of questionnaire' 'really like a sort of condensed miniature analysis each time – quite extraordinarily interesting, and exhausting too'.[29] The cardiac symptoms of effort syndrome were initially, and often tenaciously, interpreted by many patients as weakness or disease of the heart, and the treatment at Mill Hill focused in part on disabusing them of these ideas and increasing their understanding of their own condition.[30] Although Mill Hill would form the basis for Kavan's excoriating critique of psychiatry in 'The Case of Bill Williams', the psychiatric practice she was involved with there aimed to involve the patient in their own treatment. Yet, however democratic and palliative the care, its success would inevitably result in a return to combat, which sat at odds with Kavan's pacifism. As the character Bill Williams describes it, treatment at the neurosis centre is a '[b]loody racket to get sick men back into the army' (*Lazarus*, 59); the war lends urgency to Kavan's anti-psychiatric project, making her argument for resisting social conformity a matter of life and death.

Kavan had returned to England from New Zealand as a stopping-off point on her journey to join her mother in South Africa; wartime travel restrictions thwarted her plans and she found herself stranded in London. She was spared the worst excesses of the Blitz early in the war, but was living in London during the 'Baby Blitz' of early 1944. Her flat was bombed, and there are graphic evocations of air and rocket attacks in several of her stories. Experiencing the early years of the conflict from the relative safety of the United States and New Zealand, the sight of the damage done to the capital during the Blitz and the dull terror of everyday life in wartime London shocked her profoundly. She was unprepared for the relentless misery of the blackout, rationing and the atmosphere of terrible apprehension. She wrote to Hamilton: 'it's dreary here, the war and the winter, the blackout, the dismal faces, the cold, the shabbiness, the feeling of death in the air'.[31] Thus, the difficult conditions Kavan attributed to Bill Williams's war neurosis in her article – 'too little sleep, too much tension, too much danger, too much noise' (97) – applied as much to the inhabitants of Blitz-torn London as to the fighting soldier. In a letter written on Valentine's Day 1943, she described her feelings on returning to Blitz-torn London with few possessions and fewer friends:

> And then the awful force of inanimate things: a broken umbrella on the steps of a blitzed house, a barrage balloon on the ground in an empty park in the rain. It's very ridiculous that those things should make you feel as if your heart were broken up in small pieces.[32]

For Kavan, the evidence of civilian bombing brings on the feelings of a heart 'broken up in small pieces', and her metaphorically broken heart recalls the psychosomatic symptoms of the same thing in effort syndrome. This metaphorical relation between her own psychic responses to the war and that of the soldiers she worked with carries into her fictional writing and her time at Mill Hill manifests both in her direct representations of war neurosis and in more diffuse ways.

Kavan's pacifism, though less strident than Hamilton's (for she did not refuse to undertake war work), clearly influences 'Bill Williams', and her stories of this time also reflect a confluence of pacifist feelings and the politics of madness.[33] Her anti-fascist sentiments were clearly stated but, as 'Bill Williams' testifies, she interpreted any social system as totalitarian and her belief that German atrocities were echoed in the actions of the Allies, combined with her enduring feelings of exile, made her a stranger to patriotism. The misanthropic protagonist of 'Glorious Boys' reflects that she has always found it easiest 'to let people think she was a little mad' (48); after openly expressing her anti-war sentiments to a friend, she tells them not to 'take any notice of me; I suppose I'm a bit crazy'. In private, she thinks of the war as 'lunacy: we've all of us gone insane' (48), shifting pathology from the individual to society as a whole. R. D. Laing would echo this theme in his assertion that 'being out of one's mind is the condition of the normal man' and that '[n]ormal men have killed perhaps 100,000,000 of their fellow men in the last fifty years'.[34] Laing's (characteristically androcentric) diagnosis of society's mad war-mongering resonates with Kavan's, but neither denies 'the myth of mental illness' as Thomas Szasz would describe it; both embrace and subvert the category, making mental illness resistance to the mad 'normality' of world war.

Many of the themes of 'The Case of Bill Williams' echo those set forth by Virginia Woolf in 'Thoughts of Peace in an Air Raid' (1942). Woolf's pacifist scheme for ending war, composed before the Blitz in August 1940, involved subduing the 'fighting instinct' of young men and compensating them with 'access to the creative feelings', 'happiness' and freedom 'from the machine'.[35] These aspects all feature significantly in 'Bill Williams' and Kavan certainly had Woolf on her mind when she was composing the article:

> You don't realize the awful impersonal finality with which the war machine closes down on the individual. There simply aren't any individuals anymore; just anonymous parts of the machine. You've got to be part of the machinery or be smashed. And there's no way out of it. Perhaps Virginia Woolf felt something like that.[36]

Kavan thus interprets Woolf's suicide as a response to war and the politics of the times rather than as a symptom of her madness. The pacifist argument of her own article, less measured than Woolf's in both tone and ultimate solution, was also harder to support following the scale of death and destruction in the Blitz. For Kavan, the 'war machine' destroys the individual, but society will not tolerate individuality even in the 'joyous, comical fight for survival called peace' (98).

The *Asylum Piece* stories, especially those in the third person, politicise the treatment of madness; Kavan's wartime stories and journalism on the same theme suggest that madness can be a form of politics. The antagonism she articulates towards normative psychiatric treatment in 'Bill Williams' is also metonymic of a wider critique of society. The class system frequently comes under fire in British wartime writing, anticipating the social reform of the postwar period, and Kavan's empathy towards the men she worked with at Mill Hill in her personal correspondence is one example of the much-mythologised social levelling resulting from the shared sufferings and deprivation of the war.[37] But the change Kavan proposes in 'Bill Williams' is more radical in its call for an end to collective society. Her political vision thus went beyond reforms to redress class inequalities; the 'tonic epidemic of madness' she calls for would be an anarchistic overturning of the entire social order, though she offers no suggestion as to how it might be practically implemented.

Kavan's soldier-protagonists in the *I Am Lazarus* stories, recalling those in her Helen Ferguson novels, have lost elements of their humanity in their encounter with the 'war machine'; they are uncanny automata, functioning rather than feeling. The incursion of war into psychic time is explicitly illustrated by Lennie in 'Who Has Desired the Sea': 'there was nothing but the skeleton in the transparent cell, brass midriff and spine, wheels and frangible springs, the hollow man, bloodless, heartless, headless; only the crazy pendulum swinging in place of head' (25). Just as effort syndrome translates psychological trauma into physical symptoms, Lennie's psychological loss of subjective time is replaced by the physically dead mechanisation of clock-time. In 'Glorious Boys', Ken is 'an anonymous robot, padded, helmeted, hung about with accoutrements and surrounded by switches and dials, sowing catastrophe from a lighted box in the sky' (47), a cog in a larger mechanism:

> It destroyed very thoroughly this war machine, this incinerator of individuality and talent and life, forging the sensitive and creative young into the steel fabric of death, turning them out by the million, the murder men, members of Murder Inc., the big firm, the global organization. (46)

Kavan's pacifist narrator, echoing the sentiments of the 'Bill Williams' article, here explicitly associates war with organised crime, commercial capitalism and globalisation. Across her writing of this period, pacifism goes hand in hand with references to 'individualism', anti-capitalism and a rejection of organised politics and social structures. This anarchistic streak, echoed in Ian Hamilton's writing, suggests that their years living self-sufficiently in New Zealand had political foundations in implementing independence from collectivism, industrialism and state control.

Psychosomatic and Metaphorical Symptoms

The most explicit influence of Kavan's time at Mill Hill on her wartime writing can be seen in three stories which take a soldier suffering from war neurosis as their protagonist: 'Who Has Desired the Sea', 'The Blackout' and 'Face of My People'. These characters join a significant cohort of psychologically traumatised soldiers in twentieth-century British literature. Wyatt Bonikowski has identified how British writers during, and in the wake of, the First World War 'turned the figure of the shell-shocked solider into the embodiment of anxieties the war had brought to England'.[38] But as advances in mechanised warfare in the Second World War brought the action to the home front and narrowed the divide between the experiences of combatant and non-combatant, literary representations of war's psychological damage shifted emphasis away from the figure of the soldier. Mark Rawlinson has described the changing political climate precipitating this and observed how the soldier, largely peripheral to the 'People's War' of the home front, was 'a figure excluded from the great struggles and social experiments of the times, arrested in service bureaucracy and strategic limbo'.[39] Kavan's writing deviates from this tendency: the soldier – specifically the psychologically scarred neurotic case – becomes a figurehead for radical social change in 'Bill Williams' and a prominent protagonist in her stories of this period. The soldiers of *I Am Lazarus* are marginalised in compound ways; they are foreigners, madmen, excluded from both the comradeship of active service and the collectivity of the home front. Their profound isolation echoes that of the *Asylum Piece* stories and Kavan draws on the narrative techniques she had developed in the earlier collection in writing their experiences; her knowledge of effort syndrome and its psychosomatic indications further inflects her experiment – mind and body become confused and interchangeable and the symptoms of neurosis become extended metaphors for traumatic experiences.

The trauma of battle has not been the sole cause of the psychological damage of Kavan's soldier-patients; war aggravates old psychological wounds and increases the burden of social and familial pressures. Displacement, homesickness, loss of financial security, the awful responsibility for the lives of others, and an overwhelming exposure to pain and wasted life are the precipitants of their breakdown. These soldiers are exposed to the same social pressures facing civilians on the British home front, but not all are British. Memories – of happier times and emotional suffering, as well as their war experience – haunt them. In all these stories, the cause and effect of psychological trauma run into one another. The life experiences that precipitate psychological damage become conflated and confused with its manifestation; physical experience becomes a model for the experience of psychological trauma. For Kavan's protagonists, symptoms of neurosis are metaphors for the events leading up to them.

Lennie, in 'Who Has Desired the Sea', is a New Zealand sailor undergoing treatment in a British military neurosis centre located close to the coast. The noise of the waves disquiets him, reviving childhood memories of the sea and traumatic memories of his war experience. The sound of the sea in the present and thoughts of his childhood by the ocean take Lennie always back to this scene of distress; one sea flows perpetually into another. Because of this, memories of childhood and memories of war always come together, juxtaposing the sea of his youth, the sunlit water 'smooth and solid' and 'blue as sapphires', with the 'piled-up', 'ugly' grey sea of his war experiences (25). Lennie's identity has become fractured, and he is endlessly searching for someone: 'a young man with thick brown awkward hair and a small scar on his cheek' (22). The reader begins to realise, as Lennie does not, that the man he seeks is himself. He has become dislocated from his past self and, in the present, has become an automaton, functioning automatically and without feeling. Here, as in many of these stories, Kavan plays with idiomatic and metaphorical expressions of insanity. She allows Lennie's fiancée to cut unknowingly to the heart of his distress in her colloquial observation 'You've always been mad on the sea', and the narrator picks up her cue: 'Yes, the sea was the one thing he had always been crazy about' (28). The wartime sea itself marches 'in manic persistence' (28), drawing the environment into his madness. Lennie fights against reliving his wartime memories of horror, and when his feelings do swell up, they threaten to submerge him: 'The sickness had come up in his throat now and his lungs, and he could feel it strangling him and he was drowning again in the four-mile-deep icy horror of sickness or water' (30). Lennie's struggle with his anxiety, like the symptoms of effort syndrome, is experienced as physical response. His nausea and choking replay his struggle in the water; feelings of trauma and the event that precipitated it are experientially akin. As the story closes, Lennie stands on the edge of a cliff, and the reader is left on the verge of understanding.

The protagonist of 'The Blackout' is a recently conscripted soldier with no name other than 'the boy'. Persistently confining him to a childlike state, his name presages Kavan's later protagonists identified as 'the girl'. The wartime blackout of the story's title is the boy's five-day period of complete memory loss, from which a doctor is attempting to help him recover. The story is riddled with real and metaphorical tunnels; as the boy attempts to escape the consequences of the doctor's questions, his mind runs 'from side to side, seeking the unknown avenues of defence or escape' (33). In the landscape of the boy's internal world, he scrambles for cover like a trapped animal, as the reader will discover he physically fled in order to evade a too painful reality.

The blackout began on the boy's last day of leave, spent at home with his auntie, who rescued him from a childhood of poverty and squalor. When arthritis rendered her unable to work, the boy was happy that a steady wage allowed him to return the care she had given him, until the consequences of war interfered:

> Then he had been called up and he had hated it all, hated the army, hated leaving home, hated losing his good job, hated the idea of being sent overseas to fight: but most of all hated leaving her badly off now, financially insecure, bombs falling perhaps, and she alone with her crippling pains and no one reliable to take care of her. (35)

Not the horrors of battle but the economic impact of war and the danger to loved ones form the backdrop to the boy's amnesia. As the doctor continues to question him, he feels the near presence of a nameless 'thing', sensing 'danger skirmishing all about in the green-walled room' (37). The memory he represses and its emotional impact are resurfacing but he perceives this as an external threat, and the agent of this menace is the doctor who compels him towards it. The boy's resentment is counterbalanced by his fear of the force the memory might acquire if left unexposed, and he does not know 'if it were through his words or his silence that the danger would strike' (37). Memory is again a tunnel, now a dangerous one, which he hurtles into:

> Running in panic along the tunnel he remembered the alley-way, like something in a film he'd seen once, blank walls leaning nearer and nearer to suffocation, and, at the bend, a lamp-bracket sticking out with a dangling noose; only no corpse was at the end of the rope [. . .] and he remembered, further along the tunnel, scrounging about at night where a street market had been and finding, finally, in the gutter, a piece of sausage, grey, slimy, like the wrist of a dead baby. (37)

In this nightmarish scene, the metaphorical tunnel of the boy's memory cuts to the real alleyway of his recent past, and the act of remembering again echoes the experience itself. By the end of the interview, the boy has broken down, recalling almost all the time he was missing, but still repressing the final moment that prompted his blackout. The non-presence of the hanging corpse and the figurative dead baby intimate that death is close at hand. Following a pattern of absence that emerges across the *Lazarus* stories, the reader is not shown, but must infer, the death of the boy's beloved auntie.

'Face of My People', which Arthur Koestler referred to as Kavan's 'Mill-Hill story', relates most directly to her knowledge of effort syndrome and the 'Bill Williams' article.[40] Like Lennie in 'Who Has Desired the Sea', the protagonist, Kling, is a foreigner. Hailing from one of the occupied European countries, he is now an in-patient in a British Army psychiatric hospital. His war experience has been working on burial duty:

> When he thought of the war it was always the digging he thought of . . . because, seeing him so strong and used to work with a spade, they had put him on that job from the beginning; and then there were faces, wrecked or fearful or quiet or obscene faces, far too many of them; how he had laboured and toiled till his saliva ran sour, desperate to hide the faces away from the brutal light.
> How many faces had he covered with earth and stones? There surely were thousands; and always thousands more waiting: and he all the time digging demented, always the compulsive urge in him like a frenzy, to hide the ruined faces away. (58)

Kling's 'demented' digging is a madness in him, just as Lennie was always 'crazy' about the sea. His desperate covering of faces with earth and stones becomes the model for the psychological action he has performed on himself in burying his emotions, and again the lines between traumatic experience and psychological consequence blur. Kling secretly believes there to be a stone lodged inside his body, crushing his breastbone. Thinking that the stone became embedded during an accident, Kling feels it to be 'a small stone, just a dead spot, a sort of numbness under the breastbone'. But Kling had 'told the MO [Medical Officer] about it and the MO had laughed, saying there was no stone or possibility of a stone, and after then he had not spoken of it again; never once'. Later, the stone 'had grown heavier and heavier until he could not think of anything else, until it crushed out everything else, and he could only carry it by making a very great effort' (57). This 'great effort' is one indicator that Kling suffers more explicitly than any of Kavan's protagonists from symptoms that might be interpreted as effort syndrome: the sensation of weight crushing his chest, signs of excessive exertion disproportionate to his physical actions, 'choking with strangled breath' (56–7) and the feeling of a 'heaviness in his heart' (59). Condemned to carry the burden of the wanton loss of life he has witnessed, the stone under Kling's breastbone is a mechanism to suppress emotional pain. For all these soldier-protagonists, repression is both a protective instinct and painful and alienating in itself. Again, in this story, personal tragedy and war trauma become tangled up, and Kling's memory of his dead father is conflated with memories of the unknown men he has buried.

Names, and namelessness, are always significant for Kavan's characters, perhaps more so for Kling than for any other. Kling is not his original name, only the first syllable of one too difficult for English tongues to pronounce. The onomatopoeic resonance between the articulation of this inauthentic, foreshortened name and the sound of metal on rock, specifically spade on stone, initiates a hallucination:

> He heard the *Kling!* of his name being shouted, and again a second clattering *kling!* and running heard the spade *kling-clink* on the stone, he seemed to be holding it now, grasping the handle that slipped painfully in his wet hands, levering the blade under the huge ugly stone and straining finally as another frantic *kling!* came from the spade, and the toppling, heavy, leaden bulk of the stone fell and the old, mutilated face was hidden beneath. (56)

Kling experiences a mnemonic synaesthesia; he experiences hearing the sound of spade on stone as the physical act of striking it – the noise reanimates the memory. This is only one of the many tangled threads of Kling's trauma: the sound of his name and the physical work of burying bodies; the face of the dead man in the gulley and the face of his dead father; the stones he dug and the weight on his chest. Onomatopoeia or paronomasia acts as a catalyst for his memories, causing him to relive his harrowing experiences. For Kling, figurative language and lived experience become indistinguishable; words come into the world and make their presence known. As part of his treatment, the doctor injects Kling with a drug that will induce him to speak, and Kling feels 'the strangeness of sleep or sickness or death moving up on him', and the stone shifts (62). Like the boy in 'The Blackout', Kling desires to maintain his silence, instinctively sensing that his suffering will mean nothing to the medical staff. As he yields to the 'strange sleep', he sees above him 'a cloud of faces, the entire earth was no graveyard great enough for so many' (63):

> The old man bent over him and blood dripped onto his face and he could not move because of what lay on his breast, and when the old man saw he could not move he bent lower still and Kling could see the tufts of bristly hairs in his father's nostrils. He knew he would have to speak soon, and, staring wildly, with the old man's face almost on his, he could see the side of the face that was only a bloodied hole and he heard a sudden frantic gasp and gush of words in his own language, and that was all he heard because at that moment sleep reached up and covered his face. (63–4)

Kling addresses the old man he buried, who becomes, almost imperceptibly, the figure of his dead father, but no one understands the secret he reveals; no one at the hospital can translate his words and the doctor simply abandons his case. The language barrier excludes the reader along with the psychiatric staff. The narrator cannot, or will not, translate for us; the truth Kling reveals to the faces that haunt him is not knowledge we can share.

Although Mill Hill clearly influenced the *I Am Lazarus* stories, Kavan chose not to portray the hospital's progressive practices in her fiction. In her depictions of psychiatric treatment here (as in 'Bill Williams' and elsewhere in her oeuvre), there is always some degree of antagonism between her patients and the psychiatric professional, and the concept of a 'cure' remains ambiguous at best. Kavan herself had recently experienced positive results from short-term psychoanalysis at the Tavistock Clinic, which had helped with her depression soon after her return to London.[41] She would go on to embrace the unorthodox, psychoanalytically influenced psychotherapy of her longstanding psychiatrist Karl Bluth and two periods of existential analysis with Ludwig Binswanger at the Bellevue Sanatorium in Switzerland. Yet in her fiction, talking therapies are presented in the same brutal light as more invasive psychiatry. The act of narration was thus vital to Kavan as both a patient and a writer, but her soldier-protagonists achieve no respite from their psychological anguish in telling it. These characters are unwilling narrators, forced to testify to indifferent hearers, and as Kling begins to succumb to the narco-analysis, he thinks: 'They've taken everything; let them not take my silence' (63).

'The Awful Force of Inanimate Things' and 'The Rising Tide of Hallucination'

Edward Glover, the psychoanalyst who gamely gave his professional opinion of the fictional Bill Williams in *Horizon*, was a member of the committee of psychiatrists, psychologists and psychoanalysts set up in London as early as 1938 in anticipation of a war involving civilian bombardment. Their remit was to plan for 'the prospect of an epidemic of shell shock similar in type to that observed in the Army during the war of 1914–18'.[42] However, by 1941, the general conclusion reached was that there had been 'no outbreak of war neuroses in the civilian population' (133). Lyndsey Stonebridge has explored the political consequences of this outcome in figuring 'the British people as a collectivity of steadfastly sane survivors', noting its value as wartime propaganda and consequent significance for postwar social reforms.[43] Identifying Glover's frustration at a 'no-neurosis myth' that thwarted any opportunity for studying the psychological effects of the war on civilians, Stonebridge suggests that today 'the kind of psychoanalysis of anxiety that Glover sought is probably best found in the fiction of the period', citing the 'compelling strangeness of the 1940 novel' as evidence (17). Kavan's fictional writing –

compellingly strange – can be seen to contest the report's findings, as the symptoms of war neurosis experienced by her soldier-patients in *I Am Lazarus* reverberate too in the world of her civilian characters and narrators. The most fantastical of these stories are those set outside the neurosis centre, and in Kavan's representations of civilian bombing the psychosomatics of effort syndrome are augmented and expanded.

An abusive turn in the intimate relationship between body and psyche throughout the *Lazarus* collection, which manifests the confusion between the physical and psychological in effort syndrome, is explicitly articulated by the narrator of 'Glorious Boys':

> The terrifying independence of the body. Its endless opposition. The appalling underground movements of the nerves, muscles, viscera, upon which, like a hated and sadistic gauleiter, one unremittingly imposed an implacable threat of insubordination. The perpetual fear of being sabotaged into some sudden shameful exposure. (39)

Kavan's 'gauleiter' of the mind appropriates the newly horrifying idiom of the Nazi Party to illustrate the hostile alliance of body and mind; the mind's ongoing suppression of the body is likened not to the impact of German war-mongering, but to authoritarian rule inside the Third Reich. In this model of dictatorship, the threat and fear of sabotage work both ways. The body can expose the mind; it is a medium through which the psyche's privacy will be involuntarily laid bare – in effort syndrome, it manifests the symptoms of war neurosis, and treatments such as narco-analysis render it susceptible to interference from the psychiatric profession. But if the body is a vulnerable point of access to the mind, the mind's opposing threat to the body is inherent in Kavan's personal and fictional encounters with suicide.

Kavan's Valentine's Day letter, in which she describes her heart 'broken up in small pieces' and 'the awful force of inanimate things' calls attention to the peculiar status of objects in wartime London.[44] Like the 'broken umbrella' in her letter, things play a prominent role in her *Lazarus* stories and familiar, quotidian objects become poignant, significant and absurd. The un-named protagonist of 'Glorious Boys' has, like Kavan, recently arrived in war-torn London from 'the underside of the world' (40). Her attempts to communicate with other people are largely unsuccessful; instead, like Thomas Bow in 'I Am Lazarus', she feels greater empathy for inanimate objects. Unlike Mr Bow, this narrator is acutely aware that this is considered peculiar, and in turn finds it odd 'how normal people have no time except for other people' (40). She wonders: 'What is the thing about me that people never can take? . . . she knew the answer perfectly well . . . the preoccupation with non-human things, the interest in the wrong place, that was so unacceptable. People took it as an insult' (42). Her intimacy with physical objects is at its most intense when witnessing an air raid for the first time:

> She had stood watching out in the street, and while the big building burned, and she was feeling the anguish of exploded walls, burst roof, torn girders wrenching away, smoke, flames, blinding up, spouting up through the crazy avalanching of stone, the crashing ruinous death of all that mass of stone and durability struck down with a single blow. (41)

Watching the building burn, Kavan's protagonist feels the agonies of its death throes. This synaesthetic and hallucinatory perception of the city and its buildings echoes across Blitz writing.

William Sansom's 'Fireman Flower' (1944), the title story to the collection Kavan described as 'fascinating', is an account of a bombed and burning factory which becomes a Cartesian meditation on knowledge, the senses and the imagination.[45] The smoke inside the burning building throws 'a film of unreality, a distortion that exaggerated or diminished each object' and through it, Flower sees surreal and hallucinatory visions – broken cables are 'long twin tails of a poisonous fish'; 'a green curtain, torn and discoloured, lay rumpled on the floor like a drowned old woman'.[46] Doggedly pursuing the seat of the fire, Flower knows that 'the world is somersaulted at a fire. Everything can happen' (141). That not just anything, but everything, can happen, is also vital to the surreal goings-on in Kavan's air-raid stories, which exhibit and amplify the 'rising tide of hallucination' that Elizabeth Bowen would later observe in her own wartime stories, collected in *The Demon Lover and Other Stories* (1945).[47] Although Kavan's bare descriptive language sits in contrast to Bowen's linguistic convolutions, correspondences between their writing are at their most acute in these stories, with their shared gothic inflections, hauntings, unreliable narrators and emphasis on seemingly prosaic domestic objects. Kavan's and Bowen's careers align them as quintessentially mid-century writers, Bowen publishing between 1923 and 1968, Kavan between 1929 and 1967. Kavan's pacifism and Anglo-Irish Bowen's role as British informant inflect their wartime writing with political and ethical ambiguities. In one of her *Horizon* reviews, Kavan described the short story as 'like a small room in which is concentrated a brilliant light'; Bowen would also conceive of the short story as a 'small, spotlit zone'.[48] Both writers thus define the form as a spatially confined and temporally fleeting brilliance, and both directed this concentrated illumination towards blacked-out London during the Second World War.

The division between life and death which becomes indistinct at the conclusion of *Asylum Piece* is further eroded in Kavan's war stories, emphasised by the collection's titular reference to Lazarus. Leo Mellor has suggested that questions 'concerning the porous boundary between the living and the dead' animate Bowen's and Kavan's representations of the 'haunted nature of wartime London'.[49] In Bowen's *The Heat of the Day*, victims of the bombing linger after death:

> Most of all the dead, from mortuaries, from under cataracts of rubble, made their anonymous presence – not as today's dead but as yesterday's living – felt through London. Uncounted, they continued to move in shoals through the city day, pervading everything to be seen or heard or felt with their torn-off senses, drawing on this tomorrow they had expected – for death cannot be so sudden as all that.[50]

The abrupt nature of death by bombing is enough to deny (or at least postpone) it, and those living in the present tense of yesterday refuse to give up their expectations of temporal continuity. Mellor's 'porous boundary' can be observed too between sanity and madness, life and fiction, and animate and inanimate bodies in Bowen's and Kavan's wartime writing.

Bowen's war stories take human relationships as their focus. Conversely, the inhabitants of Kavan's wartime London suffer from the severe estrangement that characterises her work and have limited contact with others; they are isolated individuals, socially awkward, grieving lost family and comrades, abandoned by lovers, often considered mad or peculiar. Yet the 'preoccupation with non-human things' in Kavan's wartime stories can be seen too in what Maud Ellman terms Bowen's 'meticulous inventories of household objects, each depicted with surreal intensity'.[51] Ellman describes how in Bowen's writing 'things behave like thoughts and thoughts like things, thus impugning the supremacy of consciousness',[52] and Bowen's own observation that war 'worked as a thinning of the membrane between the this and the that' in *The Heat of the Day* captures the disintegration of barriers between people and people, and people and things, in representations of wartime London.[53]

The final story in the *I Am Lazarus* collection, 'Our City', depicts a fantastic, war-ravaged metropolis. Un-named and ungendered, its enigmatic narrator has a peculiarly intimate relationship with the anonymous city. From the outset of the story, this city is set against the narrator; its enmity can be sensed in streets with an air of meanness, malevolence and the 'smell of spite' (125). In a surreal metamorphosis, the wartime city is transformed into an octopus, a toothed animal trap, ensnaring, confining and passing sentence on the narrator, condemning them to the impossible paradox of being simultaneously its exile and its prisoner. Against the backdrop of this war-torn city, mind and body engage in ongoing conflict, affect and emotion bleed into physical landscapes, and everyday objects become animated. The confusion between bodies and things in wartime extends to the entire city; the physical damage of bombing is not the only harm London suffers in its war experience – war manifests as sickness and its symptoms are exhibited on the body of the metropolis as a 'bald, excrescent shelter' with 'a curious morbid look, like some kind of tumour that has stopped being painful and hardened into a static, permanent lump' (125–6).

Reflecting Kavan's description of the short story form as 'a small room' with 'a brilliant light', the narrator wakes just before the sound of the air-raid siren but makes no attempt to take cover and does no more throughout the attack than check the time, switch on the light and turn it off again; all the action of this scene is played out in the environment both in and outside the narrator's bedroom:

> Mobile guns grind elephantinely over me. A plane buzzes round my head. Outside the black windows the searchlights climb questing. I can feel the broad beams sawing and the narrow beams scissoring through my nerves. Then suddenly from far away over the city, dull, muffled, heavy noise. Pandemonium is starting up; is coming nearer and nearer, implacably, is here, ultimately, on top of me. (129–30)

Following the pattern of the air raid in 'Glorious Boys', in the course of the attack, the distinction between un-named city and un-named narrator becomes indistinct; what the city experiences the narrator experiences too. The room 'floats irresponsibly in the shattering noise' like 'a lighted bubble', but the integrity of its walls has become unsound (130). The air raid outside comes in, and within the room things begin to act in a peculiar way. The action that is at one moment outside the black windows, far away over the city, is in the next 'buzz[ing] round my head', 'sawing' and 'scissoring through my nerves', 'over me', 'ultimately, on top of me'. As the narrator and the city become fleetingly inseparable, the room's furnishings become fellow protagonists, responding to the air raid in their own idiosyncratic ways: the clock remains diligent and indefatigable; 'the bottles on the dressing-table snigger against one another'; 'the curtains flutter a little, but the pale blue carpet doesn't turn a hair' (130). This anthropomorphic animation adds to the scene's nightmarish quality, but in the midst of bizarre metamorphoses and absolute chaos, there is one thing the narrator cannot believe to be true: 'Impossible to imagine that people are connected in any way with the racket that's going on. It's an absolutely inhuman excess of noise, the rage of the city itself. Our city itself is ravening at the night' (130). The inhumanity of the air raid implicates the non-human. As the narrator's imagination is confounded by the reality of modern warfare, it turns instead to the curtains, the carpet and the city itself. The charm and comfort of the furnishings in 'Our City' mock the narrator's state of persecution; the relentless frivolity of the pale blue carpet gives it power to horrify, making it complicit in the bombardment. Comfort, beauty and human empathy are all denied to this inhabitant of the war-torn city, and their physical reminders are a terrible affront.

In Bowen's story 'Mysterious Kôr', the blackout both literally and metaphorically affects what people can and cannot see. To Pepita, who thinks of the fantastical 'ghost city' of Rider Haggard's *She* (1887) 'all the time' (198) in wartime London, its literary origins are interesting only inasmuch as 'what it makes me see' (199). What the war shows Pepita is: 'If you can blow whole places out of existence, you can blow whole places into it' (199), that is, if London is being literally destroyed, she and Arthur can create Kôr, and the blacked-out city becomes a nexus of fictional location, fantasy world and dream. But for Arthur, playing at bringing a story alive can go too far, and he complains: 'A game's a game, but what's a hallucination?' (213). Attempting to follow her imaginative lead, he asks Pepita 'you mean we're there now, that here's there, that now's then?' (200). Bowen's characteristically convoluted arrangement of 'heres', 'nows', 'wheres' and 'thens' demonstrates how time and place are malleable and subject to becoming confused in the blackout. What is unsettling and uncanny to Arthur is integral to Bowen's and Kavan's wartime writing; when it comes to fiction and reality, the tipping point from play into madness or hallucination is dangerously close and the grossly altered perspective induced by war might, or might not, be delusion.

In the wartime metropolis of both writers, the blacked-out night has a life of its own; in the wake of the raid in 'Our City', the turmoil is followed by a dreadful regeneration:

> The noise is over. But now something begins to happen that is in its way as sensational, as appalling. Through the darkness of the blacked-out windows I am aware of an indescribable movement throughout the city, a soundless spinning of motion in the streets and among the ruins, an unseen upward surge of building: the silence industriously, insecurely, building itself up. The silence gathers itself together in the parks and the squares and the gaps and the empty houses. Like a spider's web rapidly woven, the frail edifice mounts up quickly towards the moon. Soon the precarious work is finished, the whole city is roofed, covered in with silence, as if lying under a black cloche [. . .] every citizen crouches uneasily, peering up at the transparent black bell of silence hanging over our city. Is it going to break? (131)

The 'transparent black bell of silence', anticipating Plath's 'bell jar', maintains a parallel between the intense anxiety and depression of

Asylum Piece and the experience of living in the wartime city in this later collection; the isolation of Kavan's first-person narrator is felt by 'every citizen' crouching under it, unifying London's inhabitants in apprehension. In 'Mysterious Kôr', waiting for Arthur and Pepita to return, Callie too senses some silent tension out in the blacked-out night: 'At once she knew that something was happening – outdoors, in the street, the whole of London, the world. An advance, an extraordinary movement was silently taking place' (205). The unseen 'something' that happens in the dark silence of both stories, 'sensational' in Kavan's narrative and 'extraordinary' in Bowen's, is intensely active, rapid and urgent. Callie feels the same palpable apprehension described by Kavan's narrator: 'Once gained by this idea of pressure she could not lie down again; she sat tautly, drawn-up knees touching her breasts, and asked herself if there were anything she should do' (205). Sitting tautly, crouching uneasily, for London's inhabitants the blackout is not simply an absence of light, and often sound, but a state of being.

Building on the narrative strategies she had begun in *Asylum Piece*, Kavan's experimentalism was profoundly influenced by wartime and its political and aesthetic effects on her writing would continue throughout her career. In her *Lazarus* stories, war initiates a radical dissolution of boundaries between minds and bodies, people and things, the city and its inhabitants, the living and the dead. There is no trace here of the cultural 'myth of the Blitz' as a unifying experience, identified by Angus Calder; instead, Kavan's literary representations reveal the terrible apprehension and emotional fragility of London's inhabitants in wartime.[54] The solipsistic experiences of her psychiatric inmates in the collection bleed into the world, breaching the confines of both the asylum and the individual mind, and wartime London becomes a fantastic synthesis of psychic trauma and physical response. Kavan's contact with effort syndrome and its cardiac symptoms throws into relief the intimacy of the psychological and the physiological in her wartime writing, shaping her understanding of the hearts and minds of soldiers and civilians in the Second World War.

Notes

1. Anna Kavan to Rhys Davies, undated [1945], Anna Kavan Papers, *MFL*. Several of the stories in the collection had already appeared in journals and magazines; wartime paper shortages delayed Cape's publication schedule.
2. Cyril Connolly, 'Why Not War Writers? A Manifesto', *Horizon*, 9:22 (October 1941), p. 235.

3. Evelyn Waugh, *Put Out More Flags* [1942] (London: Penguin, 1976), p. 218.
4. Paul K. Saint-Amour, *Tense Future: Modernism, Total War, Encyclopedic Form* (Oxford: Oxford University Press, 2015).
5. Beryl Pong, *British Literature and Culture in Second World Wartime: For the Duration* (Oxford: Oxford University Press, 2020), p. 25.
6. Elizabeth Bowen, *The Heat of the Day* [1949] (London: Vintage Books, 1998), p. 174.
7. Patrick Hamilton, *The Slaves of Solitude* [1947] (London: Constable, 2006), p. 296.
8. Sara Wasson, *Urban Gothic of the Second World War: Dark London* (Basingstoke: Palgrave Macmillan, 2010), p. 61.
9. Anna Kavan to Ian Hamilton, 7 March 1943, *NLNZ*.
10. Mark Rawlinson, 'Narrating Transitions to Peace: Fiction and Film after War', in Gill Plain (ed.), *British Literature in Transition, 1940–1960: Postwar* (Cambridge: Cambridge University Press, 2019), 143–60, pp. 157–8.
11. Wartime, along with the success of *Asylum Piece*, brought Kavan into contact with diverse creative networks and individuals during her travels. In New York she forged friendships with Walker Evans and Jim Agee, and was introduced to other displaced British writers including Louis MacNiece and Sylvia Townsend-Warner. During her two years in New Zealand, she and Ian Hamilton spent time with writers Frank Sargeson, Denis Glover and Greville Texidor. In London, her Antipodean experience encouraged friendships with New Zealand artist Len Lye, and Australian writers Max Murray and Maysie Greig, and at *Horizon* she socialised with Peter Watson, Arthur Koestler and Cyril Connolly. For details of this period of Kavan's life, see letters in Hamilton Papers, and specifically for her time in New Zealand, see Jennifer Sturm (ed.), *Anna Kavan's New Zealand: A Pacific Interlude in a Turbulent Life* (Auckland: Vintage, Random House New Zealand, 2009).
12. Anna Kavan to Ian Hamilton, 24 January 1943, *NLNZ*.
13. Mollie Panter-Downes, 'Letter from London' *New Yorker*, 21 September 1940.
14. *Asylum Piece* first published 23 February 1940, see Archives of Jonathan Cape Ltd, Archives of Random House publishers, University of Reading Library, Special Collections.
15. Anna Kavan to Ian Hamilton, 20 February 1943, *NLNZ*.
16. Peter Watson, the magazine's financial backer, became Kavan's close friend, and she spent several weekends at Connolly's Sussex home. See Hamilton Papers, especially Kavan to Hamilton, 24 February 1944. She was hospitalised with heart problems in 1944.
17. For detailed histories of the journal, and brief accounts of Kavan's time there, see Michael Shelden, *Friends of Promise: Cyril Connolly and the World of Horizon* (London: Hamish Hamilton, 1989) and Jeremy Lewis, *Cyril Connolly, a Life* (London: Jonathan Cape, 1997).
18. Arthur Koestler to Cyril Connolly, 28 June 1944, Cyril Vernon Connolly Papers, *MFL*.
19. Anna Kavan to Ian Hamilton, 11 April 1943, *NLNZ*. After working with Connolly for some months she would later find him a 'really a nice guy

under that super-intellectual façade', Kavan to Hamilton, 2 December 1943, *NLNZ*.
20. Jennifer Sturm (ed.), *Anna Kavan's New Zealand: A Pacific Interlude in a Turbulent Life* (Auckland: Vintage, Random House New Zealand, 2009).
21. See Janet Wilson, 'A Pacific Sojourn: Anna Kavan and the New Zealand Connection, 1941–2', *Women: A Cultural Review*, 28:4 (Winter 2017), 285–94.
22. Anna Kavan, 'New Zealand: Answer to an Inquiry', *Horizon*, 8:45 (September 1943), 153–62, pp. 162, 159, 157.
23. Kavan, 'New Zealand: Answer to an Inquiry', p. 156.
24. Ian Hamilton, *Till Human Voices Wake Us* (Auckland: University of Auckland, 1984). This account, first published privately in 1953, resonates strongly with Kavan's 1940s writing in its focus on the individual and the value of subjective viewpoint as well as in imagery and language.
25. Kavan's novel *Guilty*, in which her protagonist's life of social alienation is inaugurated by the stigma associated with his father's pacifism, continues to explore this theme. *Guilty*, originally written in 1956, was published posthumously in 2007.
26. Maxwell Jones, *Social Psychiatry: A Study of Therapeutic Communities* (London: Tavistock Publications Ltd, 1952), p. 1.
27. For a history of effort syndrome, see Edgar Jones and Simon Wessely, 'War Syndromes: The Impact of Culture on Medically Unexplained Symptoms', *Medical History*, 49:1 (1 January 2005), 55–78; Thomas Lewis, *The Soldier's Heart and the Effort Syndrome* (London: Shaw, 1940); Ben Shephard, *A War of Nerves: Soldiers and Psychiatrists 1914–1994* (London: Jonathan Cape, 2000).
28. Maxwell Jones, *Social Psychiatry*, p. 2.
29. Kavan to Hamilton, 23 June 1943, *NLNZ*.
30. See Maxwell Jones and Aubrey Lewis, 'Effort Syndrome', *The Lancet* (28 June 1941), 813–18.
31. Kavan to Hamilton, 14 November 1943, *NLNZ*.
32. Kavan to Hamilton, 14 February 1943, *NLNZ*.
33. Jennifer Sturm's research into Kavan's time in New Zealand provides details of her relationship with Ian Hamilton, but although Kavan did not welcome her own conscription to war work in Britain, she made no resistance to it on ideological grounds.
34. R. D. Laing, *The Politics of Experience and the Bird of Paradise* (London: Penguin, 1967), p. 24.
35. Virginia Woolf, 'Thoughts on Peace in an Air Raid', in *The Death of the Moth and Other Essays* (London: Hogarth Press, 1942), 154–7, p. 157.
36. Anna Kavan to Ian Hamilton, 24 April 1943, *NLNZ*.
37. In one example, Kavan writes: 'One of the boys was telling me the other day about a traumatic experience he had when a very great pal of his was badly wounded . . . I found that very moving', Anna Kavan to Ian Hamilton, 1 August 1943, *NLNZ*.
38. Wyatt Bonikowski, *Shell Shock and the Modernist Imagination: The Death Drive in Post-World War I British Fiction* (London: Routledge, 2013), p. 2.
39. Mark Rawlinson, 'The Second World War: British Writing', in Kate McLoughlin (ed.), *The Cambridge Companion to War Writing* (Cambridge: Cambridge University Press, 2009), 197–211, p. 203.

40. See Arthur Koestler to Cyril Connolly, 28 June 1944, Cyril Vernon Connolly Papers, McFarlin Library Special Collections, University of Tulsa. Bill Williams makes a cameo appearance as a minor character in 'Face of My People'. The story first appeared in *Horizon* two months after 'The Case of Bill Williams' (see Kavan 'Face of My People', *Horizon*, 9:53, 323–35).
41. Kavan to Hamilton, 12 October 1943, *NLNZ*.
42. Edward Glover, 'Notes on the Psychological Effects of War Conditions on the Civilian Population', *International Journal of Psychoanalysis*, 22 (1941), 132–46, p. 132.
43. Lyndsey Stonebridge, *The Writing of Anxiety: Imagining Wartime in Mid-Century British Culture* (Basingstoke: Palgrave MacMillan, 2007) p. 32.
44. Kavan to Hamilton, 14 February 1943, *NLNZ*.
45. Anna Kavan, 'Reviews', *Horizon*, 9:52 (April 1944), 283–5, p. 284.
46. William Sansom, 'Fireman Flower', in *Fireman Flower and Other Stories* (London: Hogarth Press, 1944), 126–63, pp. 132, 134.
47. Elizabeth Bowen, 'Postscript by the Author', in *The Demon Lover and Other Stories* (London: Jonathan Cape, 1945), p. 218.
48. Anna Kavan, 'Reviews', *Horizon*, 9:52 (April 1944), 283–5, p. 283; Elizabeth Bowen quoted in Maud Ellmann, *The Nets of Modernism: Henry James, Virginia Woolf, James Joyce, and Sigmund Freud* (Cambridge: Cambridge University Press, 2010), p. 95.
49. Leo Mellor, *Reading the Ruins: Modernism, Bombsites and British Culture* (Cambridge: Cambridge University Press, 2011), p. 162.
50. Bowen, *The Heat of the Day*, p. 91.
51. Maud Ellman, *Elizabeth Bowen: The Shadow Across the Page* (Edinburgh: Edinburgh University Press, 2003), pp. 146–7.
52. Ellman, *Elizabeth Bowen*, p. 5.
53. Bowen, *The Heat of the Day*, p. 92.
54. See Angus Calder, *The Myth of the Blitz* (London: Jonathan Cape, 1991).

Chapter 4

The Crowding of Dreams: Postwar Time and Experimentalism

> So many dreams are crowding upon me now that I can scarcely tell true from false: dreams like light imprisoned in bright mineral caves; hot, heavy dreams; ice-age dreams; dreams like machines in the head.
>
> *Asylum Piece*

This catalogue of dreams in *Asylum Piece* anticipates the scope of Anna Kavan's fictional writing; the 'machines in the head' from her first collection of stories, the 'hot, heavy' tropical visions of *Let Me Alone* and *Who Are You?* and the 'ice-age dream' of her last and best-known work.[1] Kavan's oblique, often oneiric prose consistently resists simplified interpretations that relegate its fantastic elements to dream; her characters never wake up to reality and if her narrator can 'scarcely tell true from false', the reader is left in the same quandary. But dream and its relation to conscious life, and to fiction, is a recurring theme in her writing. Her representations of blacked-out and night-time worlds in her 1940s stories, including those induced through narcosis and narco-analysis, developed into a sustained engagement with sleep and the unconscious in *Sleep Has His House* (published in the USA as *The House of Sleep*).[2] This surrealist novel continues the gothic trope of Kavan's earlier writing and draws on existentialist and psychoanalytic theory, shaped by her close association with Karl Bluth and Ludwig Binswanger. Continuing and expanding her exploration of fractured and uncertain identity into a postwar context, Kavan pushed her linguistic and narrative experiment in new directions, but always with an eye to representations of subjective reality, inflected by her treatment with psychotropic drugs and her long-term heroin use. Time, which had begun to behave strangely in her wartime writing, also continues to take an odd turn in her postwar fiction.

In her final review for *Horizon* in early 1946, Kavan decried a cultural impulse to look backwards, which she identified as beginning during the war and continuing beyond it.[3] Her observation that an 'increase in the paper quota' had been largely allocated to reprints and that familiar works were crowding out 'new names and experimental forms' (62) identified a postwar retreat from experimentalism back towards more traditionally realist modes of writing, a narrative that would later become a critical commonplace in works such as Rubin Rabinowitz's *The Reaction against Experiment in the English Novel 1950–1960* (1967) and Bernard Bergonzi's *The Situation of the Novel* (1970). Kavan described a publishers list as 'an index of social tendencies; a chart of collective psychological trends' (62) and thus she extended her analysis to a collective 'infantile fixation' (65), 'the ultimate flight to the womb' (62). This review, like her fiction of the time, reveals both her close engagement with psychoanalytic theory and her continuing focus on reality:

> Only the most mature human beings can bear to look our present reality in the face. For the survival of the rest, some form of escape is an essential condition. Humanity looks back in search of a sanctuary, because to look in any other direction is to encounter the treacherous unknown. Only the past is finite, and, being crystallized, cannot betray. (63)

Kavan's observations elucidate her increasing experiment with narrative temporality in the postwar, reflecting experimental strategies emerging in the work of other British writers.

Kavan's preoccupation with reality, noted throughout the previous chapters of this book, continued to burgeon in both her writing and that of other British experimentalists in the postwar period, captured by Frank Kermode's description of 'the characteristic experience of serious modern fiction' as 'a radical re-appraisal' of the relation between fiction and reality in *The Sense of an Ending* (1966).[4] In the postwar of Kermode's study, 'the use of fictions for the exploration of fiction' (152) had become commonplace, and this hard look at fiction as the artistically sanctioned telling of lies was a symptom of a historically situated crisis of reality during a time in which writers and readers were 'muddled about the question of what [. . .] we could take on trust from the past' and 'morbidly aware of the nature and motive of our mendacity' (152). What Kermode describes as the 'dangerous relations' (37) between literary and other fictions were revealed by the recent history of a world war driven by the alluring narratives of nationalism and anti-Semitism, a retrospection coloured by mistrust, contrary to Kavan's description of the comfortable 'past which cannot betray' of the Victorian era. But what is common to these perceptions is that following the war, history, whether consoling or alarming, must be suspected as a fiction, and fiction is therefore implicated in shaping the horrors of the twentieth century.

Categories of postwar and experimental fiction have been under increasing scholarly pressure to expand. Gill Plain has artfully described how the notion of a 'postwar' shaped psychological and cultural life even during the conflict:

> At the heart of the culture of the 1940s is an amorphous entity called the 'postwar'. It takes hold, as a vision, almost the moment that hostilities are declared; it becomes a state of mind as the war progresses through its interminable, deadly grind; it shapes a literature of the aftermath, traumatic and troubled; it limits the possibilities of recognizing, let alone building, a concept of 'peace'[5]

Such freeing of the postwar from its chronological parameters is helpful for considering it as a concept across the mid-century, and pertinent to the ways in which time becomes both elastic and vital to the possibilities of existence in Kavan's fiction of the 1940s onwards. The difficulties and pitfalls of looking backwards as well as forwards, manifest in her wartime writing, developed into formal experiment with narrative temporality in her postwar work.

Kavan's interest in John William Dunne's popular but scientifically doubtful study, *An Experiment with Time* (1927), is evidenced in a description from the unpublished *The Cactus Sign* of 'another confirmation of Dunne's theory that you sometimes dream the future as well as the past'.[6] Dunne's model of serialism proposes that past, present and future exist simultaneously in a series of multitudinous dimensions. Based on the evidence of his own precognitive dreams, Dunne maintained that a linear understanding of time is a result of conscious processing, and that we can access time differently through the unconscious medium of dream.[7] Dunne's 'experiment' is closer to speculative fiction than to scientific fact and his theories can be seen disseminated and reflected in mid-century fiction. This constellation of dream, time and the unconscious is vital to Kavan's postwar writing; it mirrors her own exploration of the meeting points of conscious life and dream in *Sleep Has His House* (1947) and her formal experiment with temporality to explore the possibilities of existence in *Who Are You?* (1963).

Recent critical attention to postwar experimental writing has begun to address how Kavan's work sits in relation to a younger generation of British avant-garde writers such as B. S. Johnson, Ann Quin, Christine Brooke-Rose, Alan Burns and Alexander Trochi, all of whom, like Kavan, have suffered critical neglect.[8] Some of these were demonstrably familiar with Kavan's work, and she with theirs, and many of the writers featured in Giles Gordon's *Beyond the Words* (1975) echo Kavan's key concerns with reality, disconnection and de-personalisation, which she had begun to articulate before the end of the war.⁹ But, with a fidelity to linear progression that sits at odds with these writers' own rejection of rigid structures of history and temporality, criticism has tended to categorise British mid-century experimentalists as either late modernists who kept writing into the postwar period, or postwar writers who, in various ways, were responding to modernism's legacy. Julia Jordan's perceptive study of connections between these two groupings focuses on the later generation's explicitly stated response to modernism, rather than writers who were contemporaneous with both.¹⁰ To date little attempt has been made to read mid-century experimentalism as continuous across the pre/postwar divide. Although largely contradicted by recent scholarship, the critical narrative of a postwar rejection of experimentalism and turn to social realism (echoed in Kavan's own journalism, above) still shapes the genealogy of mid-century British writing.

As comparative work on Kavan increases, emphasising affinities between her writing and that of late modernists on the one hand and postwar experimentalists on the other, she increasingly becomes a critical lynchpin between these two categories. Scholarly readings that have traced connections between her experiment and those of Elizabeth Bowen, André Breton, Alan Burns, William Burroughs, Leonora Carrington, Graham Greene, Patrick Hamilton, James Joyce, Anaïs Nin, Jean Rhys, William Sansom, Muriel Spark and Rex Warner gather around her a diverse grouping of experimental writers not often assembled.¹¹ Mapping Kavan's place among her literary contemporaries thus brings together writers who established their reputation before or during the war with those who began writing after, positions neglected figures alongside more canonical experimentalists, groups literary fiction with science fiction and overall offers a fuller account of British mid-century experimental writing.

Sleep Has His House

Kavan began working on her first novel under her new name, *Sleep Has His House*, during the war.¹² Its image-laden, densely descriptive and surrealist style represents the unconscious through a fragmentary and fluid montage of images that form and disperse; the 'crowding' of dreams described by her earlier narrator. In a short forward, Kavan sets out her intentions to describe 'certain stages in the development of one individual human being' using 'the night-time language' which 'we have all spoken in childhood and in our dreams' (5). The third-person narrative is interspersed with short italicised passages in the first person, which 'indicate the corresponding events of the day' (5), in a method she later described as 'alternating objective with subjective pieces'.[13] These segments describe events in the life of a lonely child; the third-person passages of 'night-time language' are oblique, fragmentary and surrealist, presenting the dissociated images of an unconscious dreamscape. In a linguistic rendering of the type of surrealist film epitomised by Dali's dream sequence in Hitchcock's *Spellbound* (1945), Kavan paints the backdrop, lights the set and positions the reader's view 'from the air' or 'ground-level', shifting it as 'the dream angle changes a little' (20, 21, 25). As one scene cuts to another, her narrative continues to direct the shots of this filmic montage: 'Very chaotic detail [. . .] View of classrooms [. . .] Very close detail' (62). The narrator is sardonically self-aware of their cinematic approach to artistic representation: 'After all, they do these things much better on the moving pictures' (81–2) and explicitly describes its images appearing on a 'dream screen' (82), which later becomes a 'dreaming eye' (102).

Kavan identified a structural connection between *Sleep Has His House* and *Asylum Piece*, planning a later work which she described as 'short stories with a connecting thread (something like *Asylum Piece* and *The House of Sleep*)'.[14] Both works use interrelated third- and first-person voices and explore the unconscious through spatial metaphor; in *Asylum Piece*, the psyche and the institution are indistinguishable, in *Sleep Has His House*, the unconscious becomes a place of sanctuary for the narrator. But the alliterative, rhythmic prose and overloaded imagery of this novel contrasts with the stark language of the *Asylum Piece* stories, as Kavan expanded her linguistic and formal experiment in new directions. *Sleep Has His House* clearly owes a debt to late modernist texts which represent oneiric and unconscious states: Virginia Woolf's *The Waves* (1931), Djuna Barnes's *Nightwood* (1936) James Joyce's *Finnegan's Wake* (1939).[15] The mixed reception of *Sleep Has His House* has had consequences for Kavan's career and legacy. Contemporary reviews on both sides of the Atlantic were unfavourable, none more so than Diana Trilling's excoriating notice in *The Nation* which maintained from the outset that 'nothing makes it worth reading'.[16] Despite Kavan's stated intention to portray an unconscious 'language we have all spoken in childhood and in our dreams' (5), Trilling takes the novel to be representative of a growing movement within 'higher literary art' which maintains that 'madness is a normal, even a better than normal, way of life' (220, 218). Such harsh criticism was instrumental in Kavan's difficulties finding a publisher after the war.[17] Later assessments of the novel have indicated its appeal to literary critics – Jane Garrity considers it 'the most undervalued' of Kavan's novels and Geoff Ward suggests that it is her 'masterpiece'.[18]

Kavan continues the initialising convention she introduced in *Asylum Piece* and names her two protagonists arbitrarily: a woman, 'for the sake of economy she may as well be called A', and a 'little girl with fair hair – she is unmistakably the child of her mother and so could be called B' (22, 26). B is the voice telling the 'events of the day'; in the night-time segments she is sometimes found sleeping. The memory of her mother haunts both day- and night-time worlds: '*No one said anything to me about the death of my mother and I never asked anyone. It was a question which could not possibly ever be asked*' (35). Present but unstated, the spectre of suicide haunts this novel as an 'erratic but steadfast seeking, saraband and stalking of death by violence through the indifferent world' (44). The ghost of A appears through panes of glass, transparent and mirrored, in both first-person segments and dream sequences, taking the place of B's reflection and becoming her doppelganger. As B begins to find it '*hard to tell which face was my own*', her window becomes '*a magic glass*' (183) and inner and outer worlds become confused: '*Sometimes, looking out of an upstairs window, I could feel my mother looking out of my eyes*' (47). B's resemblance to Lewis Carroll's Alice and the mood and imagery of Carroll's imaginary worlds are made explicit as Kavan invokes a 'nightmare Alice-in-Wonderland inconsequence' (102) and a 'mass of papers flying, whirling through the air like Alice's pack of cards' (180). A has passed through the looking glass, inviting B to follow.

The uncertainty and mistrust experienced by the depressive psychiatric patient in Kavan's asylum stories, which had seemingly become contagious during the war, continued to increase in the postwar period, as identified by Frank Kermode. As confidence in a shared absolute reality waned, Kavan turned her attention to the reality of the unconscious in *Sleep Has His House*, but her narrative retains an awareness of the potential dangers inherent in this move. B increasingly withdraws from the daytime: '*Out of the night-time magic I built in my head a small room as a sanctuary from the day*' (87). Finding solace in '*changing my anxiety into written words*' (125), literary representation becomes a causeway into the unconscious: '*I relied on what I wrote to build a bridge which could not be cut down*' (125). But ultimately there is danger in this retreat: '*It was my own self in which I trusted, not seeing self as that last cell from which escape can only come too late*' (125). The literal blackness of the night in *Sleep Has His House* becomes a metaphor for the darkness that lurks there; although the first-person passages speak of creating a safe space of fantasy, this sanctuary becomes a prison and the third-person dreams veer towards nightmare.

The fractured identity which characterises Kavan's writing, brought about variously by psychological breakdown, the experiences of difference and displacement, and the pressures of social convention, is inflected by childhood trauma and neglect in *Sleep Has His House*; A's abandonment of B by suicide shapes her daughter's confused identity. Her mother's absence in the daytime world becomes a constant presence in the unconscious night-time, until A both surrounds and usurps her. B necessarily follows A, 'unmistakably the child of her mother' in both looks and inherited melancholy:

> *One day when I combed my hair in front of a mirror, my mother looked out at me with her face of an exiled princess. That was the day I knew I was unhappy.* (61)

B is lured away from her alienated existence in the daytime world of normalcy and conformity into the darkness of the night-time world that is permeated by her mother, but A is, at best, indifferent to her child, and the comfort she finds in this maternal home is underlain by self-destruction. The novel develops themes Kavan introduced in 'Now I Know Where My Place Is' from the *Lazarus* collection, in which the narrator's childhood self haunts their present in a place that lingers 'on the horizons' of consciousness, appearing 'in that vague twilight between sleep and waking' (119). This 'small, serious and rather lonely figure' who occupies herself with 'solitary pursuits, too grave to come into the category of games' (120) is the prototype for B in *Sleep Has His House*, and the narrator's description of a 'queer dream-plasma which flows along like a sub-life' (120) anticipates the novel's explicit representation of the unconscious. Kavan would continue to explore the psychological effects of childhood neglect again in her realist novel *A Scarcity of Love* (1956) and in *Ice*, in which the girl's fate and personality are determined by her early experiences – she was 'damaged by a sadistic mother' (8) and forced 'into a victim's pattern of thought and behaviour' (36).

As Hannah Van Hove has argued, the 'influence of surrealism on *Sleep Has His House* cannot be overstated'.[19] The novel magnifies the hallucinatory and surrealist imagery that Kavan had begun introducing in her wartime *Lazarus* stories, especially 'Our City', and develops the animal symbolism that would become increasingly vital in much of her later work. The 'slow, padded beat' of a big cat's 'cushioned paws softly approaching' (9) recurs and multiplies, turning the night into a 'tiger-garden' (43), expanding the motif of the 'Chinese lion' which stalks her unpublished collection *The Cactus Sign*. Big cats would continue to feature significantly in the later stories 'A Visit' and 'Clarita'; exhibiting varying degrees of humanity, they recall the animal/human hybrids of Kafka's fables and Leonora Carrington's stories and paintings.[20] There are sensual if not overtly sexual undertones to her protagonists' relationships with these beasts, evoking Carrington's big dogs in 'The Debutante' and 'Jemima and the Wolf', and presaging Angela Carter's reworkings of fairytale in *The Bloody Chamber* (1979). The affinities with surrealism in Kavan's 1940s writing are political as well as aesthetic, especially in the movement's position on psychiatry, evidenced explicitly in André Breton's description of psychiatrists as men who 'primarily serve the instruments of social repression'.[21] Taking pacifism as a prime example of a politically inconvenient view pathologised by psychiatry, Breton's account of mental illness as social construct anticipates Kavan's pacifist, anti-psychiatric rhetoric. Geoff Ward has identified how *Sleep Has His House* straddles interwar and postwar experimentalism by observing how it recalls 'the aerial views of 1930s' literary cartography while ushering in the neo-surrealism and science fiction interests of the postwar period', emphasising its mid-century perspective.[22] In sympathy with other postwar experimental writers such as J. G. Ballard, Angela Carter and Alan Burns, Kavan would continue to draw on surrealism, especially in stories collected in *A Bright Green Field* and *Julia and the Bazooka*, as well as in *Ice*.

Dream, Existence, Opium and the Unconscious

Jane Garrity has observed how *Sleep Has His House* is 'indebted to a psychoanalytic paradigm that privileges the nonrational, nonsequential realm of associative thought' and suggests that its fragmented and ambiguous form of communicating meaning gives it an 'allegiance to dream-work'.[23] As this suggests, Kavan's exposure to psychoanalytic theory is most evident in her postwar fiction and journalism, reflecting her treatment at the Tavistock Clinic in 1943 and her visits to Ludwig Binswanger's Bellevue Clinic in Kreuzlingen in 1947 and again 1948.[24] Bluth, who referred Kavan to the Bellevue, joined her in Kreuzlingen for a spell in 1947, and his attempts to have Binswanger's work published in English indicates its major influence on his own psychiatric method.[25] Binswanger's term *Daseinsanalyse* for his fusion of philosophy, psychiatry and psychoanalysis reveals the strong influence of both Heidegger and Freud on his thinking. However, his style of analysis deviated substantially from Freud's teachings, despite his longstanding friendship with his earlier mentor.[26] His thought remained more faithful in intention to

Heidegger's work but his interpretation of some Heideggerian concepts have been subject to charges of misinterpretation and his own evaluation of 'creative misunderstanding'.[27]

In his 1930 essay *Dream and Existence* Binswanger works through a selective cultural history, drawing on sources from Greek philosophy and drama to nineteenth-century German literature and psychoanalysis. His central tenet that dream is a state of existence, a realm that is 'nothing other than a definite mode of the Being of man', diverges considerably from the Freudian perception of dream as a window into the unconscious.[28] Going beyond Freud's interest in the relationship between fiction and the psyche, evidenced in both his engagement with classical literature and in 'Creative Writers and Day-dreaming' (1907), Binswanger places not only the substance of fiction but the form of poetic language at the core of his existential analysis in *Dream and Existence* when he claims that: 'The nature of poetic similes lies in the deepest roots of our existence (*Existenz*) where the living, spiritual form and the living, spiritual content are still bound together' (81). Thus, for Binswanger, literary metaphor and simile are not simply linguistic synthesis but an intrinsically integrated structure of meaning which express something fundamental to our existence. Binswanger applies this same model to the realm of dream; like literary figuration, the meaning of dream cannot be fully divided from its expression and its importance lies not in what it might signify but in the imaginative experience itself. Thus, for Binswanger, both dream and literary text are existential experiences which resist interpretation. In *Sleep Has His House*, the 'allegiance to dream-work' observed by Garrity is likely to have been inflected by this unorthodox interpretation of Freudian psychoanalysis, coming to Kavan both directly from Binswanger and second-hand via Karl Bluth.

Kavan's heroin addiction was an open secret among her acquaintances during her lifetime. When it was made public after her death, the glamourous associations that had accrued around recreational drug use in the 1960s led to her addiction becoming an important feature of her life story, shaping interpretations of her fiction and underlying her status as a forgotten 'cult' writer.[29] In some of these readings, as Carole Sweeney has noted, Kavan's writing has been presented as little more than 'a side-effect of drug use' and as Zadie Smith observed, for some of her readers her heroin addiction is 'at least as important' as her prose.[30] Many of the stories collected in the posthumous *Julia and the Bazooka* (1970) make explicit references to heroin use, as cultural context granted Kavan the freedom to represent characters administering, and experiencing the effects of, the drug. Aside from these, *Sleep Has His House* makes the most explicit references to opiates, taking its title and epigraph from a modernised version of John Gower's *Confessio Amantis*, which refers to the 'poppy which is the seed of sleep'.³¹ As her psychiatrist, Dr Bluth prescribed heroin to Kavan for many years.³² His letters and poems to her are ornamented with sketches and playful references to syringes, and he privately confessed to using small doses of heroin himself.³³ Bluth's writings suggest that heroin also had artistic and intellectual significance for him and Kavan's close association with him sheds light on her relationship with the drug. His *Horizon* essay 'The Revival of Schelling' (1945) traces the philosopher's place in a history of Western thought and considers the influence of opiates on the German Romantics. According to Bluth, for the Romantics 'opium was not a dangerous drug nor a symbol of delusion, but a draught of reality, and through its influence they found a way to that secret land which they thought of as their true home'.³⁴ For Schelling, he claimed, opium 'was night and the mother-womb of the unconscious into which his solitary and exiled soul longed to return' (160).

Bluth's essay resonates strikingly with the narrator's representation of the unconscious realm in *Sleep Has His House*: '*And in the night my own mother came to the window to meet me, strange, solitary; splendid with countless stars; my mother Night; mine, lovely, mine. My home*' (184). B creates her house of sleep within the night that is her mother, a literal rendering of the 'mother-womb of the unconscious' (160) described by Bluth. His description of opium as a 'draught of reality' for Schelling reverberates with Kavan's ongoing preoccupation with this concept and highlights the significance of the poppy of Kavan's epigraph to the novel as a whole. Much of Bluth's interpretation of Schelling demonstrates a preoccupation with sleep, symbolism and poetic language which invokes Binswanger's theories; he maintains that '[t]he only true wisdom was that which originated in the world of dreams' and that '[m]yths, dreams and music are symbols describing the structure of the unconscious'.³⁵ The resonances between his article and Kavan's novel align her drug writing with older cultural conceptions of opiates, rather than with post-war drug culture, an affinity reinforced by Nycole Prowse's observation that Kavan's stories of addiction make 'a gesture towards Romantic-utopianism' that 'places drugs in the order of Nature' and that they are 'not the propelling inner-nightmare of modernity but the answer to, and insulation against it'.³⁶ However, such Romantic notions of opiate use are contradicted by bleaker elements in Kavan's drug writing, both in *Sleep Has His House* and her later stories.

Readings of Kavan as a writer of addiction have universally interpreted the effects of drug use on her life and writing as positive. Her success at living with and controlling her addiction over decades, and its seemingly therapeutic effect on her severe depression, support such interpretations. But the harsher aspects of her dependence can be traced in the frequent references to health and money worries in her correspondence, including heart problems and blood clots. In *Sleep Has His House*, B's unconscious plays out the possibilities of A's final moments, a 'quick red springing wide and away' from 'the fragile exposed curve of the vulnerable white neck' (38) and a nightmare montage of self-inflicted death:

> She plunges from towers strict and terrible in their stark fragile strength, delicate as jerboa's bones on the sky, perdurable with granite and steel [. . .] the screaming skid of wheels spouting slush with her blood. Limp as an old coat not worth a hanger, she is to be found behind numbered doors in hotel bedrooms; or dangling from the trees of country churchyards [. . .] The weeds of lonely rivers bind her with clammy skeins; the tides of tropical oceans suck off her shoes; crabs scuttle over her eye sockets. Sheeted and anonymous on rubbered wheels she traverses the interminable bleakness of chloroform-loaded corridors. (44)

The sequence ends with a stiff shape under the bedclothes in a dismal room 'cluttered with glasses, cups, empty whiskey and gin bottles; syringes, scattered tablets, powders spilled from their crumpled papers, needles, empty tubes labelled diamorph' (45). Whatever the Romantic overtones of Kavan's ode to opium as the 'mother-womb of the unconscious' in Bluth's words, this image of opioid overdose in *Sleep Has His House* still invokes the dark and sordid side of drug use. This 'plunging', 'screaming', 'spouting', 'anonymous' death fills the void of the unspoken and unanswered '*question which could not possibly ever be asked*' (35) about A's death. B's bleak imaginings in this visceral scene are echoed in Kavan's posthumous story 'The Old Address' in which a newly discharged addict fantasises about their own death, becoming 'mangled, splintered, a smashed matchbox' (15) spouting blood until humanity is choked and drowned in it.[37] Although several critics, including Nycole Prowse, have observed the 'embodiment and agency' inherent in Kavan's drug writing,[38] in *Sleep Has His House* the lure and risk of death to the addict is rendered darker by what is left behind – the emptiness not only of 'whiskey and gin bottles' and 'tubes labelled diamorph', but a child's life.

Hannah Van Hove has observed the 'proliferation of violent imagery' in the night-time segments of the novel, describing how 'images of war consistently intrude into the dream world'.[39] The horrors and destruction of world events lurk in the unconscious in montages of 'confusion, danger, violence, chaos, strife' (126); the dreaming eye sees 'a city after atomic bomb hit'; 'a road crammed with panic-stricken refugees';

'a mammoth war plane' (127). Thus, there is no escape from the outside world in the house of sleep. In *A Scarcity of Love* (1956), in which Kavan returned to a style similar to her Helen Ferguson novels, her protagonist Gerda drowns herself after years of childhood neglect and emotional rejection. Her suicide is a retreat to sanctuary which echoes the imagery of *Sleep Has His House*: 'there it lay, her own world, safe and secret, beneath the dark water [. . .] Now she was nearly home. Very soon she would be in the midst of the bright insubstantial reality of her dream' (183). Death is thus a dark and beautiful home where dream and reality meet in Kavan's postwar writing; the closeness of life and death which she had begun to explore in *Asylum Piece* and which intensified in her wartime stories lingers on.

Ornithology and Ontology: *Who Are You?* and the Existential Birdcall

Like the existentialist fiction of Jean-Paul Sartre's *La Nausée* (1938) and Albert Camus's *L'Etranger* (1942), Kavan's writing emphasises experiences of meaninglessness, ontological uncertainty and deadened affect. In her novella *Who Are You?*, in which she reworks a section of her earlier Helen Ferguson novel *Let Me Alone*, she formalises the inherently existentialist aspects of her earlier writing to explore time and identity by breaking the narrative and repeating the story (see Chapter 1, this volume). The question of the novel's title explicitly invokes what Patricia Waugh describes as the 'interrogative' mode of postwar experimental writing.[40] Evoking the opening line of André Breton's novel *Nadja* (1928) – 'Who am I?' – which places the question of identity foremost, this novel demonstrates the continuing influence of surrealism on Kavan's writing. Natalie Ferris has traced parallels between the two novels, concluding that 'Kavan's articulations of a self that is incoherent, fragmented and unfamiliar, even to itself' bring her close to 'the complex female identities presented by the women artists of the surrealist movement'.[41]

John Rolph, Kavan's editor at the Scorpion Press which published the novel, suggested one major editorial change to the manuscript of *Who Are You?* to which Kavan readily agreed – the exclusion of the novel's original opening page which was an authorial message to the reader:[42]

> There's no answer to the brain-fever bird's question because the process of becoming an individual is complete only when life is. Each person has many identities, according to the changing pressures and conditions of his existence. The 'you' of one situation is not the you of another.

Who you are at any given moment in life is determined by unpredictable circumstances, beyond your control – you are the product of your environment etc.

The people in this story live through the same situations twice over. But they are not the same, and the outcome is different, because the element of nightmare which predominates in the first experience is in abeyance later. Their identities are equally real or unreal in both cases. The you of the birds' question could be either, or both of them – or neither.[43]

This discarded note lucidly demonstrates Kavan's engagement with existentialist ideas in the novel. Her principal concern with the unfixed nature of identity, placing existence before essence, is the central tenet of existentialism, yet her focus on the determining nature of circumstances 'beyond your control' does not sit easily with the notion of free will. Kavan's assertion of the differing outcomes of the two episodes is unclear, for the conclusion of the novel remains deliberately ambiguous. The only definite change is the belief of the protagonist, 'the girl', that she has any choice in her fate, though she abdicates control of it: 'On the spur of the moment, she's made up her mind that chance shall decide' (114).

The girl has a dim awareness of the narrative's double nature, surfacing most perceptibly in her conversations with the character identified by his 'Suède Boots'. Anticipating the break between the first telling of the story to the second, she feels that

> she'd like to go on forever re-living that first afternoon, having the same identical conversation ad infinitum. Though she won't admit it, at the back of her mind is a constant dread of some fatal nightmare moment when everything will have to stop. (61)

After the stop comes to pass, her awareness increases in the second iteration: 'Before I met you I used to feel as if I was in a nightmare,' she tells him, 'and that I'd never escape.' But she no longer remembers this feeling with any distinctness, and might be describing the sensations of a girl in a book' (98). The 'nightmare climax' of the story's previous incarnation references the 'element of nightmare' in Kavan's unpublished note, pressing her continuing interest in dream and existence. As a girl in a book describing the sensations of a girl in a book, the repetitive, self-reflexive nature of the two episodes continues to bring pressure to bear on the 'reality' of the text, keeping the possibility of alternative realities and differing outcomes open. She would go on to develop this use of narrative repetition and temporal impossibility in her last and best-known work, *Ice*.

As a rewriting of her Helen Ferguson novel *Let Me Alone*, *Who Are You?* is already a retelling of the sensations of the fictional 'Anna Kavan', another 'girl in a book'. The tension between determining social forces and an existentially authentic unfixed identity is already inherent in the earlier novel. Anna's sense of being divided in *Let Me Alone* is made manifest in *Who Are You?* as the girl lives out her existence in two entirely different dimensions, reframing and formalising the existential crisis she experiences in her sexually violent marriage.[44] In *Who Are You?* Mr Dog Head half recollects his infatuation with the girl he married but his former passion has turned to a 'fierce, almost insane antagonism in him, the lust to conquer her' (309). His rape of the girl is a deliberate act of punishment, a husband's attempt to assert ownership of his wife and (in the first play of events) to tie her to him by forcing her to conceive. To the girl, the attack is experienced as a death that echoes Anna's existential annihilation: 'she can't stand it another second . . . she's dying . . . being horribly murdered' (82) and in the second iteration: 'She's suffocating . . . dying . . . she's being murdered' (112). Following the pattern of *Let Me Alone*, the mutual hostility of the girl and her husband is externalised in the alien and threatening landscape; the native wildlife and vegetation are as baffling and intimidating to the girl as he is. Like the live rats that Dog Head bats towards his wife in his perverse game of tennis, the colonial backdrop of the story is repurposed as a weapon in their marital hostilities.

The existential affinities between Kavan's Helen Ferguson novels and Jean Rhys's interwar writing, especially their experimental representations of fractured identity (see Chapter 1), continued into their postwar work. Following long periods of obscurity during which both had difficulty finding a publisher, each achieved late success with their final novels in the 1960s. In 1964, towards the end of the long period Rhys spent revising and rewriting *Wide Sargasso Sea*, she wrote in a letter to Francis Wyndham:

> I've never read a long novel about a mad mind or an unusual mind or anybody's mind at all. Yet it is the only thing that matters and so difficult to get over without being dull.
> Anna Kavan's stories I like, and I have her novel *Who Are You?* Very short but what a splendid title. If only I'd thought of it – but it would have been too late in any case.[45]

Rhys's letter indicates that she was reading Kavan's novel while in the final stages of drafting her own; the title she coveted emphasises her interest in uncertain identity and in writing 'about a mind'. The protagonists of *Who Are You?* and *Wide Sargasso Sea* are both young, newly married to Englishmen and living in the tropics. The names of both couples are missing or contested; the girl's husband is only ever Mr Dog Head and

Antoinette's husband is never directly addressed, understating Rhys's intertextual engagement with Charlotte Brontë's *Jane Eyre* by avoiding the name Rochester. This man without a name takes Antoinette's from her, re-identifying her as 'Bertha' in a speech act that has radical consequence for her sense of self: 'Names matter, like when he wouldn't call me Antoinette, and I saw Antoinette drifting out of the window' (147).

Who Are You?, the 'splendid' title admired by Rhys, is also the call of the brain-fever bird which opens and closes Kavan's narrative: 'All day long, in the tamarinds behind the house, a tropical bird keeps repeating its monotonous cry, which consists of the same three inquiring notes. Who-are-you? Who-are-you? Who-are-you?' (8). Reflecting on Kavan's own use of repetition in the narrative, the unrelenting cry of the bird recurs at significant moments throughout the novel, framing the narrative's temporal schism, penetrating the girl's consciousness and creeping 'right into her head' (12). Her impression of the sound is of a perpetual and inevitable mechanism, and though it emanates from the tropical landscape, it appears to spring from some unnatural, even supernatural, source. The cry echoes a motif from 'Christmas Afternoon in Burma' in which a lizard 'calls *tick*-tack, *tick*-tack, *tick*-tack, in its queer, semi-human, Robot's voice as if counting the seconds' (631). Presaging the brain-fever bird, the native lizard's cry expresses the relentless pressure of time and the inhuman mechanism of colonial life. In *Who Are You?* the noise has become an insistent questioning of identity and to the girl its 'sole function seems to be to drive people mad' (62).

Avian provocateurs make themselves known in other mid-century texts. In Muriel Spark's story 'The Go-Away Bird' (1958), the call of the grey-crested lourie – 'go 'way, go 'way' – haunts the conflicted life and death of her white South African protagonist.[46] An interrogative bird-call also haunts *Wide Sargasso Sea*; the parrot belonging to Antoinette's mother, Annette, has a vocabulary limited to the cry 'Qui est là? Qui est là?' and the answer 'Ché Coco'.[47] Like the brain-fever bird's 'Who-are-you?', Coco's enquiring 'Qui est là?' becomes a refrain in Rhys's novel, directed towards an unknown second-person and becoming internalised by the heroine as self-doubt. In both novels, the bird is notably absent; Coco dies early in *Wide Sargasso Sea* and in *Who Are You?* the birds 'remain invisible' (10) in the branches of the tamarind trees. The bird is thus a device with which to introduce a question without a speaker, to which Kavan's nameless girl has no answer; it accumulates and intensifies as she contemplates changing her fate and at the dimensional split in the narrative, expressing her struggle with self-identity and free will.

Birds, real, imagined and metaphorical, are recurring symbols throughout Kavan's work.[48] For Binswanger too, the bird is a significant figure as it appears in both dream and literature. In *Dream and Existence* he maintains

> it is true of both ancient and modern poetry, and true of dreams and myths of all ages and peoples – that again and again we find that the eagle or the falcon, the kite or the hawk, personify our existence as rising or longing to rise and as falling.[49]

Thus, in Binswanger's schema, the grounded and elusive brain-fever bird not only gives voice to, but personifies, the girl's anguished existence. In formally existential terms, her moments of self-doubt are those of *angst*, defined by Heidegger in *Being and Time* as 'anxiety' towards that which is 'completely indefinite':[50]

> Anxiety 'does not know' what that in the face of which it is anxious is . . . it is already 'there', and yet nowhere; it is so close that it is oppressive and stifles one's breath, and yet it is nowhere. (231)

This un-situated yet omnipresent *angst* captures the indeterminate origins and insidious reach of both 'Who are you?' and 'Qui est là?' in these novels. For Heidegger 'anxiety' is nothing and nowhere, yet its nothingness is the nothingness of the world: 'That which anxiety is anxious about is Being-in-the-world itself' (232). Thus 'anxiety' is intrinsically bound up with self-awareness and its opposite, inauthentic everyday involvement in the world, characterised by Heidegger as a state of 'falling', and evoked directly in the girl's sense that '[s]omehow she seems to have lost contact with her existence' (30). But despite her seemingly direct engagement with existentialism in the novel, as elsewhere in Kavan's writing, free will appears to be denied by the difficult psychological and material circumstances of her protagonist.

Kavan's ongoing concern with identity was enhanced and matured by her exposure to existential analysis and to progressive psychiatric practices in the postwar period. Many of the concerns and inflections in both *Sleep Has His House* and *Who Are You?* correspond to psychoanalytic and existential theory, but not all were a result of the direct influence of Binswanger or Karl Bluth. Rather, their joint concerns of existential and epistemological uncertainty were characteristic of their times. Bluth's assessment that 'Freud is a materialist, Binswanger an idealist' in his review of 'Swiss Humanism', identifies Binswanger's departure from the clinical work of psychoanalysis in his writings, and the quasi-spiritual components of his theories.[51] But despite the sometimes esoteric nature of Binswanger's ideas, his blending of psychoanalytic and existential theory predicted the project of the emerging anti-psychiatry movement in the postwar period. Retrospectively, R. D. Laing would describe

The Divided Self as 'a sort of soft edge between psychoanalysis and existentialism', claiming that the 'nearest similarity was to Binswanger'.[52] The frequent association between Kavan's writing of fractured identities and R. D. Laing's theories, notably articulated in Anaïs Nin's description of her as a writer who 'entered the world of the divided self with skill and clarity', is less indicative of any direct influence than it is of their joint concerns emerging from this same 'soft edge'.[53] The popularity of *The Divided Self*, which Angela Carter described as 'one of the most influential books of the sixties', is thus testament to the legacies of existentialism and psychoanalysis throughout the mid-century, inflecting the counterculture and radical politics of the 1960s.[54]

Kavan's continuing project of experimentation kept her open to new cultural influences in the final decade of her career, indicated in her insistence that 'my writing changes with the conditions outside', including the writing of a younger generation of British postwar avant-garde writers.[55] Parallels with the collage, interpolation and interruption of writers such as Ann Quin and Alan Burns are clear in her 1960s novels. The sexual freedom and illicit drug use which had been features of Kavan's life but only vaguely alluded to in her fiction were now fitting topics for 1960s counterculture and became topics in her late and posthumously published stories. But, among a 'heterogeneous, conflicted and contradictory' decade of literature, as Sebastian Groes has described it, some of the themes and narrative experimentation that were features throughout her career found a responsive audience they had sometimes lacked.[56] The ontological uncertainty which, in affinity with Jean Rhys, had characterised her writing from the 1930s onward, had become widely disseminated by Laing's *Divided Self*. Helen Carr has observed the continuities between Rhys's pre-war novels, which struggled to find an audience, and *Wide Sargasso Sea*, maintaining that the novel's 'critique of racial, colonial and patriarchal oppression on the one hand, and [. . .] perceptive understanding of psychic breakdown on the other' were already prevalent in her early novels.[57] Carr describes how the rise of the anti-psychiatry movement and the revolutionary social politics of the 1960s increased both psychological and political awareness such that readers 'caught up, to some extent at least, with the insights and preoccupations that had always characterised Rhys' fiction', observations that might equally apply to Kavan's writing and its reception.[58]

Throughout her postwar writing, Kavan's increasing experimentation with linear temporality continued to evoke the disruption of time in her wartime writing. Her late short story 'Julia and the Bazooka', published posthumously in 1969, exemplifies her ongoing preoccupation with the Second World War into the decades that followed.[59] Spanning Julia's life and death by aerial attack, it is almost exclusively in the present tense, making every moment paradoxically coincident. Moving freely back and forth from her early life to the time of her funeral, Julia is simultaneously a small child, a schoolgirl, a grown woman and a heap of ashes. Only the second sentence moves into the past to reveal that 'Julia loved flowers' (150), and this slip ensures that Julia's past tense haunts the present of the story. During 'the time of the flying bombs' (153), Julia 'steps on to the staircase, which is not there. The stairs have crumbled, the whole house is crumbling, collapsing, the world bursts and burns' (154). The bomb effects a disconnection between the reality of one moment (staircase) and the reality of the next (no staircase), which is too sudden for Julia, and the narrative, to process. Thus, the staircase is both there and not there, present and past. The resultant break between the reality of Julia alive and Julia dead is likewise delayed, and she continues in the present tense following her death, unseen and unheard by the ARP (Air Raid Precautions) men, the doctor, the undertaker and the parson. Like the staircase, Julia both is and is not at the same time, and these two realities co-exist throughout the story until its conclusion when: 'There is no more Julia anywhere. Where she was there is only nothing' (157). The perpetual present tense of this story allows Julia to embody the existential liminality of many of Kavan's characters, permanently caught between girlhood and adulthood, life and death. Characteristic of Kavan's late 1960s fiction in its experimental narrative temporality and explicit references to drug use, 'Julia and the Bazooka' harks back to her Second World War writing in its demonstration that to live under bombardment is to inhabit time and place in peculiar ways.

Muriel Spark's *The Hothouse by the East River* (1973) takes the premise of 'Julia and the Bazooka' to a further extreme, extending the prematurely cut-off lives of the war dead to an entire novel. Both story and novel hinge on sudden death by V1 and V2 missiles. Spark's narrator muses on the metaphor 'to give someone a rocket', explaining that 'in this English spring of 1944 when rocket missiles are leaping on London [. . .] the word is one of such that you either have to bandy it about as a euphemism or sit down, weep and give up'.[60] The 'bazooka' of Kavan's story is both the weapon that kills Julia and the name she gives her syringe; like the 'rocket' of *Hothouse*, it is bandied about as euphemism while simultaneously signifying the destructive force of certain reality. Only towards the end of Spark's novel is it borne in on both reader and protagonists that its main characters were killed in the war. Paul insists he survived the bomb, but Elsa corrects him: 'That was your imagination running away with itself' (126). The nagging doubt that has dogged both Paul and reader as to who is making things up, who is mad and who is dead, is finally resolved; he explains to Elsa's analyst: 'She doesn't need treatment' . . . 'She doesn't exist' (129), Elsa explains to him that their daughter is only 'a vagary of your mind' (127). For the characters in Spark's novel, sanity, reality and existence hang on a knife edge. The postwar is a world of lives unlived and children unborn, it remains an idea and not a reality, an imagined future that never came to pass. Like Julia in Kavan's story, and the dead that haunt the streets in Elizabeth Bowen's *Heat of the Day* 'drawing on this tomorrow they had expected', in *Hothouse* the war dead claim their future.[61]

If the postwar began, in Gill Plain's words, as 'a vision', the inevitable confrontation between this dream and its reality inflected the disjoin between world and fiction in mid-century writing. Enhancing the constant pressure on reality in her writing, which Leigh Wilson has described in relation to *Ice* as a 'refusal to stabilise the mimetic gap',[62] Kavan's temporal experiments, including narrative repetitions of her own and other fiction, would develop further in her 1960s writing. Keeping the possibility of alternative realities always open, the political consequences of dream, fantasy and speculation would continue to shape her fiction.

Notes

1. Anna Kavan, 'Asylum Piece II', *Asylum Piece* (London: Jonathan Cape, 1940), p. 128.
2. Doubleday brought out the US edition in 1947 under the title *The House of Sleep* and Cassell followed with the English edition *Sleep Has His House* in 1948. Although she was happier with the production of the US edition, Kavan used the two titles interchangeably in her correspondence; the novel has been reissued posthumously in both the UK and USA as *Sleep Has His House*.
3. Anna Kavan, 'Back to Victoria', *Horizon*, 13:73 (January 1946), pp. 61–6.
4. Frank Kermode, *The Sense of an Ending: Studies in the Theory of Fiction* [1966] (Oxford: Oxford University Press, 2000), p. 132.
5. Gill Plain, *Literature of the 1940s: War, Postwar and Peace* (Edinburgh: Edinburgh University Press, 2012), p. 33.
6. Anna Kavan, *The Cactus Sign*, unpublished manuscript, Anna Kavan Papers, *MFL*, p. 387.
7. J. W. Dunne, *An Experiment with Time* (London and Basingstoke: Papermac, Macmillan Publishers, 1981).
8. See, for example, Kaye Mitchell and Nonia Williams (eds), *British Avant-Garde Fiction of the 1960s* (Edinburgh: Edinburgh University Press, 2019); Andrew Radford and Hannah Van Hove (eds), *British Experimental Women's Fiction, 1945–1975: Slipping Through the Labels* (Basingstoke: Palgrave Macmillan, 2021); Carole Sweeney, *Vagabond Fictions: Gender and Experiment in British Women's Writing, 1945–1970* (Edinburgh:

9. See Giles Gordon (ed.), *Beyond the Words: Eleven Writers in Search of a New Fiction* (London: Hutchinson, 1975). Ann Quin and Robert Sward include a quotation from *Ice* in the cut-up poem 'Living in the Present', *Ambit*, 34 (1968), 20–1. For close comparison between Kavan and Alan Burns, see Leigh Wilson, 'Anna Kavan's *Ice* and Alan Burns' *Europe After the Rain*: Repetition with a Difference', *Women: A Cultural Review*, 28:4 (Winter 2017), 327–42.
10. See Julia Jordan, *Modernism and the Avant-Garde British Novel: Oblique Strategies* (Oxford: Oxford University Press, 2020).
11. See studies by Gregory Ariail; Natalie Ferris; Andrew Gaedtke; Hannah Van Hove; Victoria Walker; Geoff Ward; Sara Wasson; Leigh Wilson.
12. A section of the novel was first published as 'The Professor', *Horizon*, 13:75 (March 1946).
13. Anna Kavan to Peter Owen, 19 September [1958], HRC.
14. Anna Kavan to Peter Owen, 24 November [1967], HRC.
15. For fuller comparisons see Jane Garrity, 'Nocturnal Transgressions in *the House of Sleep*: Anna Kavan's Maternal Registers', *Modern Fiction Studies*, 40:2 (Summer 1994), 253–77 and Hannah Van Hove, 'Exploring the Realm of the Unconscious in Anna Kavan's *Sleep Has His House*', *Women: A Cultural Review*, 28:4 (Winter 2017), 358–74.
16. Diana Trilling, *Reviewing the Forties* (New York: Harcourt Brace Jovanovich, 1978), p. 218.
17. For details of Kavan's relationship with her last publisher, Peter Owen, see Leigh Wilson 'Whose Sister? "Convenient Pigeonholes", Peter Owen and the Publishing of Anna Kavan', in Andrew Radford and Hannah Van Hove (eds), *British Experimental Women's Fiction, 1945–1975: Slipping Through the Labels* (Basingstoke: Palgrave Macmillan, 2021), 83–101.
18. See Garrity, 'Nocturnal Transgressions'; Geoff Ward, 'The Wibberlee Wobberlee Walk: Lowry, Hamilton, Kavan and the Addictions of 1940s Fiction', in *The Fiction of the 1940s: Stories of Survival*, ed. by Rod Mengham and N. H. Reeve (Basingstoke: Palgrave Macmillan, 2001), 26–45.
19. Van Hove, 'Exploring the Realm of the Unconscious', p. 365.
20. Kavan worked on 'The Cactus Sign' during the time she was travelling early in the war years, see manuscript in Anna Kavan Papers, *MFL*; 'A Visit' and 'Clarita' published in *Julia and the Bazooka*. For a note on this story's genesis see Chapter 2.
21. André Breton, 'Psychiatry Standing before Surrealism', in *Break of Day* [1934], trans. by Mark Polizzotti and Mary Ann Caws (University of Nebraska Press, Lincoln/London, 1999), p. 68.
22. Ward, 'Wibberlee Wobberlee Walk', p. 43.
23. Garrity, 'Nocturnal Transgressions', p. 260.
24. Kavan stayed at the clinic 17 March–22 April 1947 and 30 April–10 May 1948.
25. Kavan discusses her treatment at the Bellevue in letters to George Bullock in the Anna Kavan Papers, *MFL*; Bluth's letters regarding English translations of Binswanger's work in Ludwig Binswanger Archive (1947),

Universitätsarchiv, Eberhard Karls Universität Tübingen (*EKUT*); Bluth favourably reviews Binswanger's *Grundformen und Erkenntnis Menschlichen Daseins* in Karl Theodor Bluth, 'Selected Notices: Swiss Humanism', *Horizon*, 15:86 (February 1947).
26. For more on Freud and Binswanger's personal and intellectual dialogue, see Gerhard Fichtner (ed.), *Freud–Binswanger Correspondence 1908–1938* (London: Open Gate Press, 2003) and Ludwig Binswanger, *Sigmund Freud: Reminiscences of a Friendship*, trans. by Norbert Guterman (New York: Grune & Stratton, 1957).
27. For a full discussion of this, see Jacob Needleman (ed.), *Being-in-the-World: Selected Papers of Ludwig Binswanger* (New York: Basic Books, 1963).
28. Ludwig Binswanger and Michel Foucault, *Dream and Existence*, trans. by Forrest Williams and Jacob Needleman, ed. by Keith Hoeller (Seattle, WA: Review of Existential Psychology and Psychiatry, 1986), p. 85.
29. See Elizabeth Young, *Pandora's Handbag: Adventures in the Book World* (London: Serpent's Tail, 2001) and Emily Hill, 'Cult VIP/Anna Kavan: Kafka's Sister', *Dazed and Confused*, August 2010.
30. Sweeney, *Vagabond Fictions*, p. 55; Zadie Smith, 'Two Paths for the Novel', *The New York Review of Books*, 20 November 2008.
31. The book's British title is a line from the Gower epigraph, the US title is taken from Edith Sitwell's heading to the same passage in the compilation: Edith Sitwell (ed.), *Planet and Glow-Worm: A Book for the Sleepless* (London: Macmillan & Co., 1944).
32. For a detailed history of British 'white drug' sub-cultures in the mid-century, see Christopher Hallam, *White Drug Cultures and Regulation in London, 1916–1960* (Palgrave MacMillan, Basingstoke, 2018).
33. See letters from Karl Bluth to Anna Kavan in *MFL*; Binswanger revealed that Bluth had confessed his use of heroin to him – Ludwig Binswanger to Dr Ernst Lucas, 1 May 1958, *EKUT*.
34. Karl Theodor Bluth, 'The Revival of Schelling', *Horizon*, 12:69 (September 1945), p. 160.
35. Bluth, 'Revival of Schelling', pp. 167, 178.
36. Nycole Prowse, '"Out of Control": Excess, Desire and Agency in Female Drug Writing', *Hecate*, 42:2 (2016), 39–54, pp. 51, 48.
37. Anna Kavan, 'The Old Address', *Julia and the Bazooka* (London: Peter Owen, 1970).
38. Prowse, 'Out of Control', p. 49. See also Young, *Pandora's Handbag*.
39. Van Hove, 'Exploring the Realm of the Unconscious', p. 368.
40. Patricia Waugh, *Feminine Fictions: Revisiting the Postmodern* (London and New York: Routledge, 1989), p. 217.
41. Natalie Ferris, 'The Double Play of Mirrors: Anna Kavan, Autobiography and Self-Portraiture', *Women: A Cultural Review*, 28:4 (Winter 2017), 391–409, p. 403.
42. John Rolph to Anna Kavan, ND, Anna Kavan Papers, *MFL*.
43. Scorpion Press Collection, *HRC*.
44. This aspect of her novel is again echoed in Rhys's *Wide Sargasso Sea*, see Victoria Walker, 'Ornithology and Ontology: The Existential Birdcall in Jean Rhys's *Wide Sargasso Sea* and Anna Kavan's *Who Are You?*', *Women: A Cultural Review*, 23:4 (December 2012), 490–509.

45. Jean Rhys to Francis Wyndham, 7 March 1964, in *Jean Rhys: Letters 1931–66*, ed. by Francis Wyndham and Diana Melly (London: Penguin, 1985), pp. 254–5.
46. Muriel Spark, *The Collected Stories* (London: Penguin, 1994), p. 254.
47. Carole Angier's biography reveals that Coco's cry has its origins in the call of Rhys's grandmother's parrot. Carole Angier, *Jean Rhys: Life and Work* (London: André Deutsch, 1990) p. 16.
48. For fuller discussion of this see Angelos Evangelou, '"In fact I am an animal": Mental Illness, Vulnerability and the Problem of Empathy in Anna Kavan's *Asylum Piece*', *English Studies*, 2021, pp. 10–12.
49. Binswanger, *Dream and Existence*, p. 85.
50. Martin Heidegger, *Being and Time* [1927], trans. by John Macquarrie and Edward Robinson (Oxford: Blackwell Publishers Ltd, 1962), p. 231.
51. Bluth, 'Swiss Humanism', p. 149.
52. Bob Mullan, *Mad to Be Normal: Conversations with R. D. Laing* (London: Free Association Books, 1995), p. 159.
53. Anaïs Nin, *The Novel of the Future* (London: Peter Owen, 1968), p. 139. For further readings of Laing's divided self and Kavan's writing see, for example, Evangelou, '"In Fact I Am an Animal"' and Hannah Van Hove 'Anna Kavan: Pursuing the "in-between reality" hidden by the "ordinary surface of things"', in *British Avant-Garde Fiction of the 1960s*, ed. by Kaye Mitchell and Nonia Williams (Edinburgh: Edinburgh University Press, 2019) 107–24.
54. Angela Carter, 'Truly, It Felt Like Year One', in *Very Heaven: Looking Back at the 1960s*, ed. Sara Maitland (London: Virago Press, 1988), p. 215.
55. Anna Kavan to Peter Owen, 29 March [1966], *HRC*.
56. Sebastian Groes, *British Fictions of the Sixties: The Making of the Swinging Decade* (London and New York: Bloomsbury, 2015), p. 12.
57. Helen Carr, '1966 and Wide Sargasso Sea: The Climate that Made Jean Rhys Legible', in Kate Aughterson and Deborah Philips (eds), *Women Writers and Experimental Narratives: Early Modern to Contemporary* (Basingstoke: Palgrave, 2021), 139–47, p. 145.
58. Carr, p. 139.
59. First published in *Encounter*, 32:3, March 1969, later collected in *Julia and the Bazooka* (1970).
60. Muriel Spark, *The Hothouse by the East River* [1973] (London: Penguin, 1975), p. 58.
61. Elizabeth Bowen, *The Heat of the Day* [1949] (London: Vintage Books, 1998) p. 91.
62. Wilson, 'Anna Kavan's *Ice*', p. 339.

Chapter 5

Experimental Fictions: *Ice* and the Anthropocene

> I could not remain isolated from the rest of the world. I was involved with the fate of the planet, I had to take an active part in whatever was going on.
>
> *Ice*

Kavan's last and best-known novel has provoked and defied classification more than any of her other works. Letters between Kavan and her publisher Peter Owen reveal that she was unsurprised, even flattered, by a reader's report describing *Ice* (1967) as 'a mixture of Kafka and *The Avengers*' and the novel revels in the tropes of popular entertainment without relinquishing its status as 'high' literature.[1] Its non-linear, ill-defined and fantastical plot allows its three principal characters to act out scenarios borrowed from romance, porn, spy drama, action-adventure, gothic fantasy and sci-fi; but the novel's subtle misalignment of genres disturbs moral certainties, depicting a happy ending that might be a murderous abduction, a heroine who gets eaten by a dragon and a hero who longs to break her bones. This hybridity of genre has contributed to many critical assessments of the novel as being without parallel – Brian Aldiss claimed that '*Ice* is unique', Doris Lessing agreed that there is 'nothing else like it' and Jonathan Lethem affirms that '*Ice* stands alone'.[2] But Leigh Wilson has observed how even laudatory assessments of Kavan's 'literary isolation' have been inflected by assumptions about women's writing, noting that '[i]f these critics have rooted the worth of Kavan's writing in a supposed innocence of literary debate and of its provocation to conscious practice, the gender politics of this are not hard to spot'.[3]

Although *Ice* is often read in isolation, the novel was the culmination of Kavan's mid-century experimental writing career, epitomising the tropes and thematic preoccupations of her early Helen Ferguson novels, continuing the stylistic experiment she embarked upon when she began writing as Anna Kavan, and maintaining the radical politics she developed in the early 1940s. Augmenting her familiar tropes of unreliable narrator, unstable reality, nameless protagonists and temporal impossibility, the novel reflects her ongoing experiment with representations of reality while incorporating elements of the popular and counterculture of the late 1960s. The intensity of climatic and environmental conditions in her Helen Ferguson texts, especially the fantastical wintry landscapes of *The Dark Sisters*, *Goose Cross* and *Rich Get Rich*, become overwhelming as the unstoppable onslaught of a new ice age. The incestuous desire and marital rape of *Let Me Alone* and *Goose Cross* are magnified and transmogrified into a complex portrait of sexual predator and victim; the constellation of the male gaze, sexual violence and the 'unreal' in *Let Me Alone* overwhelms the world of the later text. The subtle combination of third- and first-person voices that first emerged in her early writing as Anna Kavan evolve in *Ice* into a narrator/protagonist whose perspective slips, almost imperceptibly, into that of the other characters. This narrator is as unreliable as any she had previously written. His faulty grasp of reality extends the fine balance of realism and fantasy that she began in *Asylum Piece*, foretold in the unreality, self-alienation and self-division of *Let Me Alone*. Reading Kavan's politics as key to the novel's aesthetic, this chapter argues that the experimental narrative strategies of *Ice* and the contemporary concept of the Anthropocene can be mutually illuminating.

Kavan's genre-melding in *Ice* incorporates elements of popular 1960s fiction and other media with the gothic surrealism of her earlier work, validating her insistence to her publisher in 1966 that 'my writing changes with the conditions outside', citing the importance of 'outside influences', 'environment and atmosphere'.[4] Her evident pleasure in the Peter Owen reader's reference to the British television series, *The Avengers*, indicates the clear influence of spy drama on this novel. Vague hints about her narrator's involvement in espionage, his equivocal relationship with his ostensible enemy/double and his ruthless attitude towards women all evoke the moral ambiguity of Cold War dramas such as Ian Fleming's James Bond novels and John Le Carré's *The Spy Who Came in from the Cold* (1963), along with their film adaptations. The narrator of *Ice* casts retrospective light on Kavan's career-long combination of the gothic fantastic with other genres by archly acknowledging its potentially anachronistic form: 'I had never before met anyone who owned a telephone and believed in dragons. It amused me, and also contributed to my sense of the unreal' (34). Brian Aldiss notably named *Ice* 'best sci-fi novel of 1967', but he would later claim that '*Ice* is not sci-fi, and only marginally science fiction', observing that it has 'all the virtues and very few of the vices – the pretension or the obscurity' of a 'high-SF novel' and that its 'incantatory powers move it beyond the scope of materialist science-fantasy'.[5] Kavan clearly reciprocated Aldiss's admiration, writing to a friend: 'I simply can't wait to tell you Brian Aldiss whom I admire so much has chosen ICE as best SF book of year. I'm not making it up. He doesn't know I'm a fan of his either.'[6] Her enthusiasm reinforces the influence of New Wave science fiction on aspects of her work, illuminating the novel's popularity with writers such as Aldiss, J. G. Ballard, Doris Lessing and Christopher Priest.

Ballard would later describe the 'fierce intensity' of Kavan's 'vision'[7] and his description of 'inner space fiction' in 'Time Memory and Inner Space' (1963) fits the ambiguities and contradictions of *Ice*:

> I believe that speculative fantasy, as I prefer to call the more serious fringe of science fiction, is an especially potent method of using one's imagination to construct a paradoxical universe where dream and reality become fused together, each retaining its own distinctive quality and yet in some way assuming the role of its opposite, and where, by an undeniable logic black simultaneously becomes white.[8]

This model of a fiction that hinges on both dream and reality accommodates the many paradoxes of *Ice*, whose characters are perpetually caught between love and hate, life and death. Manifesting the 'ice-age dreams' (128) predicted in *Asylum Piece* and continuing to press the relationship between dream and conscious life so central to *Sleep Has His House*, the narrator confesses that 'I dreamed [. . .] whether I was asleep or awake' (99).

Praising her 'original voice' and 'the cool lucid light' of her 'unique mind', Doris Lessing was instrumental in drawing attention to Kavan's writing in the early 2000s when it had again fallen into obscurity.[9] Lessing's fictional representations of madness, her interest in the British anti-psychiatry movement and her experiments with genre, especially science fiction, bring her mid-century fiction into alignment with Kavan's. Like Kavan, Lessing's writing of divided selves anticipated rather than simply responded to R. D. Laing's theories.[10] Lessing was not, as she has sometimes been portrayed, a disciple of Laing, meeting him only once,[11] but in fellowship with Angela Carter, J. G. Ballard and Anaïs Nin, she directly acknowledged Laing's influence on her fiction.[12] Shifting from realism to space fiction to inner space fiction and back again, her diverse oeuvre has suffered from a critical bias that segregates science fiction from literary fiction, and her *Children of Violence* and *Canopus in Argos* series have often been ignored or dismissed by critics. This prejudice, which reflects the perceived rift between the sciences and humanities set out in the 'two cultures' debates of the postwar period, elides the extent to which science relies on speculation, and fiction relates to the world around it.[13] But the proliferation of science fiction in the mid-century indicates a dialogue between the two disciplines which anticipates the retrospectively applied concept of the Anthropocene.

Considering affinities between *Ice* and her own writing of a world overcome by ice in *The Story of General Dann and Mara's Daughter, Griot and the Snow Dog* (2005), Lessing suggests that in Kavan's novel 'this *Ice* is not psychological ice, or metaphysical ice, here the loneliness of childhood has been magicked into a physical reality as hallucinatory as the Ancient Mariner's'.[14] Lessing's reading follows Ballard's paradoxical model of inner space fiction (a category she applied to her own *Briefing for a Descent into Hell* (1971)) in proposing that the world of the novel is neither metaphor, allegory nor projection of psychological damage, but a created reality with its roots in childhood neglect. Lessing's allusion to Coleridge's *Rime of the Ancient Mariner* reinforces the Romantic inflections in Kavan's writing, and the mariner's tall tale foreshadows that of Kavan's narrator, suggesting direct influence on Kavan's text. Coleridge's 'snowy cliffs' of ice, 'green as Emerauld' 'split with a Thunder-fit' prefigure the narrator's encounter with apocalypse: 'I felt the fatal chill of the ice touch me, heard its thunder, saw it split by dazzling emerald fissures'.[15] Like the mariner, the narrator somehow survives death to recount his fantastic tale, invoking the poem's lyric repetition with his recurring narrative patterns, and echoing its lesson to love well your fellow creatures or be doomed.

The Anthropocene and Mid-Century Fiction

Recounted in the past tense, *Ice* is an un-named first-person narrator's tale of his flight from the imminent catastrophe of an approaching ice age and his search for a lost, nameless girl. His journey takes him across the globe, through apocalyptic landscapes, on a voyage repeatedly broken by fantastic visions of the approaching ice and the girl he pursues. The novel can be grouped with a small sub-genre of postwar dystopian fiction depicting climate disaster, which recent critical attention has begun to reread as a precursor to the contemporary 'cli-fi' genre.[16] This apocalyptic and post-apocalyptic fiction is exemplified by J. G. Ballard's early novels *The Wind from Nowhere* (1961), *The Drowned World* (1962) and *The Burning World* (1964); Brian Aldiss's *Hothouse* (1962) and John Christopher's *The World in Winter* (1962). Such works, demonstrably responding to their recent past of the Second World War and the uncertain future of their Cold War present, now appear to a new generation of readers eerily prescient of twenty-first-century environmental disaster and climate change. This has played a role in encouraging a recent resurgence of both critical and popular interest in *Ice*, epitomised by a *New Yorker* review of the new 2017 edition describing it as 'a haunting story of sexual assault and climate catastrophe, decades ahead of its time'.[17]

Re-dating of the recently proposed Anthropocene epoch to mark its beginnings in the mid-twentieth century has piqued scholarly interest in how such mid-century literature of climate change might be read in light of this contemporary concept.[18] Thomas Davis has outlined the potential opportunities and pitfalls of such a project, asking 'how we should receive transmissions about the Anthropocene from writers and artists during the last century who were working prior to its conceptualization in our century', and cautioning that it may 'ultimately prove unsatisfactory, as it so often does, to recode earlier cultural work in the critical vernacular of the present'.[19] In representing a climatic apocalypse that is the result of human action, *Ice* evokes Anthropocenic concerns in obvious ways, but the disaster of the text is not an accurate prediction of the causes or actualities of twenty-first-century climate change; the ice of Kavan's final novel intensifies a conflation of emotional and atmospheric elements familiar in her writing from her earliest publications. Just as the narrator states openly at the beginning of the novel that 'reality had always been something of an unknown quantity to me' (6), the genesis of the ice apocalypse remains ill-defined, ambiguous and over-determined. Rumours about 'a secret act of aggression by some foreign power' (22) are never confirmed or denied; the narrator hears of 'a steep rise in radioactive pollution, pointing to the explosion of a nuclear device, but of an unknown type' and the possibility that this might lead to 'substantial climatic change' (22). Further speculation suggests that the 'melting Antarctic ice cap' might flow over the oceans, creating a 'vast ice-mass', 'reflecting the sun's rays and throwing them back into outer space' (22). These unconfirmed and unlikely-sounding reports shape or corroborate the narrator's many dreams and visions of the world destroyed by ice; an 'indestructible ice-mass [. . .] implacably destroying all life', crashing icebergs hurling 'huge boulders into the sky like rockets' and '[d]azzling ice stars' 'filling earth's core with their deadly coldness' (99). Whether the narrator foretells or imagines these scenes remains ambiguous, for nothing in *Ice* is entirely certain, not even the ice itself.

As both a geological epoch and a critical paradigm, the Anthropocene continues to be challenged from multiple perspectives. Donna Haraway's *Staying with the Trouble* (2016) has notably taken up objections to the Anthropocene as a narrative that places the human at its centre, flattening out the concept of the human overall, disregarding capitalist world systems and eliding the uneven responsibility for climate change and environmental damage. Haraway observes that the Anthropocene's apocalyptic timescale of climate emergency encourages two-fold responses of hope and despair, both of which negate the necessity for urgent action. She finds despair 'harder to dismiss' than complacent hope of salvation, describing how the certainty that 'the apocalypse is really nigh' engenders an 'abstract futurism and its affects of sublime despair and its politics of sublime indifference'.[20] This vexed relationship to the future touches on other conceptual challenges to the Anthropocene's deep geological timescales, captured in the discourse of popular science by Peter Brannen's statement that the 'Anthropocene is an event, not an epoch'.[21] Like Haraway, Brannen identifies an inherent hubris in humanity's attempt to measure its legacy on an epochal timescale of tens of millions of years, maintaining that '[g]eological time is deep beyond all comprehension' and that unless 'we fast learn how to endure on this planet, and on a scale far beyond anything we've yet proved ourselves capable of, the detritus of civilization will be quickly devoured by the maw of deep time'.[22] For Brannen, the paradox of the Anthropocene is that human life defines this new epoch, but most likely we will never see it come to pass.[23] Dipesh Chakrabarty's clear-sighted analysis of the wide-ranging Anthropocene debate elucidates this disconnect in narratives of its geological and human temporality, identifying how it 'entails a constant conceptual traffic between Earth history and world history':[24]

> From the very beginning of its career, then, the Anthropocene has had two lives, sometimes in the same texts: a scientific life involving measurements and debates among qualified scientists, and a more popular life as a moral-political issue. So long as the Anthropocene was seen mainly as a measure of human impact, though acknowledged as the impact that ushered in a new period in the planet's history, the focus remained on the force and its wielder (humanity, capitalist classes, rich nations, capitalism), and questions of geological time simply fell into the shadows.[25]

Chakrabarty demonstrates that geological time, integral to the Anthropocene's 'scientific life', is unworkable for its moral-political role simply because it is, in Brannen's terms, 'deep beyond all comprehension'.[26] To inspire human affect and consequently action, the Anthropocene must be a story in which we play a significant role, thus its geological temporality must be displaced onto the scale of human world history. Haraway's critique of the concept still concedes that 'I know that we will continue to need the term *Anthropocene*' and even Brannen admits that the 'idea of the Anthropocene is an interesting thought experiment'.[27] Whatever its problems or paradoxes, this 'thought experiment' has value in promoting discussion about the profound impact of human action on the environment and on human and non-human life, now and for the future.

Although the doubtful climatic consequences described in *Ice* sit in opposition to the reality of twenty-first-century global warming, the mood of unease with which the novel opens and the apocalyptic visions that haunt the narrator resonate with the Anthropocene anxiety of its contemporary readership. As Simon Andrew Orpana observes in his ecocritical reading of the novel and petro-culture, the narrator's descriptions of apocalypse 'capture the sense of the *unheimlich* that accompanies contemporary experiences of a changing climate'.[28] The narrator reports that politicians have banned foreign news, he senses that they 'did not know how to deal with the approaching danger, and hoped to keep the public in ignorance of its exact nature'; without political leadership, 'everything was chaotic and contradictory', the only certainties are that the 'situation was alarming, the atmosphere tense, the emergency imminent' (22). As the cold deepens, 'fuel shortage', 'power cuts' and 'the break-down of transport' lead to panic and mass migrations of climate refugees, and global conflict soon follows. Although *Ice* is often referred to as 'post-apocalyptic', the predicted catastrophe never catches up with the narrator, it is always looming. His awareness of living in end times conforms to Frank Kermode's description of a 'widely shared sense of crisis' in *The Sense of an Ending* (1966), first published a year before Kavan's novel.[29] Kermode's account of apocalyptic thought and narrative offers compelling elucidation to postwar literature's 'radical reappraisal' (132) of the relation between fiction and reality, as it attempted to grapple with the consequences of the holocaust's mythic ideology. Kermode's study of humanity's pervasive sense of living in end times is cross-historical and remains acutely resonant, but he is mindful that the innovations of postwar literary fiction are responding to the 'non-narrative contingencies of modern reality' (132) and there will always be 'changes in our reality' (179–80). Such analysis emphasises that the literary and (world) historical moment from which *Ice* emerged is in danger of being forgotten in contemporary responses which read the novel as 'ahead of' rather than simply 'of' its times. The climatic apocalypse of *Ice* sits in different relation to an Anthropocene futurity than the apocalyptic and post-apocalyptic futures represented in contemporary cli-fi, which, though arguably still shaped by the moral upheaval of the twentieth century's atrocities, are also responding to recent scientific evidence of climate change. Remaining mindful of Thomas Davis's counsel to literary scholars that '1950 as a date for the Anthropocene's onset seems a tempting and convenient gift, but it is not one we should take',[30] and resisting the urge to perceive *Ice* as prophetic ('decades ahead of its time'), this chapter reads Kavan's novel alongside some of these critiques of the Anthropocene. Rather than examining how *Ice* represents or misrepresents twenty-first century Anthropocene concerns, I consider how it enacts and predicts the same 'interesting thought experiment', sharing both the ambitions and the limitations of this contemporary concept, and suggest that *Ice* might be Anthropocene literature not in its mid-century foundations, nor in its representation of climatic change and planetary apocalypse, but in its experimental narrative form.

Aestheticising Apocalypse and Abuse

Typical of Kavan's experimental fiction, the reader of *Ice* never discovers the name of the narrator and knows little of his history or material circumstances. His actions are driven by his desire to possess the girl he pursues who is white-blonde, childlike, and has the air of a fated victim. From the outset, this last of Kavan's reliably unreliable narrators makes clear that his perception cannot be trusted. Describing the landscape of one of the many countries he visits, he remarks how it 'reminded me of a discarded film set [. . .] had no solidity, it was all made of mist and nylon, with nothing behind' (31), and such explicitly theatrical settings hint to the reader that a brazen fiction is being acted out. Told in the past tense, his entire narrative is a recollection and, as the narrator insists on reminding us, memory can be deceptive; he states boldly of the girl 'I had not seen all the things I remembered about her' (19) but he appears untroubled by this. Stumbling haphazardly through an icy fog of memory, fantasy and waking dream, he is unable to clearly distinguish between objective reality and his subjective or unconscious experience. Without clear markers between the 'reality' of the world of the novel and the narrator's fantasies, the narrative must repeatedly reset itself to shake free from his subjective visions: temporarily rescued from the approaching ice, he is struck by a 'shock, the sensation of a violent awakening, as it dawned on me that this was the reality, and those other things the dream. All of a sudden the life I had lately been living appeared unreal: it simply was not credible any longer' (72). Determined to undermine the credibility of his own narrative, at times the narrator proposes explanations for his peculiar perception – he must be dreaming, delirious, or suffering side effects from medication. Ultimately none of these justifications prevails and the key to the 'reality' of the strange world in which he operates remains elusive. Hannah Van Hove's recent work highlights how Kavan's sustained and experimental 'rejection of an absolute reality' was often poorly received in her lifetime;[31] today's 'post-truth' political climate has afforded a warmer reception for this narrative experiment. Kavan's disruption of subjective and objective realities in *Ice* predicts the Anthropocene's conceptual breakdown of a hard divide between objective scientific evidence of the natural world we live in and our subjective place in it.

The novel's third principal character, the cruel and arrogant 'warden', shares the narrator's obsession with the girl and for much of the novel she is in this man's power, abused and dominated by him, as the narrator pursues them with ambiguous intent. Lacking psychological depth, these characters take on and discard roles in an assortment of fantastic scenarios. Always, the girl is the victim and the other man is her persecutor but the narrator's subject position within the triptych is more complex and mutable; at times he plays a key part in the action but often he is only a voyeuristic bystander. Part of the peculiarity of *Ice* lies in the narrator's perspective of impossibility; he cannot be party to all that he declares to know and see. Perverting the stream of consciousness narrative, Kavan's first-person storyteller has access to the thoughts and feelings of his fellow characters, witnessing scenes at which he is not present and experiencing the sensations of both girl and warden. Slipping into the perspective of the victim, he derives pleasure from both telling her interior experience of fear and watching it from outside. The first person becomes third as the narrator describes the girl's physical and emotional responses to pursuit, intimidation and execution (49–51). Frequently, he comes back to the childhood abuse that has ordained her fate: 'Systematic bullying when she was most vulnerable had distorted the structure of her personality, made a victim of her' (50); 'Fear was the climate she lived in; if she had ever known kindness it would have been different' (49). Although the girl is frequently remote from him, always just out of reach, his passion for her is driven by his sense that she is 'a lost, essential portion of my own being' (25) and that 'like a part of me, I could not live without her' (73). His antagonism towards his nemesis the warden is also counterbalanced by moments of close identification; he experiences an indescribable affinity with him, a sort of blood-contact [. . .] so that I began to wonder if there *were* two of us' (76–7), and senses that they are 'like halves of one being' (98). In their final encounter, the narrator is captivated by the warden's powerful status and lavish lifestyle, even in the face of apocalypse: 'Drinks were brought, I was handed a tinkling glass. 'Ice! What luxury!' He glanced at my dilapidated uniform, made a grimace. 'You can't expect luxury if you insist on being a hero' (130). For the novel's villain, ice is a mere triviality that can be contained and put to use, and although the narrator likes to play the hero he is repeatedly beguiled and enchanted by its opposite. Thus, the narrator's intimate knowledge of the other characters extends to make each of them his fragment or double, and in the brutal world of the novel, the boundaries between victim, persecutor and protector are repeatedly blurred and transgressed. This ambiguous perspective anticipates an Anthropocene narrative in which humanity acts simultaneously as perpetrator, casualty and potential redeemer.

Like his associations with his fellow protagonists, the narrator's relationship to the natural world is not easy to chart. Early in his narrative, he describes his fascination with the indri lemurs, which (unacknowledged in the novel where places, like characters, remain anonymous) are indigenous to Madagascar. Animals and birds have symbolic significance in many of Kavan's texts and she often drew from the diverse cultures and habitats she had encountered living in New Zealand, Burma and the Dutch East Indies. But her knowledge of the indris almost certainly came to her via the BBC's pioneering natural history television programme, *Zoo Quest to Madagascar*, first broadcast in 1961 and presented by a young David Attenborough at the beginning of his broadcasting career. In the episode, Attenborough is shown making the first recording of the indris's call. The narrator of *Ice*, whose own recording of the indris is significant early in the novel, has studied them during his travels and reveals that the 'gentle affectionate ways and strange melodious voices of these near-legendary creatures had made a great impression on me' (9). The narrator, whose past is part-modelled on David Attenborough's activities, echoes the broadcaster's anthropomorphic description of the lemurs:

> These forests are their last home in the world and their numbers must be very restricted. They do no harm to anyone or anything [. . .] They have no natural enemies, except, possibly Man [. . .] The people who live in these forests regard them with an awe amounting to reverence, for these beautiful creatures, they say, are a gentle branch of the human race who have taken refuge in the trees to live, inoffensively, in peace.[32]

The narrator of *Ice* has taken these sentiments to heart:

> With their enchanting other-world voices, their gay, affectionate, innocent ways, they had become for me symbols of life as it could be on earth, if man's destructiveness, violence and cruelty were eliminated. (57)

For both Attenborough and narrator, the peace-loving indris represent non-human, but also near-human, life on earth, delimiting our own 'destructiveness, violence and cruelty' by embodying their opposite qualities.[33] Switching channels from *The Avengers*, Kavan drew from another instance of 1960s popular broadcasting to shape her narrative.

Attenborough's emphasis on humanity's impact on the natural world demonstrates that some of the novel's seemingly Anthropocenic anxieties were circulating in postwar culture and the prominent role that his more recent broadcasts have played in illustrating the effects of climate change to a public audience further inflects the novel's uncanny relation to the contemporary Anthropocene. Attenborough's *Zoo Quest* programme feeds the characterisation of Kavan's narrator who is adventurer, sadistic fantasist and natural historian in one. The 'almost extinct race' (9) of indris remain at the edges of the narrator's consciousness as his tale unfolds; he makes and then abandons a plan to devote his life to 'writing their history' (73) and eventually goes in search of them but finds instead another dream. His unstable relationship to non-human life on earth, sometimes passionate, sometimes indifferent, only repeats his shifting connections and antipathies to girl and warden: 'I looked at the natural world, and it seemed to share my feelings, to be trying in vain to escape its approaching doom' (122). In a period of relative calm, insulated from the approaching cold and with the girl in his clutches, he suffers a pang of conscience and decides to return to the fray of global catastrophe: 'I could not remain isolated from the rest of the world. I was involved with the fate of the planet, I had to take an active part in whatever was going on' (117). But for this narrator, an active part in apocalypse involves warfare and murder; to be 'involved' is to destroy and be destroyed. Enhancing its explicit disturbance of subjective and objective realities, *Ice* does not allow for clear distinctions between self and world or self and other; human experience and climatic or planetary happenings are intertwined and sometimes indistinguishable. This narrative innovation foreshadows one of the necessary displacements of the contemporary Anthropocene thought experiment, whose moral imperative must find a way to make humanity understand that it is 'involved with the fate of the planet' as both perpetrator and victim of destruction and as not-so-innocent bystander.

In the freezing atmosphere of *Ice*, the girl wears a thick grey loden coat that occasionally reveals its red and blue check lining; it is metonymical of the novel's bleak spectrum of greys broken by flashes of red and blue – dirt, stone, rubble, bruises on pallid skin, blood on snow, intensely cold blue eyes. Against this, the narrator's visions of ice are luminescent bursts of prismatic colour, terrifying and beautiful, accompanied by deafening noise: 'Huge ice-battlements, rainbow turrets and pinnacles [. . .] lit from within by frigid mineral fires' (147) mirror the 'stupendous sky-conflagration' of the aurora borealis, 'a blazing, vibrating roof of intense cold and colour' and '[c]old coruscations of rainbow fire' (21).

The girl takes centre stage in these dreamlike visions of the approaching ice, sharing its aura of unearthly, cosmic fantasy:

> Her albino hair illuminated my dreams, shining brighter than moonlight. I saw the dead moon dance over the icebergs, as it would at the end of our world, which she watched from the tent of her glittering hair. (99)

Although he professes concern about the girl's welfare at the hands of the other man, it rapidly becomes clear that the narrator's fascination with her is driven by his own seemingly uncontradictory desires to protect her and to cause her pain. By the third page of the novel, he is experiencing visions of 'the girl's naked body, slight as a child's, ivory white against the dead white of the snow', sees 'her mouth open, a black hole in the white face, heard her thin, agonized scream' (7–8). As he watches her figure consumed by ice, it arouses in him 'an indescribable pleasure from seeing her suffer' (8). This sadistic fantasy is the first of the novel's many scenes of the girl's intimidation, rape, murder and death by ice. The sexual violence of Kavan's earlier work, notably the marital rape in *Let Me Alone*, *Goose Cross* and *Who Are You?*, is represented in the third person, emphasising the female victim's trauma and violation. In *Ice*, the arousal and pleasure taken in the girl's anguish and fear are told from the perspective of a sadistic voyeur through a narrative that repeatedly aestheticises the image of her damaged and violated body:

> I came upon her by chance, not far away, lying face down on the stones. A little blood had trickled out of her mouth. Her neck had an unnatural twist; a living girl could not have turned her head at that angle: the neck was broken. She had been dragged by the hair, hands which had twisted it into a sort of rope had dulled its silvery brightness. On her back blood was still fresh in places, wet and bright red; in other places it had caked black on the white flesh. (54)

Forced to witness these scenes through his eyes, the girl's pain and degradation become a spectacle for reader as well as narrator and Kavan makes us complicit in his pleasure at her abuse. His visions of her annihilation by ice, in which her naked body is consumed in an orgy of apocalyptic agony, present human and planetary death as simultaneous and mutually implicated. As the narrator revels in his fantasy of sexual violence and earthy apocalypse from the comfort of his morally evasive position, he plays out Haraway's description of an Anthropocenic 'affect of sublime despair' coupled with the 'politics of sublime indifference', casting himself as the girl's saviour while enjoying a compellingly exquisite spectacle of death.

Haraway's explicitly feminist critique of the Anthropocene is apposite to a consideration of *Ice* in relation to the concept, since the novel's depictions of sexual violence demand, and pose challenges for, feminist interpretations. Reading *Ice* in a longer tradition of narratives of an 'intertwined apocalyptic destiny of self and globe', Victoria Nelson has identified the girl as the novel's main protagonist, taking the narrator as the 'symbiotic alter ego of the brutal men to whom this woman is in thrall'.[34] In her analysis of *Ice* as a psycho-topographic narrative in which 'inner psychic processes are projected sympathetically onto an exterior landscape' (45), girl and planet are destroyed by men and ice: 'The world and the woman are the same entity; the body of the planet is her body; man's sadistic misuse of both has resulted in their deaths' (62). Nelson's interpretation of *Ice* coincides neatly with Haraway's thought on the inherently masculine protagonist of the Anthropocene narrative, but it also conveniently elides the novel's difficulties. Tempting though it is to identify with girl rather than narrator, the reader's only access to her interior world is through him; *Ice* is his story and not hers, and the complexity of their relationship will not allow him to be dismissed so easily. In a more recent feminist reading, Leigh Wilson has argued compellingly that by undermining the certainties of reality, Kavan's experimental aesthetic 'force[s] the reader again and again to be aware of her imaginative engagement with the not-real and to consider the ethical effects of this', thus *Ice* ultimately 'challenges the inevitability of sexual violence in the world'.[35] Following Wilson's suggestion that the novel's disturbing aestheticisation of violence is key to the ethics of Kavan's experiment, I suggest that the discomfort these scenes provoke in the reader is another feature that brings it into close alignment with the Anthropocene.

The 'Ethical Value' of Experiment

Kavan frequently described herself as an 'egoist' and an 'individualist' in her wartime journalism and correspondence. These terms were vital to her radical politics of the time, including her anti-war sentiments expressed in the *I Am Lazarus* stories and 'The Case of Bill Williams'. In one *Horizon* review, she explicitly articulates an association between collectivism and totalitarianism:

> The word 'Collectivism' in our time has come to mean something more dangerous than group living or group thinking: it includes the concept of the organization of collective units into youth camps, labour camps, and fascist conditions in general.[36]

For Kavan, a mechanised system of society whose components must conform to collective standards necessarily denies creative and political dissidence – as she maintains in 'Bill Williams': 'the social machine is the enemy of the individual' (97). The 'tonic epidemic of madness' (98) she prescribes for modernity's systems of authoritarianism indicates the anarchistic rather than revolutionary bent to her politics; she did not propose reform of collective society, but that it should be annihilated. This political impulse towards disruption can be seen echoed in the increasing subversion of narrative conventions in her writing from the 1940s onward, matching her vision for a radically overturned social system with a dismantling of aesthetic form and genre.

Kavan's individualism did not forego responsibility towards fellow individuals. Her 1944 *Horizon* review of James Agee and Walker Evans's *Let Us Now Praise Famous Men* (1941), indicative of her personal campaign to find a British publisher for the book, reveals her interest in the ethics of this 'study in words and pictures of three Alabama "poor white" tenant families'.[37] Associating depression-era poverty with postwar deprivation, Kavan states that 'the problem raised' by the book is 'universal' 'and of the utmost urgency to us all':

> It is a terrifying fact that the post-war world will be full of damaged and helpless human beings with whose fate, if any values are to survive, the whole human race must realize itself involved. Any experiment whatsoever, which may shock people into awareness of their responsibility to those undefended ones is of supreme importance. The ethical value of this book can hardly be exaggerated in that it tends, in disturbing the reader's emotional norm, to force upon him acknowledgement of his own profound implication in the matter.[38]

Kavan's description of Evans and Agee's work, again applying 'experiment' as a term of approbation, emphasises the ethical potential of their project in stressing the responsibility of 'the whole human race' towards 'damaged', 'helpless' and 'undefended' individuals. I suggest that this is Kavan's sort of experiment, and the tendency to 'force upon' the reader 'acknowledgement of his own profound implication' in the fate of others is something she herself intended, perhaps most explicitly in *Ice*. Further, the ethical imperative of this experiment is analogous with what Chakrabarty describes as the Anthropocene's role as 'a moral-political issue'.[39]

Kavan's use of a first-person narrator in her final novel brings the reader into an uncomfortable intimacy with him, augmenting the narrative technique she had initiated in *Asylum Piece*. Its scenes of violence succeed in 'disturbing the reader's emotional norm' by presenting them through his eyes, and the 'ethical value' of this experiment lies in forcing them to inhabit his morally ambiguous and unaccountable subject position. Journeying with the self-deluding narrator of *Ice*, like him, the reader becomes a bystander to violence and death. His confusion about his own identity implicates his honesty as much as his sanity, combining the existential doubts that plagued Kavan's earlier protagonists with postwar deceptions over identity and political allegiance, which were the major theme of fictions such as Max Frisch's *I'm Not Stiller* (1958) and Kurt Vonnegut's *Mother Night* (1962), whose protagonists are tried and condemned as people they claim not to be.

In one episode, the narrator is arrested and undergoes a trial by unseen authorities: 'The case was that a girl had vanished, supposed kidnapped, possibly murdered' (75). This judicial device prompts the reader to interrogate more closely his 'visions' of the girl lying with her neck snapped or flung into the sea; if these are the waking dreams he has claimed them to be, he is to be tried for his imaginings rather than his actions. The trial thus formalises the reader's dilemma; should the narrator be convicted or acquitted of the crimes of his desires? Is he a murderous sadist or merely a sadistic fantasist? Is he a collaborator or a bystander? The scenes in the court are intercut with others in which the narrator intimidates and assaults the girl, vying for her with the other man; in the next moment he claims to the jury that he did not find her. His answers to the questions put to him in the courtroom imply that much of the novel's previous action never took place, but it is difficult to determine whether he is lying to the jury, to the reader, or to himself. His role as a 'witness' to the abuse of the girl turns out to have no foundation in a court of law. Faced with scepticism about his story, he can only maintain, with uncharacteristic certainty: 'That is the truth' (75). The invisible judges have no faith in the reliability of his evidence; faceless voices in the courtroom state that he is 'a psychopath, probably schizoid' (77) and the trial is abandoned. This reprieve on the grounds of diminished responsibility proves the success of the defence the narrator has been pleading to the reader throughout the novel; his repeatedly stated confusion over his sanity and sensory acuity making his 'horrible dreams' (8) involuntary and unconscious, denying culpability for his fantasies and disavowing his terrible desire. At the end of the novel, the narrator is surprised by the girl's accusations of mistreatment at his hands, as though the scenes in which he bullied and intimidated her were no more real than his prolific fantasies of her abuse. The revelation presents 'a view of myself I much preferred not to see' (154) but he accepts the charges and feels himself 'justly accused' (157).

Allan Hepburn has described the 'specific literary lineage' of the trial 'from the 1930s through to the 1960s', including representations responding to the Stalinist show trials and the Nuremburg and Eichmann trials.[40] Hepburn observes that mid-century 'literary representations respond to the understanding of the trial itself as an instrument of punishment, not justice, in which ideological stances and perceived treacheries are judged. In such instances, innocence or guilt is beside the point' (133). For Kavan, the wider historic impact of these mid-century tribunals was also clearly inflected by her attachment to Kafka's *The Trial*; by her earlier writing of severe depression with its associated feelings of guilt and persecution; and by Ian Hamilton's unmistakably flawed Appeal Board hearing, during which clear evidence of his pacifism was discounted and he was sentenced to imprisonment not as a conscientious objector but as a military defaulter.[41] The trial of the narrator in *Ice*, ostensibly to determine whether he is guilty of murdering the girl who may, or may not, still be alive, echoes the ambiguities of mid-century war trials.

Even before the onslaught of cold, the world of *Ice* is in ruins, scarred by conflicts both ancient and recent. As civilisation breaks down, mobs of refugees loot and murder in scenes of desperate brutality and the intimate violence done to the girl within the novel's triptych reverberates throughout human society. These features support Doris Lessing's suggestion that *Ice* was Kavan's 'Second World War novel'.[42] Kavan's reflections on the global situation in the immediate aftermath of the war are revealing; in a letter from early 1946 she wrote:

> Talking of war guilt, the Nuremburg trials are something of a farce even apart from Hiroshima – I suppose there's almost no crime on the sheet (except possibly the Belsen range) which hasn't been duplicated by the accusers.[43]

Laying aside the atomic bomb and the death camps as the outer limits of the war's atrocities, Kavan's anti-war and anti-nationalist sentiments inflect her belief that all involved in fighting the war were guilty. In *Ice*, the narrator, too, observes humankind's 'collective guilt' in bringing about their own and the world's annihilation by ice:

> Instead of my world, there would soon be only ice, snow, stillness, death; no more violence, no war, no victims: nothing but frozen silence, absence of life. The ultimate achievement of mankind would be, not just self-destruction, but the destruction of all life; the transformation of the living world into a dead planet. [. . .] I was oppressed by the sense of universal strangeness, by the chill of approaching catastrophe, the menace of ruins suspended above; and also by the enormity of what had been done, the weight of collective guilt. A frightful crime had been committed, against nature, against the universe, against life. (142)

The ice itself implements just punishment for the 'frightful crime' that humankind has perpetrated; collectively suicidal, they have called into being 'icy giant battalions, marching in relentless order across the world, crushing, obliterating, destroying everything in their path' (92), 'ghostly avengers coming to end mankind' (153). Although the destruction of the planet, relentless and seemingly unstoppable, is the collective responsibility of humankind, the narrator has no agency to change its destiny; his responsibility for the girl's fate, which at times he chooses to acknowledge, at others deny, translates this accountability onto the scale of individual action. *Ice* plays out the shared feelings which Anthony Burgess identified as shaping the sensibilities of readers and writers at midcentury: 'a powerful and desperate guilt since the revelations of Belsen and the blasting of Hiroshima'[44] which Allan Hepburn describes as a 'pervasive atmosphere of postwar culpability'.[45]

Rebecca West's account of 'the historic peep show' of the Nuremburg Trials in *The New Yorker* (1946) employed much of the language of mechanisation that Kavan drew on in 'Bill Williams': 'A machine is running down, a great machine, the greatest machine that has ever been created – the war machine, by which mankind, in spite of its infirmity of purpose and its frequent desire for death, has defended its life.'[46] This invocation of the death drive echoes Kavan's own description of '[h]ow crazy the human race has become with its passion for death' at the end of the war.[47] But for Kavan, the war machine was not a weapon of defence but the manifestation of this desire, and to her the 'atomic bomb [. . .] seems the consummation of the global death wish'.[48] Over twenty years later, in *Ice*, the narrator dreams of a benign being who describes 'the end of the human race', its 'collective death-wish' and 'fatal impulse to self-destruction' (123). The narrator's sentiment in the novel's closing line that 'the weight of the gun in my pocket was reassuring' (158) echoes the logic of postwar nuclear armament, but it is a flimsy weapon with which to fend off apocalypse. West describes how 'every trial is flawed by the same imperfection' – 'every accused person is suffering the injustice of being tried by people who, in the economic and social struggles which have worsted him, have come off best, to the extent of being on the bench while he is in the dock'. Echoing Kavan's sentiment that 'the Nuremburg trials are something of a farce', this 'tribunal set up in the hope of superseding war by law' relies upon the impartiality of those who are equally culpable.[49] The trial of the narrator in *Ice* is also something of a farce, a distraction from the real judgement of the novel; there is no tribunal to determine the guilt of humankind, no possibility of reprieve, only judgement in the form of ice.

Bouts of heavy snowfall in *Ice* make place indistinguishable, obliterating detail; the individual character of cities and landscapes is wiped out, the achievements of humanity and the diversity of nature eradicated. As the girl and narrator chase through these wastelands in continual flight and pursuit, she is brutally assaulted, threatened and killed time and again along the way, her bodily and emotional violation described with repetitively recurring imagery, accumulating to a disturbing monotony of language, place and deed. The cold and ice continue to advance and the novel's spatial and temporal scope contract as both time and inhabitable areas of the globe run out. As the world increasingly disappears in blizzard, the falling snow provides a model for the plot of both narrator and human life as a whole:

> the snowflakes whirled madly in all directions, filled the night with their spectral chaos. I seemed to feel the same feverish disorder in myself, in all my pointless rushing from place to place. The crazily dancing snowflakes represented the whole of life [. . .] In the delirium of the dance, it was impossible to distinguish between the violent and the victims. (152–3)

Snow and ice swallow up the world of the novel spreading 'a sheet of sterile whiteness over the face of the dying world, burying the violent and their victims together in a mass-grave, obliterating the last trace of man and his works' (146). This shroud for the planet and its destroyers is a blank page un-inscribing the novel's meaning. In this nihilistic apocalypse, the novel's characters and their actions are ultimately of no more consequence than 'an infinity of snowflakes like ghostly birds, incessantly swooping past from nowhere to nowhere' (157), like humanity's ultimate insignificance on the scale of deep time. Mirroring conventional narrative roles of hero, heroine and villain, the novel's three principal characters embody and subvert the archetypes of popular fiction. The perverted narrator's knowledge of, and identification with, the subject positions of all three makes it 'impossible to distinguish between the violent and the victims' (153), exposing the complexity and multiplicity of the human character. His dilemma embodies Kavan's disillusionment with humanity in the wake of the Second World War; all are guilty, all can be tempted by cruelty and dominance, or silent in the face of it. Thus, *Ice* undermines the concepts of good and evil and their narrative personifications, stressing humankind's shared culpability in atrocity, and reluctance to take individual responsibility.

Ice ends where it began, with the narrator behind the wheel of a car driving through dark and snow; but now the girl is by his side, rescued from the cold death of fantasy. As the end comes closer, he becomes acutely aware of living in the moment, and the narrative's past tense becomes more perplexing:

> The past had vanished and become nothing; the future was the inconceivable nothingness of annihilation. All that was left was the ceaselessly shrinking fragment of time called 'now'. (153)

Recounted from the 'inconceivable nothingness of annihilation', the narrative's impossible future plays out the same paradox Brannan identifies in his critique of the Anthropocene's epochal status; the narrator is the protagonist of an apocalypse that he cannot survive, speaking from a future in which he does not exist. Chakrabarty's analysis of Anthropocene temporality offers some elucidation for the temporal perversity of *Ice*. We cannot comprehend time in which we play no role; for the Anthropocene's moral-political plot to have any effect we must be in the story, even if that means effecting a necessary displacement in its timescale. As with *Ice*, the Anthropocene is a narrative in which we are the protagonists, dominating the planet and perhaps casting ourselves as its saviour – but are we hero, villain or victim? Can we make such easy distinctions? Thus, *Ice* is 'Anthropocene fiction' in the sense that its experimental narrative exhibits the concerns and enacts the paradoxes of the Anthropocene in its temporal peculiarities, its self-absorbed perspective, and its ethical urgency. *The New Yorker* review of *Ice* concludes that a 'half century after its first appearance, Kavan's fever dream of a novel is beginning to seem all too real', suggesting that the gap between the narrator's fantasy and the reader's reality appears to be closing.[50] But if Kavan's postwar experiment in *Ice* is to succeed ethically as well as aesthetically, in the same way she describes the effects of *Let Us Now Praise Famous Men*, the reader's emotional norm should not be disturbed simply by the recognition that this past-tense fantasy somehow aligns with our real-life apocalyptic future; we should acknowledge our 'own profound implication in the matter'. In the same way that Kavan perceived the significance of Evans and Agee's representation of depression-era poverty to the plight of postwar refugees, her own experimental narrative is most intimate with the plot of the Anthropocene in a common attempt to encourage 'the whole human race' to recognise their involvement with the crisis before them. The Anthropocene is an experimental fiction that is ethically necessary even if scientifically problematic or nonsensical, constructed to meet the reality of the current climate emergency. Like the narrator of *Ice*, we are 'involved with the fate of the planet', its climate, its possible futures, and the destinies of the other individuals living upon it.

Kavan began describing her own writing as 'experimental' in the 1940s. She continued to explore the term in her story of the same name, published posthumously in *Julia and the Bazooka*, in which her married protagonist invites a near-stranger to a sexual encounter, a 'small experiment' (38) to determine whether she can rediscover the pleasure she has lost in her marriage, for 'even an unsuccessful experiment is to be preferred to [. . .] emptiness and isolation' (38). Her feelings of unreality begin even before she fills her syringe, one of the explicit references to drug use that pepper Kavan's posthumous stories, and early on, she realises: 'This was just a stupid mistake on my part, not even an experiment, just something I had to get through' (39). Kavan's insistence on applying a term predominantly associated with scientific methodology to fictional writing and, as this story suggests, to ways of living, repudiates the division of the 'two cultures' of the sciences and humanities; her continuing allegiance to it demonstrates that her approach to experiment brings her closer to an Anthropocenic model in which the two are mutually implicated. Responding to the 'environment', 'atmosphere' and 'outside influences' of the mid-twentieth century, pursuing the artistic and ethical 'value' of the writing she most admired, Kavan's ongoing and evolving experiment to explore the relationship between fiction and reality was an endeavour shared with many of her contemporaries, resulting in a diverse body of work characteristic of the complex and hybrid nature of mid-century fiction.[51]

Notes

1. Anna Kavan to Peter Owen, 24 March 1966, HRC. The reference is to the British television series which ran from 1961–1969 on ITV.
2. Brian Aldiss, 'Introduction', in Anna Kavan, Ice (London: Picador, 1973), 14–21, p. 9. Doris Lessing, 'Anna Kavan', in *Time Bites* (London: Harper Perennial, 2005), p. 143; Jonathan Lethem, 'Gazing at *Ice*' (Foreword) in Anna Kavan, Ice (New York: Penguin, 2017), p. viii.
3. Leigh Wilson, 'Anna Kavan's *Ice* and Alan Burns' *Europe After the Rain*: Repetition with a Difference', *Women: A Cultural Review*, 28:4 (Winter 2017), 327–42, p. 328.
4. Anna Kavan to Peter Owen, 29 March [1966], Peter Owen Ltd. Records, HRC.
5. Brian Aldiss, 'Kafka's Sister', in *The Detached Retina* (Liverpool: Liverpool University Press, 1995), p. 142; Brian Aldiss, 'Introduction' to *Ice* (London: Picador, 1973), pp. 7–8, p. 9.
6. Anna Kavan to Raymond Marriott, 'Thursday' [1967], MFL.
7. J. G. Ballard to Peter Owen, 15 January 2001, Peter Owen Ltd. Records, HRC.

8. J. G. Ballard, 'Time, Memory and Inner Space', *The Woman Journalist*, Spring 1963, 10–11, p. 10.
9. Doris Lessing, 'Ice in an Outlaw's Heart', Review of *A Stranger on Earth* by Jeremy Reed, *The Independent*, Friday 7 July 2006, p. 25.
10. See, for example, Marion Vlastos, 'Doris Lessing and R. D. Laing: Psychopolitics and Prophecy', *PMLA*, 91:2 (March 1976), 245–58.
11. Lesley Hazelton's article which claimed that at one time 'Laing, Doris Lessing and the American radical writer Clancy Sigal formed a circle of almost incestuous mutual influence' has been widely quoted but is shown in other sources to be a serious overstatement. See Lesley Hazelton, 'Doris Lessing on Feminism, Communism and "Space Fiction"', *The New York Times*, 25 July 1982, and alternative accounts in Bob Mullan, *Mad to Be Normal: Conversations with R. D. Laing* (London: Free Association Books, 1995), p. 303 and Carole Klein, *Doris Lessing: A Biography* (London: Gerald Duckworth & Co., 2000).
12. Works specifically acknowledged to engage with Laing's ideas include Carter's *Several Perceptions* (1968), Lessing's *Briefing for a Descent into Hell* (1971), and Ballard's stories in *The Wind from Nowhere* (1962). Nin cites the influence of Laing in *The Novel of the Future* (1968).
13. See C. P. Snow, *The Two Cultures* [1959] (Cambridge: Cambridge University Press, 1998).
14. Doris Lessing, *Time Bites* (London: Harper Perennial, 2005), pp. 143–4.
15. Samuel Taylor Coleridge, 'The Rime of the Ancyent Marinere' [1798] in *Lyrical Ballads*, ed. W. J. B. Owen (Oxford: Oxford University Press, 1969) p. 9, lines 52–67; Kavan, *Ice*, p. 147.
16. See, for example, Adrian Tait, 'Nature Reclaims Her Own: J. G. Ballard's *The Drowned World*', *Australian Humanities Review*, 57 (2014), 25–41; Simon Andrew Orpana, 'The Prism of Petrol: Drive, Desire and the Energy Unconscious in Anna Kavan's *Ice*', *Inscriptions*, 12:1 (2019).
17. Jon Michaud, 'A Haunting Story of Sexual Assault and Climate Catastrophe, Decades Ahead of its Time', *The New Yorker*, 30 November 2017.
18. See, for example, Thomas S. Davis, 'Fossils of Tomorrow: Len Lye, J. G. Ballard, and Planetary Futures', *Modern Fiction Studies*, 64:4 (2018), 659–79; Stephanie LeMenager, 'Climate Change and the Struggle for Genre', in Tobias Menely and Jesse Oak Taylor (eds), *Anthropocene Reading: Literary History in Geologic Times* (Pennsylvania: Pennsylvania State University Press, 2017), 220–38; Tait, 'Nature Reclaims Her Own'; Orpana, 'The Prism of Petrol'.
19. Davis, 'Fossils of Tomorrow', p. 661.
20. Donna Haraway, *Staying with the Trouble: Making Kin in the Chthulucene* (Durham, NC and London: Duke University Press, 2016), pp. 3, 4.
21. Peter Brannen, 'The Anthropocene is a Joke', *The Atlantic* (13 August 2019), <https://www.theatlantic.com/science/archive/2019/08/arrogance-anthropocene/595795/> (accessed 13 December 2019).
22. Brannen, 'The Anthropocene is a Joke'.
23. In a later article, Brannen modifies his position by conceding that the consequences of human action for the planet are so far-reaching that if 'we wipe ourselves out tomorrow it will still be the Anthropocene a million years from now, even if very little of our works remain'. Peter Brannen, 'What

Made Me Reconsider the Anthropocene', *The Atlantic*, 11 September 2019, <https://www.theatlantic.com/science/archive/2019/10/anthropocene-epoch-after-all/599863/> (accessed 13 December 2019).
24. Dipesh Chakrabarty, 'Anthropocene Time', *History and Theory*, 57:1 (2018), 5–32, p. 6.
25. Chakrabarty, 'Anthropocene Time', p. 9.
26. Brannen, 'The Anthropocene is a Joke'.
27. Haraway, *Staying with the Trouble*, p. 47; Brannen, 'The Anthropocene is a Joke'.
28. Orpana, 'The Prism of Petrol', p. 6.
29. Frank Kermode, *The Sense of an Ending: Studies in the Theory of Fiction with a New Epilogue* (Oxford: Oxford University Press, 2000) [1966], p. 16.
30. Davis, 'Fossils of Tomorrow', p. 676.
31. Hannah Van Hove, 'Anna Kavan: Pursuing the "in-between reality" hidden by the "ordinary surface of things"', in Kaye Mitchell and Nonia Williams (eds), *British Avant-Garde Fiction of the 1960s* (Edinburgh: Edinburgh University Press, 2019), 107–24, p. 114.
32. 'Episode 5', *Zoo Quest to Madagascar* (1961), BBC, first broadcast 30 June 1961.
33. Cyril Connolly would describe how the lemurs that appear throughout the pages of *The Unquiet Grave* represent 'strength and beauty' 'as well as the innocent paradise', an equivalent significance to the Indri lemurs in *Ice* which suggests the enduring influence of his work on Kavan's. Cyril Connolly, 'Introduction', in *The Unquiet Grave: A Word Cycle by Palinurus*, revised edition (London: Hamish Hamilton, 1951), p. xv.
34. Victoria Nelson, 'Symmes Hole, or the South Polar Romance', *Raritan*, 17:2 (1997), 136–66, pp. 42, 61.
35. Wilson, 'Anna Kavan's *Ice*', p. 341.
36. Anna Kavan, 'Reviews', *Horizon*, 10:59 (November 1944), 359–62, p. 360.
37. Kavan knew Evans and Agee in New York earlier in the war and discussed the possibility of collaborating on a book with Evans, who also took a series of photographs of her, now held in the Walker Evans Archives, Metropolitan Museum of Art, New York.
38. Anna Kavan, 'Reviews', *Horizon*, 9:52 (April 1944), 283–5, p. 285.
39. Chakrabarty, 'Anthropocene Time', p. 9.
40. Allan Hepburn, 'Trials and Errors, *The Heat of the Day* and Postwar Culpability', in Kristen Bluemel (ed.), *Intermodernism: Literary Culture in Mid-Twentieth-Century Britain* (Edinburgh: Edinburgh University Press, 2009), 131–49, p. 132.
41. See Ian Hamilton, *Till Human Voices Wake Us* (Auckland: University of Auckland, 1984) and Jennifer Sturm, *Anna Kavan's New Zealand: A Pacific Interlude in a Turbulent Life* (Auckland: Vintage, Random House New Zealand, 2009).
42. Doris Lessing, 'Ice in an Outlaw's Heart', Review of *A Stranger on Earth* by Jeremy Reed, *The Independent*, Friday 7 July 2006, 25.
43. Anna Kavan to Ian Hamilton, 24 January 1946, NLNZ.
44. Anthony Burgess, *The Novel Now: A Student's Guide to Contemporary Fiction* (London: Faber & Faber, 1967), p. 34.
45. Allan Hepburn, 'Trials and Errors' p. 131.

46. Rebecca West, 'Extraordinary Exile', *The New Yorker*, 7 September 1946.
47. Anna Kavan to Ian Hamilton, 1 September 1945, *NLNZ*.
48. Anna Kavan to Ian Hamilton, 1 September 1945, *NLNZ*.
49. Anna Kavan to Ian Hamilton, 24 January 1946, *NLNZ*.
50. Michaud, 'A Haunting Story'.
51. Anna Kavan to Peter Owen, 29 March [1966], *HRC*; Anna Kavan, 'Back to Victoria: Selected Notices', *Horizon*, 13:73 (January 1946), 61–6, p. 65; Anna Kavan, 'Reviews', *Horizon*, 9:52 (April 1944), 283–5, p. 285.

Bibliography

Archival Sources

Anna Kavan Papers; Cyril Vernon Connolly Papers: McFarlin Library, University of Tulsa (*MFL*)
Peter Owen Ltd. Records; William A. Bradley Literary Agency Records; Scorpion Press Collection; Francis Henry King Collection: Harry Ransom Center, University of Texas at Austin (*HRC*)
Walter Ian Hamilton Papers, Alexander Turnbull Library, National Library of New Zealand, Wellington (*NLNZ*)
Archives of Jonathan Cape Ltd, Archives of Random House publishers, University of Reading Library, Special Collections (*JC*)
Ludwig Binswanger Archive, Universitätsarchiv, Eberhard Karls Universität Tübingen (*EKUT*)

Works By Anna Kavan

Fiction

As Helen Ferguson

A Charmed Circle (London: Jonathan Cape, 1929)
The Dark Sisters (London: Jonathan Cape, 1930)
Let Me Alone (London: Jonathan Cape, 1930)
A Stranger Still (London: John Lane, 1935)
Goose Cross (London: John Lane, 1936)
Rich Get Rich (London: John Lane, 1937)
'Martin's Wife', *Home and Country*, July 1937, 365–7
'Christmas Afternoon in Burma', *Home and Country*, December 1937, 629–31
'Wives' Encounter', *Home and Country*, October 1938, 407–8

As Anna Kavan

Asylum Piece (London: Jonathan Cape, 1940)

Change the Name (London: Jonathan Cape, 1941)
I Am Lazarus (London: Jonathan Cape, 1945)
The House of Sleep (Garden City, NY: Doubleday, 1947) [*Sleep Has His House*. London: Cassell & Co., 1948]
The Horse's Tale, with Karl Theodor Bluth (London: Gaberbocchus Press Limited, 1949)
A Scarcity of Love (Southport and London: Angus Downie, 1956)
Eagle's Nest (London: Peter Owen, 1957)
A Bright Green Field (London: Peter Owen, 1958)
Who Are You? (Lowestoft: Scorpion Press, 1963)
Ice (London: Peter Owen, 1967)

Posthumous

Julia and the Bazooka (London: Peter Owen, 1970)
My Soul in China (London: Peter Owen, 1975)
Mercury (London: Peter Owen, 1994)
The Parson (London: Peter Owen, 1995)
Guilty (London: Peter Owen, 2007)
Anna Kavan's New Zealand: A Pacific Interlude in a Turbulent Life (Stories), ed. by Jennifer Sturm (Auckland: Vintage, Random House New Zealand, 2009)

Journalism

'New Zealand: Answer to an Inquiry', *Horizon*, 8:45 (September 1943), 153–62
'The Case of Bill Williams', *Horizon*, 9:50 (February 1944), 96–107
'Reviews' [Peter De Polnay; Philip Toynbee; Mary McCarthy; Ruthven Todd], *Horizon*, 9:50 (February 1944), 138–41
'Reviews' [Virginia Woolf; William Sansom; H. A. Manhood; James Hanley; Katharine Butler Hathaway; James Agee and Walker Evans], *Horizon*, 9:52 (April 1944), 283–5
'Reviews' [Robert Neumann; Alex Comfort], *Horizon*, 10:59 (November 1944), 359–62
'Reviews' [Woodrow Wyatt; Elizabeth Bowen; Henry Miller; Rosamond Lehmann; essays by German writers], *Horizon*, XI; 62 (February 1945), 143–6
'Reviews' [Harry Brown; Glenway Westcott; Denton Welch; L. P. Hartley; Henry Green; Aldous Huxley], *Horizon*, 12:67 (July 1945), 63–9
'Back to Victoria: Selected Notices', *Horizon*, 13:73 (January 1946), 61–6

Other Works

Abel, Elizabeth, 'Women and Schizophrenia: The Fiction of Jean Rhys', *Contemporary Literature*, 20:2 (Spring 1979), 155–77
Agee, James and Walker Evans, *Let Us Now Praise Famous Men* [1941] (London: Peter Owen, 1965)

Aldiss, Brian, *The Detached Retina* (Liverpool: Liverpool University Press, 1995)
Aldiss, Brian, 'Introduction', in Anna Kavan, *Ice* (London: Picador, 1973), 14–21
Aldiss, Brian, 'Kafka's Sister', *Journal of the Fantastic in the Arts*, 3:2 (1991), 14–21
Aldiss, Brian (ed.), *My Madness: The Selected Writings of Anna Kavan* (London: Picador, 1990)
Alvarez, A., *The Savage God: A Study of Suicide* (London: Penguin, 1974)
American Psychiatric Association, *Diagnostic and Statistical Manual of Mental Disorders, Fifth Edition (DSM-5)* (Washington DC: American Psychiatric Publishing, 2013)
Anderson, Amanda, Rita Felski and Toril Moi, *Character: Three Inquiries in Literary Studies* (Chicago and London: University of Chicago Press, 2019)
Angier, Carole, *Jean Rhys: Life and Work* (London: André Deutsch, 1990)
Arendt, Hannah, *Eichmann in Jerusalem: A Report on the Banality of Evil* [1963] (London: Penguin, 1994)
Arendt, Hannah, 'Nathalie Sarraute', *The New York Review of Books*, 5 March 1964, 5–6
Ariail, Gregory, *Kafka's Copycats: Imitation, Fabulism, and Late Modernism* (University of Michigan, 2018)
Armitt, Lucie, *Contemporary Women's Fiction and the Fantastic* (Basingstoke: Macmillan Press, 2000)
Armstrong, Tim, *Modernism, Technology, and the Body: A Cultural Study* (Cambridge: Cambridge University Press, 1998)
Astbury, Jill, *Crazy for You: The Making of Women's Madness* (Melbourne: Oxford University Press Australia, 1996)
Aswell, Mary Louise (ed.), *The World Within: Fiction Illuminating Neuroses of Our Time* (New York: McGraw-Hill Book Co., 1947)
Auden, W. H., 'The I Without a Self', in *The Dyer's Hand and Other Essays* (London: Faber and Faber, 1962), 159–67
Auerbach, Erich, *Mimesis: The Representation of Reality in Western Literature*, trans. by Willard R. Trask [1946] (Princeton, NJ: Princeton University Press, 1968)
Aughterson, Kate and Deborah Philips (eds), *Women Writers and Experimental Narratives: Early Modern to Contemporary* (Basingstoke: Palgrave, 2021)
Ballard, J. G., *The Drowned World* [1962] (London: Harper Perennial, 2008)
Ballard, J. G., 'Time, Memory and Inner Space', *The Woman Journalist*, Spring 1963, 10–11
Ballard, J. G., *A User's Guide to the Millennium: Essays and Reviews* (London: HarperCollins, 1996)
Barnes, Djuna, *Nightwood* [1936] (London: Faber and Faber, 1996)
Barthes, Roland, 'The Death of the Author' [1967] in *Image, Music, Text*, trans. by S. Heath (London: Fontana, 1977), 142–8
Barthes, Roland, *The Rustle of Language*, trans. by Richard Howard (Oxford: Blackwell, 1986)
Baxter, Jeannette, *J. G. Ballard's Surrealist Imagination: Spectacular Authorship* (Farnham: Ashgate, 2009)
Beauvoir, Simone de, *The Second Sex* [1949], trans. by Constance Borde and Sheila Malovany-Chevallier (London: Jonathan Cape, 2009)

Beck, Aaron T. and Brad A. Alford, *Depression: Causes and Treatment, Second Edition* (Philadelphia: University of Pennsylvania Press, 2009)
Benjamin, Walter, 'On Some Motifs in Baudelaire' and 'The Work of Art in the Age of Mechanical Reproduction', in *Illuminations*, trans. by Harry Zorn (London: Pimlico, 1999)
Berger, John, *Ways of Seeing* [1972] (London: Penguin, 2008)
Bergonzi, Bernard, *The Situation of the Novel* (London: Macmillan, 1970)
Berrios, German E. and Roy Porter (eds), *A History of Clinical Psychiatry: The Origin and History of Psychiatric Disorders* (London: The Athlone Press, 1995)
Berry, Ellen E., *Women's Experimental Writing: Negative Aesthetics and Feminist Critique* (London: Bloomsbury, 2016)
Binswanger, Ludwig, *Being-in-the-World: Selected Papers of Ludwig Binswanger*, ed. by Jacob Needleman (New York: Basic Books, 1963)
Binswanger, Ludwig, *Sigmund Freud: Reminiscences of a Friendship*, trans. by Norbert Guterman (New York: Grune & Stratton, 1957)
Binswanger, Ludwig and Michel Foucault, *Dream and Existence*, trans. by Forrest Williams and Jacob Needleman, ed. by Keith Hoeller (Seattle, WA: Review of Existential Psychology and Psychiatry, 1986)
Bluemel, Kristen (ed.), *Intermodernism: Literary Culture in Mid-Twentieth-Century Britain* (Edinburgh: Edinburgh University Press, 2009)
Bluth, Karl Theodor, *Andante: Gedichte* (Weimar: Wolf von Kornatzki, 1918)
Bluth, Karl Theodor, 'Leibnitz, the European', in *In Tyrannos: Four Centuries of Struggle against Tyranny in Germany*, ed. by Hans J. Rehfisch (London: Lindsay Drummond Ltd, 1944)
Bluth, Karl Theodor, 'The Revival of Schelling', *Horizon*, 12:69 (September 1945), 156–78
Bluth, Karl Theodor, 'Selected Notices: Swiss Humanism', *Horizon*, 15:86 (February 1947), 144–50
Bluth, Karl Theodor and Peter Herzog, 'Im Exil', *Monatshefte*, 76:3 (1984), 246–8
Bonikowski, Wyatt, *Shell Shock and the Modernist Imagination: The Death Drive in Post-World War I British Fiction* (London: Routledge, 2013)
Booth, Francis, *Amongst Those Left: The British Experimental Novel 1940–1980* (Author, 2012)
Booth, Francis, *Stranger Still: The Works of Anna Kavan* (Author, 2012)
Boss, Medard, *Psychoanalysis and Daseinsanalysis* (New York: Da Capo Press, 1982)
Bowen, Elizabeth, *The Demon Lover and Other Stories* (London: Jonathan Cape, 1945)
Bowen, Elizabeth, *The Heat of the Day* [1949] (London: Vintage Books, 1998)
Bowen, Elizabeth, 'Introduction: The Short Story', in *The Faber Book of Modern Stories* (London: Faber & Faber, 1937), 7–19
Bowen, Elizabeth, *Listening In: Broadcasts, Speeches, and Interviews by Elizabeth Bowen*, ed. by Allan Hepburn (Edinburgh: Edinburgh University Press, 2010)
Bowen, Elizabeth, *The Mulberry Tree*, ed. by Hermione Lee (London: Vintage, 1999)
Bowles, Jane, *Plain Pleasures* (London: Peter Owen, 2004)

Bradbury, Malcolm, *No, Not Bloomsbury* (London: Andre Deutsche, 1987)
Brannen, Peter, 'The Anthropocene is a Joke', *The Atlantic* (13 August 2019), <https://www.theatlantic.com/science/archive/2019/08/arrogance-anthropocene/595795/> (accessed 13 December 2019).
Brannen, Peter, 'What Made Me Reconsider the Anthropocene', *The Atlantic* (11 September 2019), <https://www.theatlantic.com/science/archive/2019/10/anthropocene-epoch-after-all/599863/> (accessed 13 December 2019).
Bray, Joe, Alison Gibbons and Brian McHale (eds), *The Routledge Companion to Experimental Literature* (London: Routledge, 2012)
Breton, André, *Nadja* [1928], trans. by Richard Howard (New York: Grove Press, 1960)
Breton, André, 'Psychiatry Standing before Surrealism', in *Break of Day* [1934], trans. by Mark Polizzotti and Mary Ann Caws (Lincoln/London: University of Nebraska Press, 1999)
Brewster, Scott, 'Seeing Things: Gothic and the Madness of Interpretation', in *A New Companion to the Gothic*, ed. by David Punter (Chichester: Wiley-Blackwell, 2012), 481–95
Broe, Mary Lynn and Angela Ingram (eds), *Women's Writing in Exile* (Chapel Hill, NC: University of North Carolina Press, 1989)
Brooke-Rose, Christine, *A Rhetoric of the Unreal: Studies in Narrative and Structure, Especially of the Fantastic* (Cambridge: Cambridge University Press, 1981)
Brooke-Rose, Christine, *Stories, Theories and Things* (Cambridge: Cambridge University Press, 1991)
Burgess, Anthony, *The Novel Now: A Student's Guide to Contemporary Fiction* (London: Faber & Faber, 1967)
Burkhart, Charles, *Herman and Nancy and Ivy: Three Lives in Art* (London: Victor Gollancz, 1977)
Burns, Alan, *Europe after the Rain* (London: John Calder, 1965)
Burns, Alan and Charles Sugnet (eds), *The Imagination on Trial: British and American Writers Discuss their Working Methods* (London and New York: Allison and Busby, 1981)
Burston, Daniel, *The Wing of Madness: The Life and Work of R. D. Laing* (Cambridge, MA: Harvard University Press, 1996)
Byrne, Janet, 'Moving toward Entropy: Anna Kavan's Science Fiction Mentality', *Extrapolation*, 23:1 (1982), 5–11
Calder, Angus, *The Myth of the Blitz* (London: Jonathan Cape, 1991)
Callard, David, 'Bitter Pilgrimage: The Life of Anna Kavan', *London Magazine*, 1989, 48–61
Callard, David, *The Case of Anna Kavan: A Biography* (London: Peter Owen, 1992)
Camus, Albert, *The Myth of Sisyphus*, trans. by Justin O'Brien (London: Penguin, 2000)
Canfield, Cass, *Up and Down and Around: A Publisher Recollects the Time of His Life* (London: Collins, 1972)
Carr, Helen, '1966 and Wide Sargasso Sea: The Climate that Made Jean Rhys Legible', in Kate Aughterson and Deborah Philips (eds), *Women Writers and Experimental Narratives: Early Modern to Contemporary* (Basingstoke: Palgrave, 2021), 139–47

Carr, Helen, *Jean Rhys* (Plymouth: Northcote House, 1996)
Carrington, Leonora, *The Complete Stories of Leonora Carrington*, ed. by Kathryn Davis (St Louis, MO: Dorothy, 2017)
Carrington, Leonora, *Down Below* (New York: New York Review Books, 2017)
Carter, Angela, *The Bloody Chamber* [1979] (London: Vintage, 1995)
Carter, Angela, *The Sadeian Woman* (London: Virago, 1979)
Carter, Angela, 'Truly, It Felt Like Year One', in *Very Heaven: Looking Back at the 1960s*, ed. Sara Maitland (London: Virago Press, 1988)
Centing, Richard R., 'Anna Kavan's Shout of Red', *Under the Sign of Pisces: Anaïs Nin and her Circle*, 1:3 (Summer 1970), 1–9
Chakrabarty, Dipesh, 'Anthropocene Time', *History and Theory*, 57:1 (2018), 5–32
Chakrabarty, Dipesh, 'The Climate of History: Four Theses', *Critical Inquiry*, 35:2 (2009), 197–222
Chesler, Phyllis, *Women and Madness*, revised and updated edition (New York and Basingstoke: Palgrave Macmillan, 2005)
Christopher, John, *The World in Winter* (London: Eyre and Spottiswoode, 1962)
Coleman, Emily Holmes, *The Shutter of Snow* (Normal, IL: Dalkey Archive Press, 1997)
Connolly, Cyril, 'Comment', *Horizon*, 20:120–1 (December 1949–January 1950), 359–62
Connolly, Cyril (ed.), *Horizon Stories* (London: Faber and Faber, 1943)
Connolly, Cyril, *The Unquiet Grave: A Word Cycle by Palinurus* [1944], revised edition with an Introduction (London: Hamish Hamilton, 1951)
Connolly, Cyril, 'Why Not War Writers? A Manifesto', *Horizon*, 9:22 (October 1941)
Cooper, David, *Psychiatry and Anti-Psychiatry* (London: Tavistock Publications, 1967)
'Correspondence: The Case of Bill Williams', *Horizon*, 9:51 (March 1944), 286–8
Crosland, Margaret, *Beyond the Lighthouse: English Women Novelists in the Twentieth Century* (London: Constable, 1981)
Cunningham, Valentine, *British Writers of the Thirties* (Oxford: Oxford University Press, 1988)
Cvetkovich, Ann, *Depression: A Public Feeling* (Durham, NC: Duke University Press, 2012)
Davies, Rhys, 'Anna Kavan', *Books and Bookmen*, February 1971, 7–9
Davies, Rhys, 'The Bazooka Girl: A Note on Anna Kavan', *London Magazine*, 1970, 13–16
Davies, Rhys, 'A Lady and a Leopard: Anna Kavan', *Queen*, March 1970, 43–5
Davies, Rhys, *Honeysuckle Girl* (London: Heinemann, 1975)
Davis, Thomas S., *The Extinct Scene: Late Modernism and Everyday Life* (New York: Columbia University Press, 2016)
Davis, Thomas S., 'Fossils of Tomorrow: Len Lye, J. G. Ballard, and Planetary Futures', *Modern Fiction Studies*, 64:4 (2018), 659–79
Deleuze, Gilles and Félix Guattari, *Anti-Oedipus: Capitalism and Schizophrenia*, trans. by Robert Hurley, Mark Seem and Helen R. Lane (London: Continuum, 2004)
Derrida, Jacques, 'Cogito and the History of Madness', *Writing and Difference*, trans. by Alan Bass (London: Routledge, 2001)

Dicks, H. V., *Fifty Years of the Tavistock Clinic* (London: Routledge & Kegan Paul, 1970)
Dinesen, Isak, *Seven Gothic Tales* (London: Putnam, 1934)
Dorr, Priscilla Diaz, 'Anna Kavan: A Critical Introduction' (University of Tulsa, 1988)
Dorr, Priscilla Diaz, 'Anna Kavan: A Critical Introduction' (University of Tulsa, 1988)
Dorr, Priscilla Diaz, 'Archives: Women Writers in Mcfarlin Library Special Collections', *Tulsa Studies in Women's Literature*, 5:1 (1986), 133–7
Dowds, Barbara, *Depression and the Erosion of the Self in Late Modernity: The Lesson of Icarus* (London and New York: Routledge, 2018)
Drewery, Claire, *Modernist Short Fiction by Women* (Farnham: Ashgate, 2011)
Driscoll, Lawrence, 'Planet Heroin: Women and Drugs', in *Reconsidering Drugs: Mapping Victorian and Modern Drug Discourses* (Basingstoke: Palgrave, 2000), 101–27
Dunne, J. W., *An Experiment with Time* (London and Basingstoke: Papermac, Macmillan Publishers, 1981)
Ellmann, Maud, *Elizabeth Bowen: The Shadow Across the Page* (Edinburgh: Edinburgh University Press, 2003)
Ellmann, Maud, *The Nets of Modernism: Henry James, Virginia Woolf, James Joyce, and Sigmund Freud* (Cambridge: Cambridge University Press, 2010)
Emery, Mary L., *Jean Rhys at World's End: Novels of Colonial and Sexual Exile* (Austin: University of Texas Press, 1990)
Evangelou, Angelos, '"In fact I am an animal": Mental Illness, Vulnerability and the Problem of Empathy in Anna Kavan's *Asylum Piece*', *English Studies*, 2021
Felman, Shoshana, *Writing and Madness (Literature, Philosophy, Psychoanalysis)*, trans. by Shoshana Felman, Martha Noel Evans and Brian Massumi (Palo Alto, CA: Stanford University Press, 2003)
Ferris, Natalie, 'The Double Play of Mirrors: Anna Kavan, Autobiography and Self-Portraiture', *Women: A Cultural Review*, 28:4 (Winter 2017), 391–409
Ferris, Natalie, 'A Precarious Vision: Hallucination and the Short Story in Post-War Britain', *British Experimental Women's Fiction, 1945–1975: Slipping Through the Labels*, ed. by Andrew Radford and Hannah Van Hove (London: Palgrave, 2021)
Fichtner, Gerhard (ed.), *Freud–Binswanger Correspondence 1908–1938* (London: Open Gate Press, 2003)
Foucault, Michel, *Madness and Civilization*, trans. by Richard Howard (London and New York: Routledge, 2001)
Foucault, Michel, *Mental Illness and Psychology*, trans. by Alan Sheridan (Berkeley: University of California Press, 1987)
Foucault, Michel, *Psychiatric Power: Lectures at the Collège De France, 1973–4* (Basingstoke: Palgrave Macmillan, 2003)
Foucault, Michel, 'What is an Author?' [1969], trans. by Josue V. Harari, in *The Foucault Reader*, ed. by Paul Rabinow (London: Penguin, 1984)
Frame, Janet, *Faces in the Water* [1961] (London: Virago, 2009)
Francis, Samuel, *The Psychological Fictions of J. G. Ballard* (London and New York: Continuum, 2011)
Freeman, Hugh and German E. Berrios (eds), *150 Years of British Psychiatry, 1841–1991* (London: Gaskell, 1991)

Freeman, Hugh and German E. Berrios (eds), *150 Years of British Psychiatry: Volume II, the Aftermath* (London: Athlone Press, 1996)
Freud, Sigmund, *The Standard Edition of the Complete Psychological Works*, trans. by James Strachey, 24 vols (London: Hogarth Press, 1995)
Friedman, Ellen G. and Miriam Fuchs (eds), *Breaking the Sequence: Women's Experimental Fiction* (Princeton, NJ: Princeton University Press, 1989)
Frisch, Max, *I'm Not Stiller* [1954], trans. by Michael Bullock (London and New York: Abelard-Schuman, 1958)
Fromm, Erich, *The Sane Society* (London: Routledge & Kegan Paul, 1956)
Frow, John, *Character and Person* (Oxford: Oxford University Press, 2014)
Gaedtke, Andrew, *Modernism and the Machinery of Madness: Psychosis, Technology and Narrative Worlds* (Cambridge: Cambridge University Press, 2017)
Gambaudo, Sylvie, 'Melancholia in Janet Frame's *Faces in the Water*', *Literature and Medicine*, 30:1 (Spring 2012), 42–60
Gamble, Sarah, *Angela Carter: A Literary Life* (Basingstoke: Palgrave, 2006)
Gardiner, Judith Kegan, 'Good Morning, Midnight: Good Night, Modernism', *boundary 2* 11:1/2 (1983), 233–51
Garrity, Jane, 'Nocturnal Transgressions in *the House of Sleep*: Anna Kavan's Maternal Registers', *Modern Fiction Studies*, 40:2 (Summer 1994), 253–77
Gasiorek, Andrzej, *Post-War British Fiction: Realism and After* (London: Edward Arnold, 1995)
Gee, Maggie and Lisa Appignanesi, 'The Contemporary Writer: Gender and Genre', in *Writing: A Woman's Business: Women, Writing and the Marketplace*, ed. by Judy Simons and Kate Fullbrook (Manchester: Manchester University Press, 1998)
Gifford, James, *A Modernist Fantasy: Modernism, Anarchism and the Radical Fantastic* (Victoria, BC: ELS Editions, 2018)
Gilbert, Sandra M. and Susan Gubar, *The Madwoman in the Attic: The Woman Writer and the Nineteenth-Century Literary Imagination* (New Haven and London: Yale University Press, 2000)
Gilman, Charlotte Perkins, *The Yellow Wallpaper and Selected Writings* (London: Virago Press, 2009)
Gilman, Sander L., *Seeing the Insane* (Lincoln and London: University of Nebraska Press, 1996)
Glover, Edward, 'Notes on the Psychological Effects of War Conditions on the Civilian Population', *International Journal of Psychoanalysis*, 22 (1941), 132–46
Glover, Edward, *War, Sadism and Pacifism* (London: George Allen & Unwin Ltd, 1933)
Glynn, Raewyn, 'Anna Kavan on Ice: An Encounter with Anna Kavan's Wartime Writing Via New Zealand and the Arctic Imaginary' (University of Auckland, 1997)
Goffman, Erving, *Asylums: Essays on the Social Situation of Mental Patients and Other Inmates* (London: Penguin, 1968)
Gordon, Giles (ed.), *Beyond the Words: Eleven Writers in Search of a New Fiction* (London: Hutchinson, 1975)
Gornick, Vivian, *The End of the Novel of Love* (London: Virago, 1999)
Gornick, Vivian, 'The Great Depression of Anna Kavan', *The Village Voice*, 2–8 December 1981, 49–113

Gray, Nancy, *Language Unbound: On Experimental Writing by Women* (Chicago: University of Illinois Press, 1992)
Green, Henry, *Caught* [1943] (London: Hogarth Press, 1978)
Greene, Graham, *The Ministry of Fear* [1943] (London: William Heinemann and the Bodley Head, 1973)
Groes, Sebastian, *British Fictions of the Sixties: The Making of the Swinging Decade* (London and New York: Bloomsbury, 2015)
Guy, Adam, *The nouveau roman and Writing in Britain after Modernism* (Oxford: Oxford University Press, 2019)
Hallam, Christopher, *White Drug Cultures and Regulation in London, 1916–1960* (Palgrave MacMillan, Basingstoke, 2018)
Hamilton, Ian, *Till Human Voices Wake Us* (Auckland: University of Auckland, 1984)
Hamilton, Patrick, *The Slaves of Solitude* [1947] (London: Constable, 2006)
Hanley, James, *No Directions* [1943] (London: Nicholson & Watson, 1946)
Haraway, Donna, *Staying with the Trouble: Making Kin in the Chthulucene* (Durham, NC and London: Duke University Press, 2016)
Hayter, Alethea, *Opium and the Romantic Imagination: Addiction and Creativity in De Quincey, Coleridge, Baudelaire and Others* (London: Faber and Faber, 1968)
Hazelton, Lesley, 'Doris Lessing on Feminism, Communism and "Space Fiction"', *The New York Times*, 25 July 1982
Head, Dominic, *The Cambridge Introduction to Modern British Fiction, 1950–2000* (Cambridge: Cambridge University Press, 2002)
Heidegger, Martin, *Being and Time* [1927], trans. by John Macquarrie and Edward Robinson (Oxford: Blackwell Publishers Ltd, 1962)
Hepburn, Allan, 'Trials and Errors: *The Heat of the Day* and Postwar Culpability', in Kristen Bluemel (ed.), *Intermodernism: Literary Culture in Mid-Twentieth-Century Britain* (Edinburgh: Edinburgh University Press, 2009), 131–49
Hewison, Robert, *Under Siege: Literary Life in London 1939–1945* (London: Weidenfeld and Nicolson, 1977)
Hill, Emily, 'Kafka's Sister', *Dazed and Confused*, II:88 (August 2010), 107–9
Hill Rigney, Barbara, *Madness and Sexual Politics in the Feminist Novel: Studies in Bronte, Woolf, Lessing and Atwood* (Wisconsin: University of Wisconsin Press, 1978)
Hilton, Claire, 'Mill Hill Emergency Hospital: 1939–1945', *The Psychiatric Bulletin*, 30 (2006), 106–8
Hodgson, Andrew, *The Post-War Experimental Novel: British and French Fiction, 1945–75* (London: Bloomsbury Academic, 2020)
Hoff, Ann, '"I Was Convulsed, Pitiably Hideous": Convulsive Shock Treatment in Leonora Carrington's "Down Below"', *Journal of Modern Literature*, 32:3 (Spring, 2009), 83–98
Horsley, J. Stephen, *Narco-Analysis: A New Technique in Short-Cut Psychotherapy: A Comparison with Other Methods: And Notes on the Barbiturates* (London: Oxford University Press, 1943)
Houlden, Kate, 'Queering the World or Worlding the Queer? New Readings of Anna Kavan's *Who Are You?*', *Women: A Cultural Review*, 28:4 (Winter 2017), 295–311

Ingersoll, Earl G. (ed.), *Doris Lessing: Conversations* (Princeton, NJ: Ontario Review Press, 1994)
Jackson, Rosemary, *Fantasy: The Literature of Subversion* (London: Routledge, 1988)
James, David (ed.), *The Cambridge Companion to British Fiction Since 1945* (Cambridge: Cambridge University Press, 2015)
Jefferson, Ann, *Nathalie Sarraute, Fiction and Theory: Questions of Difference* (Cambridge: Cambridge University Press, 2000)
Johnson, Erica L. and Patricia Moran (eds), 'Introduction: The Haunting of Jean Rhys', *Jean Rhys: Twenty-First-Century Approaches* (Edinburgh: Edinburgh University Press, 2015)
Jones, Clara, '"Mystery at the Lilacs": Elizabeth Bowen's Thriller Serial for Home and Country Magazine', *Literature and History*, 27:1 (2018), 3–27
Jones, Edgar, 'War and the Practice of Psychotherapy: The UK Experience 1939–1960', *Medical History*, 48 (2004), 493–510
Jones, Edgar and Simon Wessely, 'War Syndromes: The Impact of Culture on Medically Unexplained Symptoms', *Medical History*, 49:1 (1 Jan 2005), 55–78
Jones, Maxwell, *Social Psychiatry: A Study of Therapeutic Communities* (London: Tavistock Publications Ltd, 1952)
Jones, Maxwell and Aubrey Lewis, 'Effort Syndrome', *The Lancet* (28 June 1941), 813–18
Jordan, Clive, 'Among the Lost Things', *The Daily Telegraph*, 25 February 1972, 39–46
Jordan, Clive, 'Icy Heroin', Review of *Julia and the Bazooka*, *The New Statesman*, 6 March 1970
Jordan, Julia, *Late Modernism and the Avant-Garde British Novel: Oblique Strategies* (Oxford: Oxford University Press, 2020)
Jordan, Julia, *Late Modernism and the Avant-Garde British Novel: Oblique Strategies* (Oxford: Oxford University Press, 2020)
Jordan, Julia, 'Late Modernism and the Avant-Garde Renaissance', in *The Cambridge Companion to British Fiction Since 1945*, ed. by David James (Cambridge: Cambridge University Press, 2015), 145–59
Kafka, Franz, *The Castle* [1926] (London: Martin Secker, 1930)
Kafka, Franz, *Metamorphosis and Other Stories* [1915] (London: Minerva, 1992)
Kafka, Franz, *The Trial* [1925] (London: Vintage, 1999)
Kavan, Anna, *Machines in the Head: Selected Short Writing*, ed. by Victoria Walker (London: Peter Owen, 2019)
Kennedy, Sue and Jane Thomas (eds), *British Women's Writing, 1930 to 1960: Between the Waves* (Liverpool: University of Liverpool Press, 2020)
Kermode, Frank, *The Sense of an Ending: Studies in the Theory of Fiction with a New Epilogue* (Oxford: Oxford University Press, 2000)
Kime Scott, Bonnie (ed.), *The Gender of Modernism: A Critical Anthology* (Bloomington and Indianapolis: Indiana University Press, 1990)
King, Francis, *Yesterday Came Suddenly: An Autobiography* (London: Constable, 1993)
Klein, Carole, *Doris Lessing: A Biography* (London: Gerald Duckworth & Co., 2000)

Kohlmann, Benjamin and Matthew Taunton (eds), *A History of 1930s British Literature* (Cambridge: Cambridge University Press, 2019)
Kristeva, Julia, *Black Sun: Depression and Melancholia*, trans. by Leon S. Roudiez (New York: Columbia University Press, 1989)
Laing, R. D., *The Divided Self* (London: Penguin, 1965)
Laing, R. D., *The Politics of Experience and the Bird of Paradise* (London: Penguin, 1967)
Laing, R. D. and A. Esterson, *Sanity, Madness and the Family* (London: Tavistock Publications, 1964)
Le Carré, John, *The Spy Who Came in from the Cold* [1963] (London: Penguin, 2020)
LeMenager, Stephanie, 'Climate Change and the Struggle for Genre', in Tobias Menely and Jesse Oak Taylor (eds), *Anthropocene Reading: Literary History in Geologic Times* (Pennsylvania: Pennsylvania State University Press, 2017), 220–38
LeNoble, Catherine, *Anna K* (Orléans: HYX, 2016)
Lessing, Doris, *Briefing for a Descent into Hell* [1971] (London: HarperCollins Publishers, 2002)
Lessing, Doris, 'Ice in an Outlaw's Heart', Review of *A Stranger on Earth* by Jeremy Reed, *The Independent*, Friday 7 July 2006, 25
Lessing, Doris, 'Ice Maiden Stung by a Spider', *The Independent*, 5 June 1993, 28
Lessing, Doris, Review of *The Parson*, *The Times Literary Supplement*, 7 December 2001, 10
Lessing, Doris, *The Memoirs of a Survivor* [1974] (London: Harper Perennial, 2007)
Lessing, Doris, *Time Bites* (London: Harper Perennial, 2005)
Lethem, Jonathan, 'Gazing at *Ice*' (Foreword) in Anna Kavan, *Ice* (New York: Penguin, 2017)
Lewis, Jeremy, *Cyril Connolly, a Life* (London: Jonathan Cape, 1997)
Lewis, Thomas, *The Soldier's Heart and the Effort Syndrome* (London: Shaw, 1940)
Light, Alison, *Forever England: Femininity, Literature and Conservatism Between the Wars* (London: Routledge, 1991)
Lodge, David, 'The Novelist at the Crossroads' [1969], in *The Novel Today: Contemporary Writers on Modern Fiction*, new edition, ed. Malcolm Bradbury (London: Fontana, 1990)
Lukács, Georg, *The Meaning of Contemporary Realism*, trans. by John and Necke Mander (London: Merlin Press, 1963)
MacCarthy, Desmond, 'Madness and Art', Review of *Asylum Piece*, *The Times*, 10 March 1940, 4
MacKay, Marina, 'The Literary Novel', in *The Cambridge Companion to British Literature of the 1930s*, ed. by James Smith (Cambridge: Cambridge University Press, 2019)
MacKay, Marina and Lyndsey Stonebridge (eds), *British Fiction after Modernism: The Novel at Mid-Century* (Basingstoke: Palgrave, 2007)
McLoughlin, Kate, *Authoring War: The Literary Representation of War from the Iliad to Iraq* (Cambridge: Cambridge University Press, 2011)
Magot, Céline, 'The Palimpsest Girl in *Ice* by Anna Kavan', *Miranda*, 12 (2016), <https://miranda.revues.org/8675> (accessed 9 September 2018).

Marcus, Laura, *Auto/Biographical Discourses* (Manchester and New York: Manchester University Press, 1994)
Maslen, Elizabeth, *Political and Social Issues in British Women's Fiction, 1928–1968* (Basingstoke: Palgrave, 2001)
Maynard, Jessica, '"Too Much Blue, Too Much Purple, Too Much Green": Reading *Wide Sargasso Sea* in the Sixties', *The Jean Rhys Review*, 11:2 (2001)
Meckel, Christoph, *The Figure on the Boundary Line: Selected Prose*, ed. by Christopher Middleton (Manchester: Carcanet Press, 1983)
Mellor, Leo, *Reading the Ruins: Modernism, Bombsites and British Culture* (Cambridge: Cambridge University Press, 2011)
Menely, Tobias and Jesse Oak Taylor, *Anthropocene Reading: Literary History in Geologic Times* (Pennsylvania: Pennsylvania State University Press, 2017)
Michaud, Jon, 'A Haunting Story of Sexual Assault and Climate Catastrophe, Decades Ahead of its Time', *The New Yorker* (30 November 2017)
Miller, Gavin, *R. D. Laing* (Edinburgh: Edinburgh Review, 2004)
Miller, Tyrus, *Late Modernism: Politics, Fiction, and the Arts Between the Wars* (Berkeley: University of California Press, 1999)
Mitchell, Juliet, *Psychoanalysis and Feminism* (London: Pelican Books, 1975)
Mitchell, Kaye, 'The avant-garde must not be romanticized. The avant-garde must not be dismissed', in Kaye Mitchell and Nonia Williams (eds), *British Avant-Garde Fiction of the 1960s* (Edinburgh: Edinburgh University Press, 2019), 107–24
Mitchell, Kaye, 'Introduction: The Gender Politics of Experiment', *Contemporary Women's Writing*, 9:1 (1 March 2015), 1–15
Moorhead, Joanna, *The Surreal Life of Leonora Carrington* (London: Virago, 2017)
Muir, Edwin, Review of *Asylum Piece*, *The Listener*, 21 March 1940, 597
Mullan, Bob, *Mad to Be Normal: Conversations with R. D. Laing* (London: Free Association Books, 1995)
Nelson, Victoria, *The Secret Life of Puppets* (Cambridge, MA: Harvard University Press, 2001)
Nelson, Victoria, 'Symmes Hole, or the South Polar Romance', *Raritan*, 17:2 (Fall 1997), 136–66
Nin, Anaïs, *House of Incest* (Athens, OH: Swallow Press/Ohio University Press, 1994)
Nin, Anaïs, *The Journals of Anaïs Nin*, 7 vols (London: Peter Owen, 1980)
Nin, Anaïs, *The Novel of the Future* (London: Peter Owen, 1968)
'Novelist Anna Kavan Found Dead at Home', *Daily Telegraph*, 6 December 1968
'Obituary: Anna Kavan', *The Times*, 6 December 1968
Orpana, Simon Andrew, 'The Prism of Petrol: Drive, Desire and the Energy Unconscious in Anna Kavan's *Ice*', *Inscriptions*, 12:1 (2019)
Orwell, George, *Burmese Days* [1934] (London: Secker & Warburg, 1949)
Owen, Peter, 'Publishing Anna Kavan', *Anaïs: An International Journal*, 3 (1985), 75–6
Owen, Peter and James Nye, *Peter Owen, Not a Nice Jewish Boy: Memoirs of a Maverick Publisher* (London: Fonthill, 2021)

Palko, Abigail, 'Colonial Modernism's Thwarted Maternity: Elizabeth Bowen's *The House in Paris* and Jean Rhys's *Voyage in the Dark*', *Textual Practice*, 27:1 (2013), 89–108

Panter-Downes, Mollie, 'Letter from London', *New Yorker*, 21 September 1940

Parrinder, Patrick, *Nation and Novel: The English Novel from Its Origins to the Present Day* (Oxford: Oxford University Press, 2006)

Perriam, Geraldine, '"Impudent Scribblers": Place and the Unlikely Heroines of the Interwar Years' (unpublished doctoral thesis, University of Glasgow, 2011)

Periyan, Natasha, *The Politics of 1930s British Literature: Education, Class, Gender* (London: Bloomsbury Academic, 2018)

Pick, Daniel, *The Pursuit of the Nazi Mind* (Oxford: Oxford University Press, 2012)

Piette, Adam, *Imagination at War: British Fiction and Poetry 1939–45* (London: Macmillan, 1995)

Plain, Gill (ed.), *British Literature in Transition, 1940–1960: Postwar* (Cambridge: Cambridge University Press, 2019)

Plain, Gill, *Literature of the 1940s: War, Postwar and Peace* (Edinburgh: Edinburgh University Press, 2012)

Plath, Sylvia, *The Bell Jar* [1963] (London: Faber and Faber, 1966)

Pong, Beryl, *British Literature and Culture in Second World Wartime: For the Duration* (Oxford: Oxford University Press, 2020)

Porter, Roy, *A Social History of Madness: The World Through the Eyes of the Insane* (London: Weidenfeld & Nicolson, 1987)

Priest, Christopher, *The Affirmation* (London: Gollancz, 2006)

Prowse, Nycole, '"Out of Control": Excess, Desire and Agency in Female Drug Writing', *Hecate*, 42:2 (2016), 39–54

Quin, Ann, *Berg* [1964] (Normal, IL: Dalkey Archive Press, 2001)

Quin, Ann, *Three* [1969] (Sheffield/London/New York: And Other Stories, 2020)

Quin, Ann, *The Unmapped Country: Stories and Fragments* (Sheffield/London/New Haven: And Other Stories, 2018)

Quincey-Jones, Steven, 'Herbert Read's Egoist Roots', *Modernism/Modernity* 25:2 (April 2018), 389–405

Rao, Eleonora, 'The "Black Sun": Anna Kavan's Narratives of Abjection', *Textus*, IV (1991), 119–46

Rabinowitz, Rubin, *The Reaction against Experiment in the English Novel 1950–1960* (New York and London: Columbia University Press, 1967)

Radford, Andrew and Hannah Van Hove (eds), *British Experimental Women's Fiction, 1945–1975: Slipping Through the Labels* (Basingstoke: Palgrave Macmillan, 2021)

Rawlinson, Mark, 'Narrating Transitions to Peace: Fiction and Film after War', in Gill Plain (ed.), *British Literature in Transition, 1940–1960: Postwar* (Cambridge: Cambridge University Press, 2019) 143–60

Rawlinson, Mark, 'The Second World War: British Writing', in Kate McLoughlin (ed.), *The Cambridge Companion to War Writing* (Cambridge: Cambridge University Press, 2009), 197–211

Read, Herbert, 'Art and Crisis', *Horizon*, IX, no. 53 (1944, May), 336–50

Read, Herbert, 'Mood of the Month – X: The Two Cultures: An Intellectual Replies', *The London Magazine*, 6:8 (August 1959)

Read, Herbert, 'The Politics of the Unpolitical', in *The Politics of the Unpolitical* (London: Routledge, 1943)
Reed, Jeremy, *A Stranger on Earth: The Life and Work of Anna Kavan* (London: Peter Owen, 2006)
Robbe-Grillet, Alain, *Snapshots and Towards a New Novel*, trans. by Barbara Wright (London: Calder and Boyars, 1965)
Rhys, Jean, *After Leaving Mr Mackenzie* [1930] (London: Penguin, 2000)
Rhys, Jean, *Good Morning, Midnight* [1939] (London: Penguin, 2000)
Rhys, Jean, *Jean Rhys: Letters 1931–66*, ed. by Francis Wyndham and Diana Melly (London: Penguin, 1985)
Rhys, Jean, *Tigers Are Better-Looking with a Selection from the Left Bank* (London: Penguin, 1972)
Rhys, Jean, *Voyage in the Dark* [1934] (London: Penguin, 2000)
Rhys, Jean, 'The Whistling Bird', *The New Yorker*, 11 September 1978, 38–9
Rhys, Jean, *Wide Sargasso Sea* [1966] (London: Penguin, 1968)
Riquelme, John Paul, 'Toward a History of Gothic and Modernism: Dark Modernity from Bram Stoker to Samuel Beckett', *Modern Fiction Studies*, 46:3 (Fall 2000), 585–605
Rose, Jacqueline, *The Haunting of Sylvia Plath* (London: Virago, 2013)
Rubenstein, Roberta, 'Briefing on Inner Space: Doris Lessing and R. D. Laing', *Psychoanalytic Review*, 63 (1976), 83–93
Russell, Denise, *Women, Madness and Medicine* (Cambridge: Polity Press, 1995)
Sage, Lorna, *Women in the House of Fiction: Post-War Women Novelists* (Basingstoke: Macmillan, 1992)
Saint-Amour, Paul K., *Tense Future: Modernism, Total War, Encyclopedic Form* (Oxford: Oxford University Press, 2015)
Sansom, William (ed.), *Choice: Some New Stories and Prose* (London: Progress Publishing, 1946)
Sansom, William, *Fireman Flower and Other Stories* (London: Hogarth Press, 1944)
Sarraute, Nathalie, 'The Age of Suspicion' [1950], in *The Age of Suspicion: Essays on the Novel*, trans. by Maria Jolas (New York: George Braziller, 1963)
Sartre, Jean-Paul, *Being and Nothingness*, trans. by Hazel E. Barnes (London: Routledge, 2003)
Sartre, Jean-Paul, *Sketch for a Theory of the Emotions*, trans. by Philip Mairet (London: Routledge, 2002)
Sass, Louis A., *Madness and Modernism: Insanity in the Light of Modern Art, Literature, and Thought* (Cambridge, MA: Harvard University Press, 1992)
Saunders, Max, *Self Impression: Life-Writing, Autobiografiction, and the Forms of Modern Literature* (Oxford: Oxford University Press, 2010)
Schwass, Margot, *All the Juicy Pastures: Greville Texidor and New Zealand* (Wellington, NZ: Victoria University Press, 2019)
Seiler, Claire, *Midcentury Suspension: Literature and Feeling in the Wake of World War II* (New York: Columbia University Press, 2020)
Shelden, Michael, *Friends of Promise: Cyril Connolly and the World of Horizon* (London: Hamish Hamilton, 1989)

Shephard, Ben, *A War of Nerves: Soldiers and Psychiatrists 1914–1994* (London: Jonathan Cape, 2000)
Shorter, Edward, *A History of Psychiatry: From the Era of the Asylum to the Age of Prozac* (New York: John Wiley and Sons, 1997)
Showalter, Elaine, *The Female Malady: Women, Madness and English Culture 1830–1980* (London: Virago, 1987)
Showalter, Elaine, *A Literature of Their Own: From Charlotte Brontë to Doris Lessing* (London: Virago Press, 1999)
Showalter, Elaine, 'R. D. Laing and the Sixties', *Raritan*, 1:2 (Fall 1981), 107–27
Sinfield, Alan, *Literature, Politics and Culture in Postwar Britain* (London: Continuum, 2004)
Sitwell, Edith (ed.), *Planet and Glow-Worm: A Book for the Sleepless* (London: Macmillan & Co., 1944)
Smith, Andrew and Jeff Wallace (eds), *Gothic Modernisms* (Basingstoke: Palgrave, 2001)
Smith, Zadie, 'Two Paths for the Novel', *The New York Review of Books*, 20 November 2008
Snow, C. P., *The Two Cultures* [1959] (Cambridge: Cambridge University Press, 1998)
Spark, Muriel, *The Collected Stories* (London: Penguin, 1994)
Spark, Muriel, *The Comforters* [1957] (London: Virago, 2009)
Spark, Muriel, *The Hothouse by the East River* [1973] (London: Penguin, 1975)
Spark, Muriel, *Loitering with Intent* [1981] (London: Virago, 2014)
Spender, Stephen, *The Creative Element: A Study of Vision, Despair and Orthodoxy Among Some Modern Writers* (London: Hamish Hamilton, 1953)
Spender, Stephen, *The Destructive Element: A Study of Modern Writers and Beliefs* (London: Jonathan Cape, 1935)
Stephenson, Gregory, 'An Inward Ice-Age: A Reading of Anna Kavan's *Ice*', *Foundation*, 40:113 (Winter 2011), 20–8
Stewart, Victoria, *Narratives of Memory: British Writing of the 1940s* (Basingstoke: Palgrave, 2006)
Stonebridge, Lyndsey, *The Writing of Anxiety: Imagining Wartime in Mid-Century British Culture* (Basingstoke: Palgrave MacMillan, 2007)
Stuhlmann, Gunther, 'Anna Kavan Revisited, the Web of Unreality', *Anaïs: An International Journal*, 3 (1985), 55–64
Sturm, Jennifer, 'Anna Kavan Meets a New Zealand Writer on His Special Day', *Kōtare*, 5:1 (2004)
Sturm, Jennifer (ed.), *Anna Kavan's New Zealand: A Pacific Interlude in a Turbulent Life* (Auckland: Vintage, Random House New Zealand, 2009)
Sturm, Jennifer, 'Fictionalising the Facts: An Exploration of the "Place" of Aotearoa/New Zealand in the Post-War Autobiographical Fiction of Anna Kavan' (Unpublished doctoral thesis: University of Auckland, 2006)
Sward, Robert and Ann Quin, 'Living in the Present', *Ambit*, 34 (1968), 20–1
Sweeney, Carole, 'Cadaverised Girls: The Writing of Anna Kavan', *Textual Practice*, 34:4 (April 2020), 647–68
Sweeney, Carole, '"Keeping the Ruins Private": Anna Kavan and Heroin Addiction', *Women: A Cultural Review*, 28:4 (Winter 2017), 312–26
Sweeney, Carole, *Vagabond Fictions: Gender and Experiment in British Women's Writing, 1945–1970* (Edinburgh: Edinburgh University Press, 2020)

Szasz, Thomas, *The Myth of Mental Illness: Foundations of a Theory of Personal Conduct*, Revised Edition (New York: Harper & Row, 1974)

Tait, Adrian, 'Nature Reclaims Her Own: J. G. Ballard's *The Drowned World*', *Australian Humanities Review*, 57 (2014), 25–41

Tew, Phillip, 'Postwar Renewals of Experiment 1945–1979', in *The Cambridge History of the English Novel* , ed. by Robert L. Caserio and Clement Hawes (Cambridge: Cambridge University Press, 2012), 757–73

Todorov, Tzvetan, *The Fantastic: A Structural Approach to a Literary Genre*, trans. by Richard Howard (Ithaca, NY: Cornell University Press, 1975)

Tonkin, Maggie, '"The Time of the Loony": Psychosis, Alienation, and R. D. Laing in the Fictions of Muriel Spark and Angela Carter', *Contemporary Women's Writing*, 9:2, November 2015, 366–84

Tookey, Helen, *Anaïs Nin, Fictionality and Femininity: Playing a Thousand Roles* (Oxford: Clarendon Press, 2003)

Treichler, Paula A., 'Escaping the Sentence: Diagnosis and Discourse in "The Yellow Wallpaper"', *Tulsa Studies in Women's Literature*, 3:1/2 (Spring–Autumn 1984), 61–77

Trexler, Adam, *Anthropocene Fictions: The Novel in a Time of Climate Change* (Charlottesville and London: University of Virginia Press, 2015)

Trilling, Diana, *Reviewing the Forties* (New York: Harcourt Brace Jovanovich, 1978)

Ussher, Jane M., *Women's Madness: Misogyny or Mental Illness?* (Hemel Hempstead: Harvester Wheatsheaf, 1991)

Valentine, Kylie, *Psychoanalysis, Psychiatry and Modernist Literature* (Basingstoke: Palgrave, Macmillan, 2003)

Van Hove, Hannah, 'Anna Kavan: Pursuing the "in-between reality" hidden by the "ordinary surface of things"', in *British Avant-Garde Fiction of the 1960s*, ed. by Kaye Mitchell and Nonia Williams (Edinburgh: Edinburgh University Press, 2019) 107–24

Van Hove, Hannah, 'Exploring the Realm of the Unconscious in Anna Kavan's *Sleep Has His House*', *Women: A Cultural Review*, 28:4 (Winter 2017), 358–74

Vetter, Lara, 'Journeys without Maps: Literature and Spiritual Experience', in *British Literature in Transition, 1920–1940: Futility and Anarchy*, ed. by Charles Ferrall and Dougal McNeill (Cambridge: Cambridge University Press, 2018), 68–83

Vlastos, Marion, 'Doris Lessing and R. D. Laing: Psychopolitics and Prophecy', *PMLA* 91:2 (March 1976), 245–58

Vonnegut, Kurt, *Slaughterhouse-Five* [1969] (London: Vintage, 2000)

Walker, Betty, 'New Novels: *Let Me Alone*', *Times Literary Supplement* (4 December 1930), 1036

Walker, Victoria, 'Anna Kavan's *Ice*: Postwar Experimentalism and the Fiction of the Anthropocene', *British Experimental Women's Fiction, 1945–1975: Slipping Through the Labels*, ed. by Andrew Radford and Hannah Van Hove (London: Palgrave, 2021), 153–72

Walker, Victoria, 'Hearts and Minds: War Neurosis and the Politics of Madness in Anna Kavan's *I Am Lazarus*', *Women: A Cultural Review*, 28:4 (Winter 2017), 375–90

Walker, Victoria, 'An Introduction to Anna Kavan: New Readings', *Women: A Cultural Review*, 28:4 (Winter 2017), 285–94

Walker, Victoria, 'Ornithology and Ontology: The Existential Birdcall in Jean Rhys's *Wide Sargasso Sea* and Anna Kavan's *Who Are You?*', *Women: A Cultural Review*, 23:4 (December 2012), 490–509

Ward, Geoff, 'The Wibberlee Wobberlee Walk: Lowry, Hamilton, Kavan and the Addictions of 1940s Fiction', in *The Fiction of the 1940s: Stories of Survival*, ed. by Rod Mengham and N. H. Reeve (Basingstoke: Palgrave Macmillan, 2001), 26–45

Wasson, Sara, *Urban Gothic of the Second World War: Dark London* (Basingstoke: Palgrave Macmillan, 2010)

Waugh, Evelyn, *Officers and Gentlemen* [1955] (London: Methuen, 1986)

Waugh, Evelyn, *Put Out More Flags* [1942] (London: Penguin, 1976)

Waugh, Patricia, *Metafiction: The Theory and Practice of Self-Conscious Fiction* (London: Methuen, 1984)

Waugh, Patricia, *Feminine Fictions: Revisiting the Postmodern* (London and New York: Routledge, 1989)

West, Rebecca, 'Extraordinary Exile', *The New Yorker*, 7 September 1946

Wheeler, Kathleen, *A Critical Guide to Twentieth-Century Women Novelists* (Oxford: Blackwell, 1997)

White, Antonia, *Strangers* (London: Virago Press, 1981)

Williams, Nonia 'About/of Madness: Ann Quin's *The Unmapped Country*', *Textual Practice*, 34:6 (2020), 903–20

Williams, Raymond, 'Realism and the Contemporary Novel', *Universities and Left Review*, 4, Summer 1958, 22–5

Wilson, Janet, 'A Pacific Sojourn: Anna Kavan and the New Zealand Connection, 1941–2', *Women: A Cultural Review*, 28:4 (Winter 2017), 343–57

Wilson, Leigh, 'Anna Kavan's *Ice* and Alan Burns' *Europe After the Rain*: Repetition with a Difference', *Women: A Cultural Review*, 28:4 (Winter 2017), 327–42

Wilson, Leigh, 'Whose Sister? "Convenient Pigeonholes", Peter Owen and the Publishing of Anna Kavan', in Andrew Radford and Hannah Van Hove (eds), *British Experimental Women's Fiction, 1945–1975: Slipping Through the Labels* (Basingstoke: Palgrave Macmillan, 2021), 83–101

Winterson, Jeanette, 'Introduction', *Oranges Are Not the Only Fruit* (London: Vintage, 2014)

Woolf, Virginia, *Mr Bennett and Mrs Brown* (London: Hogarth Press, 1924)

Woolf, Virginia, *A Room of One's Own/Three Guineas* (London: Penguin, 1993)

Woolf, Virginia, 'Thoughts on Peace in an Air Raid', in *The Death of the Moth and Other Essays* (London: Hogarth Press, 1942) 154–7

World Health Organization, International Statistical Classification of Diseases and Related Health Problems (ICD-11): 6A71 Recurrent depressive disorder Foundation URI: <https://icd.who.int/browse11/l-m/en#/http%3a%2f%2fid.who.int%2ficd%2fentity%2f1194756772> (accessed 6 November 2022)

Young, Elizabeth, *Pandora's Handbag: Adventures in the Book World* (London: Serpent's Tail, 2001)

Zambreno, Kate, 'Anna Kavan', *Context: A Forum for Literary Arts and Culture*, 18 (September 2007)

Zola, Émile, *The Experimental Novel and Other Essays*, trans. by Belle M. Sherman (New York: The Cassell Publishing Co., 1893)

Zultanski, Steven, 'K for KAVAN', *Public*, 28:56 (October 2017), 87–97

Index

absurdism, 47, 58
affect, 38, 40, 41, 45, 62, 104, 120, 126
Agee, Jim, 90n, 128, 133
Aldiss, Brian, 47, 66n, 115, 116–17, 118
alienation, 28, 35, 60, 61, 63, 64, 65
Anderson, Amanda, 3
animal(s), 47, 62, 99–100, 124
Anthropocene, 8, 10, 116, 117, 118–34
anti-psychiatry, 51–2, 54, 57, 75, 100, 108–9, 117; *see also* politics of madness
apocalypse, 70, 118–23, 126–7, 131–3
Arendt, Hannah, 5
Ariail, Gregory, 48
artwork, 26–7, 37
asylum, 45–65, 69, 71, 89, 97, 98
atomic bomb, 103, 119, 130, 131
Attenborough, David, 124–5
Auden, W. H., 47
Auerbach, Erich, 6
Aughterson, Kate, 13
authenticity, 2–3, 37
autobiography, 1, 13, 54, 57
automata, 30, 31, 59–60, 64, 77, 79

Ballard, J. G., 31, 100, 117, 118
Barnes, Djuna, 97
Barthes, Roland, 5, 8, 36
Basaglia, Franco, 5
Beck, Aaron T., 63
Benjamin, Walter, 26, 37
Berger, John, 21
Bergonzi, Bernard, 94
Bildungsroman, 1, 31
Binswanger, Ludwig, 49, 52, 57–8, 83, 93, 100–1, 107–9
 Bellevue Clinic, 49, 57, 83, 100

biography, 1, 2, 5–6, 11–12, 14
Bluth, Karl, 49, 57, 66n, 83, 93, 100–2, 108
Bonikowski, Wyatt, 78
Bowen, Elizabeth, 4, 16, 69, 70, 85–6, 88–9, 96, 111
Bradbury, Malcolm, 6
Bradley, William, 28, 29
Brannen, Peter, 120, 133
Breton, André, 96, 100, 104
Brewster, Scott, 60
British Empire, 21, 24, 27, 31–2, 38
Britton, D. J., 16n
Brontë, Charlotte, 107
Brooke-Rose, Christine, 11, 12, 38, 95
Burgess, Anthony, 131
Burma, 23, 25, 27, 32, 33, 38, 39, 40, 124
Burns, Alan, 7, 31, 48, 95, 96, 100, 109
Burroughs, William, 96

Calder, Angus, 89
Callard, David, 17n, 28
Camus, Albert, 104
Cape, Jonathan, 22, 23
Carr, Helen, 109
Carrington, Leonora, 48, 54, 56, 96, 100
Carroll, Lewis, 98
Carter, Angela, 31, 100, 109, 117
Centing, Richard R., 19n
Chakrabarty, Dipesh, 120, 128, 133
character *see* fictional character
Christianity, 30, 72
Christopher, John, 118
cinema, 71–2, 80, 97
class politics, 24, 38, 76–7
cli-fi, 118, 121

Coleridge, Samuel Taylor, 118
colonialism, 15, 22, 27, 32–3, 107
Connolly, Cyril, 50, 69, 72, 72, 90n
Cooper, David, 52
Cowper Powys, John, 30
Cunningham, Valentine, 30

Dali, Salvador, 97
Davies, Rhys, 10, 16n, 14, 22, 23
Davis, Thomas S., 60, 119, 121
Dawson, Jennifer, 54
Day-Lewis, Cecil, 23
de-realisation, 10, 21, 22, 65, 72
'death of the author', 4, 5–7, 36
Deleuze, Gilles, 52
delusion, 46, 62, 63, 88
depression, 21, 22, 24, 25, 41, 46, 53, 55, 57, 58, 60–5, 69, 70, 74, 83, 88, 103, 130; *see also* psychiatric diagnosis (major depression)
Dicks, Henry, 49, 66n
dream, 26, 27, 46, 73, 88, 93–111, 117, 119, 122, 125
Dunne, John William, 95
Dutch East Indies, 32, 124
dystopia, 48, 69, 71, 118

Edmonds, Helen, 2, 23, 72; *see also* Kavan, Anna
effort syndrome *see* psychiatric diagnosis
electroconvulsive therapy/electric shock treatment *see* psychiatric treatment
Eliot, T. S., 9, 60
Ellmann, Maud, 86
Emery, Mary L., 34
Evangelou, Angelos, 58, 62–3
Evans, Walker, 90n, 128, 133
exile, 26, 32, 76, 86
existential analysis, 52, 57, 83, 108
existential angst, 108–9
existentialism, 5, 52, 93, 104–5, 108–9
experimental writing, 4–10, 12–16, 37–8, 41, 45–7, 54, 61, 64–5, 69, 94–6, 100, 104, 109, 115, 127–9, 133–4

fantastic, 22, 29, 38, 64, 71, 84, 88, 89, 93, 123
fantasy, 23, 27, 69, 99, 111, 122
Felski, Rita, 3
feminism, 12, 13, 14

feminist criticism, 9, 11–12, 34, 52, 127
Ferguson, Donald, 23
Ferguson, Helen, 1–2, 8–10, 14, 16n, 21–41, 46, 64, 116; *see also* Kavan, Anna
Ferris, Natalie, 42n, 104
fictional character, 1–6, 13, 27, 36, 37, 41, 51, 52, 65
fictionality, 27, 34–5
Flaubert, Gustave, 36
Fleming, Ian, 116
Foucault, Michel, 51, 52, 55–6
Foucault/Derrida debate, 54
Frame, Janet, 54, 58
Freud, Sigmund, 5, 100–1, 108
Frisch, Max, 129
Frow, John, 6

Gaedtke, Andrew, 14, 17n, 64–5
Gambaudo, Sylvie, 54
Garrity, Jane, 3, 9, 18n, 98, 100–1
Gasiorek, Andrzej, 8
gender politics, 13, 24, 31, 38, 46, 52, 115
genre, 8, 14, 27, 29, 38, 115, 117
Glover, Edward, 50, 51, 66n, 83
Glynn, Raewyn, 42n, 66n
Goffman, Erving, 52
Gogol, Nikolai, 36
Gornick, Vivian, 42n
Gordon, Giles, 95
gothic, 11, 24, 25, 29, 33, 46, 59, 60, 69, 85, 93, 115, 116
Gower, John, 102
Green, Henry, 70
Greene, Graham, 7, 96
Groes, Sebastian, 109
Guattari, Félix, 52
guilt, 45, 47, 48, 58, 62, 73, 130–2
Guy, Adam, 44n

Haggard, Rider, 88
hallucinatory imagery, 39, 69, 71, 83, 85, 86, 88, 99, 118
Hamilton, Ian, 1, 23, 47, 72, 73, 75, 77, 130
Hamilton, Patrick, 7, 70, 96
Hanley, James, 69
Haraway, Donna, 119–20, 126–7
Head, Dominic, 38
Heidegger, 100–1, 108
Hepburn, Allan, 130, 131

heroin, 11, 49, 61, 93, 101–4, 109, 134; *see also* opium
Hitchcock, Alfred, 97
Home and Country magazine, 23, 29
Home Counties, 15, 22, 27, 28, 30
Horizon, 35–6, 50, 51, 69, 72, 74
Houlden, Kate, 42n
humour, 57, 58

identity, 3, 5, 6–7, 10, 12, 13, 33, 45, 49, 93, 99, 104–9, 129
inanimate objects, 30, 59–60, 75, 83–7, 89
incestuous desire, 25, 26, 30, 116
individualism, 73, 76, 77, 127
inner space fiction, 117–18

Jaspers, Karl, 64
Johnson, B. S., 95
Johnson, Erica L., 33, 34
Jones, Clara, 29, 42n
Jones, Maxwell, 49, 50, 51, 52, 74
Jordan, Julia, 4, 18 n 30, 38, 96
Joyce, James, 96, 97

Kafka, Franz, 9, 36, 47–8, 57, 66n, 71, 100, 115, 130
Kavan, Anna
  asylum incarceration, 5, 11
  childhood, 32
  depression, 2, 11, 49, 50, 60–1, 103
  heroin addiction, 2–5, 11, 49, 61, 72, 101–3
  illness, 72, 103
  journalism, 10, 12, 14, 72, 76
  name change, 1–3, 8–9, 11–13, 34, 41, 72
  pacifism, 75–6
  painting, 42n
  politics, 14, 24, 24, 51, 54, 76–7
  life as Helen Edmonds, 23
  posthumous publications, 14, 109
  psychiatric history, 49
  suicide attempts, 11, 61, 72
  travelling and living abroad, 23, 31–2, 71–2, 75
  treatment at the Bellevue, 57–8
  work at *Horizon*, 72, 74
  work at Mill Hill Emergency Hospital, 49, 50
  works:
    A Bright Green Field, 100
    'A Certain Experience', 53

A Charmed Circle, 9, 23, 24, 27, 28
A Scarcity of Love, 23, 99, 104
A Stranger Still, 23, 26, 27, 29, 64
'A Visit', 100
'An Unpleasant Reminder', 56–7
'Annunciation', 33
Asylum Piece, 1, 2, 8, 15, 23, 37, 45–8, 52–7, 61–5, 69, 70, 71, 72, 76, 78, 85, 89, 93, 97–8, 116, 117, 128
'Back to Victoria: Selected Notices', 36, 93–4
Change the Name, 3, 23, 27
'Christmas Afternoon in Burma', 29, 32
'Clarita', 100
Eagle's Nest, 14
'Experimental', 134
'Face of My People', 51, 58–9, 75, 78, 80–1, 92n
'Glorious Boys', 76, 77, 84, 87
Goose Cross, 23, 24, 26, 27, 30, 38, 116, 126
Guilty, 14, 91n
'I Am Lazarus', 59–60, 84
I Am Lazarus, 8, 15, 45, 53, 57, 59–60, 63, 64, 69–89, 100, 127
Ice, 8, 9, 14, 15, 24, 26, 31, 35, 38, 39, 48, 70, 93, 99, 100, 105, 111, 115–33
'Julia and the Bazooka', 109–10
Julia and the Bazooka, 100, 101, 109–10, 134
'Just Another Failure', 64
Let Me Alone, 1, 21, 23–6, 30, 32, 35, 39–41, 48, 65, 93, 104–6, 116, 126
'Machines in the Head', 64
'Martin's Wife', 29
Mercury, 14
My Soul in China, 3, 14
'New Zealand: Answer to an Inquiry', 72–3
'Now I Know Where My Place Is', 99
'Our City', 86, 88, 99
'Palace of Sleep', 59
'Rather Kafka', 66n
'Reviews' in *Horizon*, 35–6, 72, 85, 93–4, 127, 128
Rich Get Rich, 23, 24, 27, 31, 116
Sleep Has His House, 9, 15, 16, 55, 93–104, 108, 111n, 117

'The Blackout', 78–80, 82
The Cactus Sign, 22, 42n, 95, 99
'The Case of Bill Williams', 3, 49–51, 56, 60, 73–5, 78–80, 83, 127–8, 131
The Dark Sisters, 23, 24, 27, 28, 116
'The Heavenly Adversary', 63
The Horse's Tale, 15, 45, 47, 49, 57–9
The House of Sleep see *Sleep Has His House*
'The man with two faces', 33
'The Old Address', 103
The Parson, 23
Who Are You?, 15, 22, 24, 26, 39–41, 93, 95, 104–11, 126
'Who Has Desired the Sea', 77–9
'Wives' Encounter', 29
see also Ferguson, Helen
Kermode, Frank, 94, 98, 121
Kesey, Ken, 58
Koestler, Arthur, 72, 80, 90n
Kristeva, Julia, 61

Laing, R. D., 10, 52, 56, 76, 108–9, 117
Lane, John, 23
Lawrence, D. H., 28
Le Carré, John, 116
Lenoble, Catherine, 16n
Lessing, Doris, 4, 115, 117, 130
Lethem, Jonathan, 115
Lowry, Malcolm, 7
Lye, Len, 90n

MacCarthy, Desmond, 47
MacKay, Marina, 9, 31
McLeod, Aorewa, 42n, 66n
MacNeice, Louis, 90n
madness, 21, 24, 30, 35, 48, 50, 54, 55, 60, 62–5, 69, 76, 97, 117, 128
  politics of madness, 14, 49–65, 69, 73–6; see also anti-psychiatry
Magot, Celine, 42n
male gaze, 21, 116
Maudsley Hospital, 73
mechanisation, 24, 31, 60, 64, 76, 77, 107, 128, 131
  mechanical reproduction, 37
  social machine, 50, 64, 128
Meckel, Christoph, 48, 66n
Mellor, Leo, 86

memory, 70, 78–80, 82, 98, 122
metafiction, 2, 3, 4, 8, 11, 13, 47, 54
mid-century fiction, 4–10, 14, 22, 24, 36–8, 41, 45, 48, 65, 96, 111
Mill Hill Emergency Hospital, 49, 50, 73–7, 80, 83
Miller, Tyrus, 9, 30
miscarriage, 30, 34
Mitchell, Kaye, 12, 18
modernism, 9–10, 13–14, 70, 96
  intermodernism, 9, 10
  late modernism, 4, 9, 10, 24, 30, 38, 96, 97
Moi, Toril, 3
Moran, Patricia, 33, 34
morphia, 11; see also heroin; opium
Muir, Edwin, 47–8
Muir, Willa, 47

narco-analysis see psychiatric treatment
narcosis see psychiatric treatment
narrative repetition, 8, 39, 104–7, 111, 118
narrative temporality, 39, 40, 69–71, 94–6, 105, 107, 109–11, 120, 133–5; see also time
Nelson, Victoria, 127
neurosis see psychiatric diagnosis
New York, 32, 72, 90n
New Zealand, 32, 33, 72–3, 75, 77, 79, 90n, 124
Nijinski, Vaslav, 57
Nin, Anaïs, 12–13, 19n, 96, 109, 117
nouveau roman, 37
Nuremburg trials, 130–1

opium, 100–3; see also heroin
Orpana, Simon Andrew, 121
Orwell, George, 32, 57
outsiders, 13, 14, 22, 29, 71
Owen, Peter, 10, 14, 20n, 115

pacifism, 31, 69, 73, 75–7, 85, 100, 127, 130
  conscientious objection, 73, 130
Panter-Downes, Mollie, 72
parody, 58, 62
patriotism, 30, 76
Philips, Deborah, 13
Pick, Daniel, 66n
Plath, Sylvia, 11, 54, 58, 88
Plain, Gill, 95, 111
politics of madness see madness

Pong, Beryl, 70
Porter, Roy, 54
postmodernism, 13
postwar avant-garde, 4, 10, 38, 109
postwar fiction, 9, 31, 35–6, 93–7
postwar literary debates/publishing, 37–8, 93–6
Priest, Christopher, 117
Prowse, Nycole, 102, 103
psychiatric treatment, 45–65, 69, 71, 74, 77–83, 100
  electroconvulsive therapy/electric shock treatment, 50, 56, 57, 58
  narco-analysis, 57, 58–9, 82, 83, 84, 93
  narcosis, 57, 59, 93
  psychiatric diagnosis, 51, 52, 61, 64, 74; dementia praecox, 59; effort syndrome, 73–4, 78–81, 84, 89, 91n; major depression, 21, 22, 24, 60–3; see also depression; neurosis, 50, 51, 71, 72, 74, 75
  psychiatric drugs, 45, 56–8, 93; amphetamines, 49; benzedrine, 50, 57; sodium amytal, 57, 58
  talking therapies, 45, 59, 83
psychoanalysis, 49, 50, 51, 66n, 83, 93, 94, 100, 101, 108–9; see also Tavistock Clinic

Quin Ann, 31, 54, 95, 109, 112n

Rabinowitz, Rubin, 94
race, 33
Rao, Eleonora, 35, 61
rape see sexual violence
Rawlinson, Mark, 71, 78
realism, 11, 15, 23, 24, 27, 35–8, 41, 45, 46, 54, 69, 71, 94, 117
reality, 4, 6, 10, 11, 15, 16, 27, 35–8, 41, 45, 46, 49, 61, 64, 65, 70, 71, 93, 94, 98, 102, 105, 110–1, 117–18, 121, 122, 127
Reed, Jeremy, 16n, 17n, 66n
Rhys, Jean, 4, 7, 33–5, 96, 106–7, 109
Robbe-Grillet, Alain, 37
Rolph, John, 19n, 104
romance, 24, 34, 115
Romanticism, 102–3, 118
Rose, Jacqueline, 12

Saint-Amour, Paul K., 70
Sansom, William, 48, 69, 85, 96

Sarraute, Nathalie, 5, 37, 45, 65
Sartre, Jean-Paul, 104
satire, 57, 58
Schelling, Friedrich Wilhelm Joseph, 102
science fiction, 11, 96, 100, 115, 116–17
Scorpion Press, 104
Seiler, Claire, 10
sexual violence, 22, 26, 34, 106, 116, 119, 126–7; see also violence
  rape, 25, 26, 30, 106, 116, 126
shell-shock, 30, 78, 83
sleep, 58–62, 75, 82, 98–9
Smith, Zadie, 2–3, 5, 37, 101
soldiers, 30, 31, 50, 71, 73–89
South Africa, 32, 33, 75
Spark, Muriel, 4, 7, 11, 96, 107, 110–11
speculative fiction, 95, 117
Stonebridge, Lyndsey, 9, 83
Sturm, Jennifer, 72–3
subjectivity, 4, 16, 24, 31, 33, 45, 55, 63
suicide, 56, 60, 62, 64, 72, 84, 98, 103, 104, 131
supernatural, 30, 38
surrealism, 11, 93, 96–7, 99–100, 104
surveillance, 46, 53, 63, 64
Sweeny, Carole, 3, 11, 18n, 19n, 38, 42n, 61, 101
Szasz, Thomas, 52, 76

Tavistock Clinic, 49, 66n, 83, 100
Texidor, Greville, 90n
time, 47, 61, 70–1, 77, 88, 93, 95, 104, 109–10, 120, 132–5; see also narrative temporality
Todd, Ruthven, 47
Toller, Ernst, 23
Tookey, Helen, 19n
Townsend Warner, Sylvia, 30, 90n
Trevelyan, Julian, 66n
trial, 47, 129–31
Trilling, Diana, 97
Trochi, Alexander, 2, 95
two cultures debate, 117, 134

uncanny, 24, 30, 59, 60, 88
uncertainty, 7, 10, 22, 38, 39, 55, 63, 104, 108, 109
unconscious, 55, 58, 59, 93, 95, 96–8, 100–3

unreality, 21–3, 26, 32, 34, 35, 38, 39, 53, 65, 72, 85, 134

Van Hove, Hannah, 9, 18n, 18n, 99, 122
Vetter, Lara, 33
violence, 12, 31, 62, 64, 98, 103, 128–30, 132; *see also* sexual violence
Vonnegut, Kurt, 129

war, 27, 104
  Cold War, 116, 118
  First World War, 5, 24, 29, 30, 31, 78, 83
  Second World War, 5, 10, 24, 29, 31, 32, 47, 50, 69–89, 93, 109–11, 130; blackout, 70, 75, 79–80, 85, 88–9; Blitz, 69–89; bombing, 69–72, 75, 110–11
  total war, 69, 72
  war-machine, 69, 76, 77, 131
Ward, Geoff, 18n, 20n, 58, 62, 98, 199

Warner, Rex, 23, 48, 96
Wasson, Sara, 18n, 20n, 68n, 71
Watson, Peter, 90n
Waugh, Evelyn, 70
Waugh, Patricia, 3–4, 6, 104
West, Rebecca, 131
White, Antonia, 53, 56
Williams, Nonia, 18n, 54
Williams, Raymond, 37
Wilson, Janet, 27, 43n, 72
Wilson, Leigh, 14, 18n, 20n, 47, 48, 62, 111, 115, 127
Winterson, Jeanette, 13
women's experimental writing, 12–13, 38, 47
Woods, Helen, 25; *see also* Kavan, Anna
Woolf, Virginia, 4, 5, 6, 11, 31, 38, 45, 73, 76, 97
Worthington, Marjorie, 23
Wyndham, Francis, 106

Zola, Émile, 36, 37

EU representative:
Easy Access System Europe
Mustamäe tee 50, 10621 Tallinn, Estonia
Gpsr.requests@easproject.com

www.ingramcontent.com/pod-product-compliance
Lightning Source LLC
Chambersburg PA
CBHW051128160426
43195CB00014B/2391